Dec. 2001

Jenn.

A wonderful book by a

wonder of a woman

Enjoy.

With love.

Judy & Bryan

NOVELS

Digging Out

Up the Sandbox

Long Division

Torch Song

Lovingkindness

The Pursuit of Happiness

If You Knew Me

NONFICTION

Generation Without Memory:
A Jewish Journey Through Christian America

Your Child's Mind
(with Dr. Herman Roiphe)

A Season for Healing:
Reflections on the Holocaust

Fruitful

ANNE ROIPHE

1185 PARK AVENUE

A MEMOIR

THE FREE PRESS

THE FREE PRESS
A Division of Simon & Schuster Inc.
1230 Avenue of the Americas
New York, NY 10020

THE FREE PRESS and colophon are trademarks of
Simon & Schuster Inc.

Designed by Pei Loi Koay

Manufactured in the United States of America

10   9   8   7   6   5   4   3   2   1

Library of Congress Cataloging-in-Publication Data

Roiphe, Anne Richardson, 1935–
    1185 Park Avenue : a memoir / Anne Roiphe.
      p.   cm.
    1. Roiphe, Anne Richardson, 1935–   —Childhood
and youth.   2. Women novelists, American—20th
century—Family relationships.   3. Women novelists,
American—20th   century—Biography.   4. Jewish
families—New York (State)—New York.   5. Jews—
New York (State)—New York—Biography.   6. New
York (N.Y.)—Social life and customs.   7. Roiphe,
Anne Richardson, 1935–   —Family.   8. Park Avenue
(New York, N.Y.)—Biography.   I. Title.
PS3568.053Z463   1999
813'.54—dc21
    [B]   98-51939
                                                      CIP

ISBN 0-684-85731-6

TO

BLANCHE PHILLIPS ROTH,

1910–1962

author's note   The names and other identifying details of some of the characters in this memoir have been changed, and a few of the stories told to me by my mother have been compressed, keeping the actual spirit of each but avoiding beating a point to death. These and the other stories in this book are told as I remember them; although through the decades some incidental details may have become slippery as wet stones, icy streets and inclining slopes, they have become part of my truth.

1185 PARK AVENUE

1

the neighborhood   Later when we would drive in from our
country house along Bruckner Boulevard in the Bronx or out to visit a friend
on Long Island and we'd drive through Queens, after tunnels or bridges, after streets of warehouses and factories smelling of glues and yeast, we'd
pass the small two-family attached houses that lined the road before the
city would slide into suburb. We'd see the striped awnings on each little
brick house, the chairs on the porches where flowerpots vied for space with
barbeque grills, the small iron gates, behind which blue and white painted
statues of the Virgin watched as the cars going or coming from Manhattan
flowed by. From rooftops Santa Claus sometimes waved and near the garage
door ceramic spotted deer grazed on closet-sized lawns. My mother would
be smoking, ashes falling in her lap, she would be sitting on a cushion so
she could see over the driving wheel. She would be wearing her dark glasses
to hide the puffiness of her eyes, the circles beneath them. She would drive
slowly so she could look at the houses carefully. Cars would honk and pass
and some would open their windows and yell at her. "Get a horse," "Woman
drivers." Then my mother would sigh, a deep sigh, "If only your father and
I lived in one of those houses and we worked together in our candy store,

I

then maybe—" and she would sigh again. "If only I lived like this," she would say and wave her hand across the Bronx or over Queens. But she didn't. We, my father, my mother, my brother and I, our nurse, Greta, our cook, Emma, our maid, either Bernice or Ingrid, or Bridget, lived in apartment 8C at 1185 Park Avenue. Blanche Phillips Roth, daughter of the late Isaac Phillips, of the Phillips Van Heusen Shirt company, and her husband, Eugene Frederick Roth, had moved into the building, right after their honeymoon trip. The year was 1931.

In the last days of the nineteenth century the New York Metropolitan map marked the place as Goat Hill. There were a few farms, shrubs, fences, and animals with long tails brushing away the flies in the summer heat. Then as the city pushed at its edges, as the rich and the poor found their appointed places it became the almost falling-off far end of Park Avenue: a broad elegant street, the kind you saw in Paris, in Rome, more sedate of course, more sober, fewer gargoyles, stone angels, wreaths and marble inlays. The almost simplicity of the buildings, their dignified height, their white stone, their red bricks, their portly girths, their well-groomed awnings of dark green and dark wine supported by gleaming brass poles suited the American burgher's need to hide the transparent immaturity of his land.

By the late 1930s a commuter train to the new suburbs in Westchester ran night and day beneath the iron-fenced center islands that were planted with ivy to disguise the access grates. Sometimes the boys waiting for a school bus would run into the middle of the avenue and leap over the iron fence. Lying down on their stomachs, with the cars passing on either side, they would peer down into the ground watching the cinders floating upward, staring at the soot-blackened wooden beams, at the ash-stained walls that plunged way down to the tracks below. They would hear the sound of metal wheels, the rush of sparks, a constant pulse from the trains passing out of or returning to Grand Central Station. A few blocks farther uptown from our building, the railroad tracks appeared in the open air, and every so often a train would rumble out of the ground following the uphill slope till it became an elevated train from which its passengers could stare into the windows of the tenements that lined this part of the never aptly named Park Avenue. Then the sun would light the dusty train windows or rain would splash down on the interlocking chains that held the railroad cars together leaving pools of dirty water around the darkened railroad ties.

Standing on the overpass on 97th Street you could look back at Park Avenue or ahead to the tilting fire escape laced four-story, laundry-flapping, cabbage-smelling buildings that pressed against the stone walls that lifted the tracks into the sky. The overpass was a line drawn in cement. It marked the formal end of Park Avenue and the true beginning of Harlem. The children from Park Avenue knew never to cross that line.

In the 1930s buildings along Park Avenue stood firm no matter what befell their inhabitants. Doormen with white gloves and gold braid on their hats opened the taxi doors. Elevator men with Irish names and shining shoes pushed levers forward or backward and the elevators, made of burnished wooden panels, trimmed in shining brass, rose and fell, rose and fell, like yo-yos on an invisible string. In the large windowless basements with gray stone walls Negro laundresses washed clothes by hand in white enamel tubs and hung the clothes on wooden racks. Behind the tubs rows of long ironing boards sat like so many coffins after a disaster. From eight in the morning till six at night the steam rose from the heavy pressing irons, ten, twenty laundresses at a time bending, standing, the smell of human sweat mingling with soap powders hanging in the wet and heavy air.

German and Irish nannies carefully pushed stately carriages, English prams with shining silver wheels and dark blue wood sides in and out the doors. Babies slept on monogrammed linen sheets and leaned their small heads against lace pillows propped against the gray canvas hoods. There were closets full of Spode and delft, of gold-handled water pitchers and silver platters etched with portraits of nymphs and satyrs gamboling beneath laurel trees. There were draperies on the windows of velvet and damask. There were Chinese screens and tapestries brought back from trips to France and Belgium. There were dark green walls and deep red walls hung with landscapes or still lifes or ringed with silver Aztec designs. There were black and white marble squares across the foyer floor and candelabras with their golden arms extended outward. There were crystal chandeliers hanging from the ceiling. There were jade picture frames on the pianos. There were Chippendale desks and art deco bowls. There were Bauhaus chairs, silver lilies around the mirror frames, vases from Tiffany's, glass from Steuben. There were shimmering silk nightgowns trimmed in Swiss lace in the drawers and monogrammed and hand-embroidered tablecloths from Belgium in the cupboards.

1185 Park Avenue took up the entire block of 93rd Street to 94th Street. There were three pairs of Gothic wedding cake gray stone arches at each of the entrances. There were three long thin columns supporting each arch and the arches formed shadowed aisles, an intentional echo of the mighty cathedrals of Europe. The main arch led to a dark cavernous courtyard that was half a city block deep. At the center there was a water-splashing stone fountain encircled by plantings. The sun did not reach down there and the pachysandra and ivy would die, would need to be replaced again and again. Heavy gray cobblestones formed a circular path around six entryways each with its own eighteenth-century sconces and an iron-worked marquee. All of the lobbies were decorated with green and white marble squares, art deco mirrors, and vases filled with fresh flowers resting on skinny black tables with legs shaped like bent lilies. There were geometric shapes on the wallpaper. Chauffeurs drove their cars inside the courtyard to pick up passengers. All deliveries were made through the basement's long corridors with entrances on the side streets. Maids and cooks, window washers, grocery boys, and nannies also used the basement to come and go.

This was one of the few buildings on Park Avenue where Jews in the early thirties could rent and so they did in large numbers. It was also the only building on the street that looked like a mock fortress, a combination cathedral and castle, secure, imposing, a tribute to American engineering. On duty there were always at least two Irish doormen at the front and one at each entryway, their uniforms similar to police uniforms and at their waists they carried billy sticks, and around their necks hung silver whistles. Every elevator had its own white-gloved attendant whose duties included ferrying tenants up and down and maintaining a perfect polish on the mirrors and the decorative brass. After midnight the black iron gates with their sharp points at the top were closed tight and locked across all three arched entrances.

The apartments contained long hallways, dining rooms and dens, built-in bars, sewing rooms and music rooms. In each there were maids and cooks who lived in the narrow divided area behind the kitchen. The servants shared a small bath and from the ceiling in the back of the apartment above each of their beds a bare bulb hung down from a chain. The heating pipes were exposed in those rooms and you had to be careful not to touch them in the dead of winter or else you might get burned.

Farther downtown on Park Avenue the Episcopalian non-Jews lived inside their own buildings. Their children went to their own kindergartens and they had their own hospitals and pediatricians, orthodontists, orthopedists, stockbrokers, funeral homes, and charity balls. They drove up on weekends to their own country clubs. Their city clubs were furnished with shabby overstuffed chairs that had been used for many generations. Their oriental rugs had worn patches from resting under a great aunt's piano or a grandfather's parlor table. Their sons spent an afternoon or so each month marching in the Knickerbocker Greys, pretending to be soldiers while practicing for future roles of leadership. Their daughters rode horses at private stables in Long Island and Connecticut. They had coming-out parties and predance dinners for offspring of those who knew someone who had gone to school with the far-from-admired Franklin or Eleanor Roosevelt. They had a polo club in New Jersey. They had a Junior League with a membership whose names were all listed in *The Social Register* that did good works for the poor with the funds received from their annual Christmas bazaar. Their summer homes were in East Hampton, Newport, or Bar Harbor Maine. They belonged to the Harvard Club and the Yale Club and their sons went to Groton and Exeter and Andover and St. Paul's. They wore the same clothes as everyone else but not quite. They didn't wear socks with their moccasins. They knew each other instantly on sight.

If society is a pyramid in which the top comes to a point, they were the point. They did not so much cast a shadow over the rest as provide a source of constant anxiety for the others. That is the place where you weren't wanted. That is the restricted hotel on this block. That is the hospital that doesn't allow Jewish doctors to admit patients. That is the school you won't bother to apply to. "Them" was the word spoken with a touch of awe and a spark of anger. Who are "they" really to think they own the world and are so much better than "us"? The big businesses, the big banks, the big fortunes, the big givers to charity, the big owners of boxes at the opera: all of them were "them." They didn't want "us." Who cared. In America who cared. And besides one could imitate them or at least try.

What they had, what they looked like, what they owned from a kind of haircut or color, to a kind of stock, to a kind of nose, to the shade of their eyes, is what everybody else desired. Of course you can't have a decent social pyramid without an equally decent shimmer of envy rising like transparent heat waves from its base.

Although we were on the Harlem end, the falling-off end, of Park Avenue Jews had a few of our own apartment buildings. Just as nice, maybe nicer because we made sure the lobby was redecorated every few years. We occupied nearly the same geographic space, but not exactly. Certainly two Park Avenues side by side coexisted if not with particular grace or kindness or mutuality at least without significant outward disturbance.

Several blocks farther east over on Second Avenue the chimneys of Ruppert Breweries spewed great swirls of smoke into the air. On a day when the wind was blowing off the East River the heavy sour sulfurous smell of malt floated up from the boiling vats inside the fortress-thick factory and drifted over Park Avenue. Then even in summer the maids would rush to close the windows and pull the drapes and the residents would put handkerchiefs over their mouths as they went in and out.

Downtown (you could ride there in a double-decker bus on Fifth Avenue or take the Third Avenue El) at the end of the 1930s in New York there were communists endlessly arguing on campuses and German intellectuals at the New School and socialists with stars in their eyes and a grim set to their lips. There were artists in Greenwich Village drinking and brawling. Edna St. Vincent Millay was burning her candle at both ends. The unions were building apartments for their workers over in the west twenties and union organizers shouted from soapboxes in Bryant Park behind the 42nd Street Library. Uptown there were jazz clubs in Harlem and across the bridge Irish pubs and Italian clubs in Queens. In Yorkville on 85th Street there were weekly bund meetings, swastikas on raised arms right there, in the Jaeger house tavern. There was a Father Divine preaching at 125th Street and on the radio a Father Coughlin blamed the entire litany of social ills on the greed of Jewish bankers.

This was a city that knew how to have a good time: tickertape parades down Wall Street, smoke from the Camel billboard on Times Square, ice skating at Rockefeller Center, bonnets at the Easter parade, tourists at the Empire State Building, bad guys, wannabes on the make at The Stork Club, 21, The Little Club, The El Morocco, drinking the night away watching the Copa girls lift their long legs, greeting the morning with cheesecake at Lindy's.

The city brimmed with mafia and gamblers, enforcers and astrologists all admired by columnists who crawled the clubs at night and told the public who was spotted where. There was no lack of ministers or loansharks. Broadway was lit up like a hopeful whore and she did good business. You could sit at a drugstore counter and sip a chocolate malted. You could meet a date under the clock at the Biltmore. Sardi's was where you went after theater. Damon Runyan told the truth but made up his happy endings. No one had ever heard of a theme park. Hollywood was where you went to sell out.

On our Park Avenue the men wore fedoras and left the house each day with a clean white cotton handkerchief in their breast pocket. The women wore hats with veils and Chanel suits and tight corsets and their silk stockings were held up by garter belts that left raw red marks on the upper thigh. They played mah-jongg on card tables fitted with a green velvet cloth. Their jewelry was gold. Their coats were mink. They lunched at the Plaza, they drank martinis after five o'clock, and on Saturdays they hopped in their cars and played a round of golf at their clubs in Westchester or New Jersey.

Off Park Avenue there were communists not just under the bed but on top of it too. There were Stalinists and Trotskyites who black-balled each other and carried on in the pages of small magazines and big publishing houses. There was Clifford Odets and Martha Graham. A person could have been reading Henry Miller and James Joyce.

At the end of the thirties the Abraham Lincoln Brigade was off fighting for justice in Spain and some people (no one I was related to) would not cross a picket line. But where I lived the uniformed doormen tipped their hats, the governesses wrote letters home, the elevator men drank beer in the basement. Yes, in other places there was a lot of talk about class society and the evils that followed in its wake but the people at 1185 were almost united in the belief that industry was our destiny, that money was the root of all good living, and the absence of money was the pit of despair, the face of the monster everyone feared. Anyway my parents didn't actually know any real communists. Later they did know a pinko or two.

On Park Avenue, a single generation away from the streets of Lvov, Lublin, Odessa, Vilna, Kiev, no one considered whether the children might be better off if the servants were fewer. Most of the men played squash or cards at their clubs. All the women had their hair done, permed, dyed, set in curlers, and dried and combed out twice a week, and a lady came to the house to wax their legs and a traveling salesman came to the door with his suitcase of fine linens imported, who knows how, from war-torn Europe. Eugene and Blanche Roth lived at 1185 Park Avenue in New York City all during the depression when wind and dust drove farmers to leave their homes and migrate to the edge of America and workers sold apples on street corners and banks closed and even the gangsters met with hard times.

But don't forget poor King Midas who couldn't taste the juice of one sweet pear.

Somewhere else in America a *Saturday Evening Post* Norman Rockwell child was baiting his safety pin hook with a worm and leaning over a brook. He had a big golden dog by his side and a fishing pole made from a whittled-down branch of a tree. He intended to bring a fish home for dinner.

2

the stork   In December 1935, in the middle of a sorrowful decade,
I came into the world.

After several miscarriages, before the Nazis had invaded Poland and
Czechoslovakia, but after Marie Bonaparte had arranged for the safe trans-
port of the elderly Freud and his wife and daughter, after the Rising Sun
shone down on Manchuria my mother gave birth to my brother in a private
hospital in New York. It was August 5, 1939. The baby was drugged and
slightly blue at birth. In accordance with the common practice my mother
had been given a large dose of anesthetic so she was unconscious throughout the delivery. As was the custom my mother stayed in the hospital for the
full twelve days, recovering, visiting with her sister, propped up on lace pillows brought from her own linen closet. Slowly she regained her physical
strength. Her breasts were bound tightly but despite that they ached until
the milk no longer flowed. The baby was not to be fed from the breast. It
wasn't done. It wasn't advised. The nurse would take over the chore of feeding the infant. Breast feeding was considered a holdover from primitive
times unsuitable for a woman who lived on Park Avenue in the city that
everyone knew was up to date. Science meant you could flush the toilet,

9

flick on the light, shut your door, ride up to the top of the Empire State in an elevator, order your groceries over the telephone, and you didn't have to nurse your own baby. Baby at the breast, baby with mouth at the nipple, how sanitary could that be? Baby at the breast was altogether too close to the dust of the barnyard. Women who had won the vote were not cows.

Big puffed-up breasts were for grown men to dream about not for babies to claim as their own. Thank God, psychologists had learned that it was better to feed your baby exactly every four hours and never pick him up till the schedule called for it. The crying infant was always in danger of being spoiled. From the first pull of air into the tiniest of lungs, each child must learn discipline, order, its place on life's assembly line. The nursery like the factory ran on reason, causality, science marching forward to make life better and better. (If only the stock market would behave as reasonably and the unions pipe down.)

My father had not been in the delivery room, had not spent his days watching his son in the newborn nursery. He sent his wife flowers and kept his appointments, went to his club and played squash and had a massage. He behaved in a perfectly usual way attracting no attention, revealing to no one but his wife a certain indifference, a chronic restlessness intensified by the embarrassment that the physical necessities of birth evoked, with its disturbing reminder of the raw, the barbaric, the uncontrollable, the feminine realm of blood and ooze, ripeness and eruption.

We were sitting on the steps that August, waiting for the baby, my baby brother, to arrive. She was wearing a white uniform and a net covered her hair. A Victorian ivy-covered house had been rented for the summer near the beach in a town called Lawrence on Long Island. The woman in the uniform was Greta, my governess, a German woman who had tended most of my elder cousins until their teen years, a woman who despite her fifteen years in this country mispronounced words like *onion* and *windmill*, who kept a small brass cross on the wall behind her bed and prayed to Jesus every Sunday at early mass, kneeling on a cold stone floor, while the light strained through the blues and reds of the rounded glass window that showed St. Francis feeding the birds.

At least twice a month I went with her to the post office and waited in a long line. She was sending packages home to her family who lived in Bavaria on a farm. She was sending gloves, woolen socks, caps, thick stockings, shoes, needles, thread, yarn. They needed everything. They were not lucky. That she told me.

Greta believed in washing. She washed her hands and my hands after each visit to the bathroom. She washed doorknobs and bed frames. She washed in the cracks of the body where bacteria might hide. She washed with strong soap that smelled of turpentine and stained the skin yellow, purifying down to the bone. She used alcohol products, disinfectants, household lye. Germs were everywhere, on bathroom doors, on money exchanged at the store, on the surfaces of sinks and only exceptional vigilance, perfect cleanliness, personal hygiene could hold them at bay. Polio and pneumonia, mastoid infections, rheumatic fever, scarlet fever, meningitis, diphtheria, danced in the air. In a world without antibiotics germs, invisible germs, were eternally poised at the foot of the bed, on the thumb that wandered into the mouth, multiplying freely, they overran, they overreached, and like low-flying pilots strafing suitcase-carrying men, women, and children along the long roads, they knew no mercy.

In front of Greta on the steps was a white wicker bassinet. Greta had a large roll of satin blue ribbon in her lap. Her hands did not have dark red fingernail polish like my mother's. Her lips were free of artificial color. Her shoes did not have heels or small straps around the ankle. She wore no gold jewelry. She worked the ribbon carefully through the ridges in front of her. She had knitted a blue blanket that was folded at the end of the white sheet of the bassinet. I was not allowed to touch the ribbon, not allowed to touch the new blanket, not to touch the white bassinet. I was to sit still and wait. The blue ribbon was the color of the afternoon sky. Like a robin's egg it was smooth and sleek. Could I have a piece of ribbon for my hair? I could not. Blue is for boys. Blue is for the brother coming home from the hospital. Blue is the color of desire. Blue is my favorite color. Blue is not for girls. The ribbon caught the sunlight and turned pale and shimmered in the air, more than just silk, gift of worms from China, the ribbon was the sacrament, an offering for the holy child.

The time passed. How long a time? In a child's mind it was months, in reality an afternoon. I felt uneasy, as if the distance between me and Greta had grown immense. I sat on the top step of the familiar porch. Down the street a dog in a yard barked. The cook was sitting at the kitchen table fanning herself with a newspaper. There were beads of moisture on the water pitcher. I watched an ant make its way across a long step. I appeared to be an eager older sister, three and a half years old, waiting patiently for the arrival of her younger brother, but in my small heart erupted the first shoots of toxic envy, the first blossoms of warm guilt, the rudimentary design of my soul, bending itself to circumstance, trying to be good, but knowing that love, the love you should feel for your baby brother, stings, brings tears to the eye. If a passerby had seen on that porch a woman in her mid-thirties, a plain-faced uniformed woman, a large mole on her chin, with her charge, a little curly-haired girl, sweet in a red polka dot pinafore, white sandal shoes and white socks folded just so to the ankle bone, a red plastic barrette in the shape of a bird on the left side of the part, anchoring down the brushed and shining thick brown hair and said to himself, the child looks like an angel, he would have been entirely mistaken. The angel was falling and would soon fall further.

After Kristallnacht, after the Anschluss, but before the *St. Louis* had been turned back from the New York harbor, before the closing of the gates of the Warsaw Ghetto, before the Japanese ambassador in Riga had issued as many visas as he could to the stateless horde who waited outside his office, who clung to the running board of the car that was taking him to the train, at a time in America when young men knew that courage might not be a personal choice, my brother came home from the hospital and Greta held him in her arms, her new responsibility, a thin baby, frail perhaps, a baby to kept away from drafts, a circumcised boy, with the same name as his father.

This was not the custom among Jewish families, who by tradition named their children only after the already dead, but was done now because this family, members of the Inwood Beach Club on Long Island, the Oakridge Country Club in Scarsdale, The City Athletic Club on 54th Street in New York City, determined to be American, new world, a part of things, not set apart as they had been before, modern as my mother's Camel's cigarette ashes continually in nervous flight around her. Greta placed the baby in the bassinet with the blue ribbons running round the sides.

Life—wheezing, excreting, sucking, urinating, blemished, eyes blinking, pulse in the scalp beating, sour smell of regurgitation, legs useless, too large head that hangs on a bony blue-veined body, dried brown fragment of a cord pressed against a belly button, a blood-red scratch from a fingernail on the cheek, eyes puffed and barely open: a miracle. Eugene Frederick Roth Jr. wrapped in a blue blanket slept while his older sister watched but was not allowed to touch for fear of germs and his nurse rocked the bassinet gently. Hope in defiance of the facts ran high as it always does at the beginning. The baby was called Johnny so he wouldn't be confused with his father.

There was no formal bris, there were no Hebrew prayers said. The circumcision was for reasons of health and because a Jewish boy could simply not be a Jewish boy with a foreskin. This was removed to remember Isaac bound on the altar, demonstrating the perfect faith of the father. Also, according to Freud, the offering of the piece of the baby's skin was a comment on the murderous impulses that yo-yo back and forth between father and son. The ritual of snipping the tiny penis was created to subdue and control, admit and deny the impulse to human sacrifice. Of course Freud was spinning his own tales and all we know in fact is that the baby boy loses his foreskin to honor the covenant with his God who once in time past demanded a cruel and excessive loyalty but did indeed substitute a ram at the last minute, or so it was said and said again, down through the generations by those whom this American generation would humor while passing on to other more pressing and certainly more scientific and urgent matters.

The toilet was not presented when the child showed signs of understanding the process of waste and its removal. There was no gentle forgiving of accidents or respect for independence wishes. Children were trained by shame and force and usually soon after their first birthdays. Disobedient children were wrapped up in their soiled sheets and left in their beds for hours. Disobedient children could be enclosed naked in a closet. You trained a child the way you trained a puppy. This was not cruelty. This was common practice, considered to be good for the child.

A stork, Greta told me, had brought my brother directly down from heaven. *Freud* after all, although he had evaded the Nazis in a last-minute manner that revealed that he might not have taken his own aggression theories as seriously as he ought, had not yet become as much of a household word as *Jack Benny* or *Dick Tracy* or the *Rockettes*. Children in America were not to be improved by truth; they were to be protected from it. There was an algae growth of shame, a murky brew of embarrassment over the entire matter of procreation. You did not look a child in the eye and speak of copulation. If a child's hand strayed down to a genital you slapped his face or shook her till she pleaded with you to stop. On the matter of the stork I had my doubts. I had seen many babies but not one stork except in a picture book. Even the baby Jesus was brought to his manger by a stork, Greta told me.

Euphemism made for mystery and mystery convinced most of us that pain and blood, grief and horror surrounded the body, leeched onto its surface, shadowing the more ordinary matters of the day. As if they were ghosts in a cemetery, the facts of life, the reality of the body grasped at us with fog fingers, waiting for the moment we would sink and become prey.

The summer sky over Lawrence, Long Island, was deep blue, the nearby ocean lapped at the sand near the cabanas of the beach club, the purple hydrangea that erupted in gardens August after August as if they, mere root and stem, eaters of sunlight, dwellers in the dirt, understood that time was both longitudinal and cyclical and history was made from variations on form, curved their petals upward. But God, who perhaps authors all things or all good things including the good things we don't understand are good because we are mere mortals, was there when my brother came home from the hospital or was not. If it is true that God is the creator, if Adam was the first man and Eve was made from Adam's rib then God was present at my brother's birth. If all that is mere fable, human inventions meant to keep away the evil eye about whose existence there really is no doubt, well then God was not present.

the family   In the fall we returned from Long Island to 1185 Park Avenue to a new larger apartment 8C, in the front of the building. Our mother's brother, Sy, also lived with his wife and two children at 1185 Park. They had the apartment 9D on the floor above and our mother's sister Libby lived ten blocks downtown at 944 Park Avenue and her sister Sylvia lived in an even larger apartment at 1095 Park.

My mother's source of support was the family shirt business, which had just survived a depression-era comeuppance, and was at the time of my brother's birth beginning to recover. Our father was the lawyer for the company. He was awarded that position when he married my mother.

The Van Heusen, Phillips Jones shirt business had begun as our mater-

1185 Park Avenue

nal grandfather with his father, our great grandfather, in dire need, rented a pushcart on the Lower East Side. My brother and I were the great grandchildren of a man named Moses Phillips who had studied in a yeshiva in a small town in Poland, come to America and worked as a sexton, a janitor in the house of worship, until with his more enterprising but never attending school ten-year-old son he began to sell shirts, to make shirts, to become a real American, or so my mother told me.

We have pictures of Moses Phillips dour and black hatted, a long shapeless black coat covering his body, a sad oval-faced man trying to stay erect while a great wind is blowing. The picture comes from the breaking of ground for the new Beth Israel Hospital downtown in the year 1912. The family was one of the major contributors to this hospital that promised kosher food for the sick and a place for doctors of Russian Jewish origins to admit their patients. A portrait of Moses's son Isaac hangs in the lobby today. They did not forget, this grandfather and great-grandfather of ours, that they belonged to the community, the endangered community. They knew that Cossacks on horseback had driven their people to flight, that laws had prevented them from owning land, living where they would, making and growing in the old country. They knew that even here in the new land they were despised for being themselves, that each moment was perilous and the only way to survive was with your people, to care for them as well as yourself. They did not behave like outlaws or criminals or free agents. They gave to the community, a place for the elderly, the Daughters of Sarah and Jacob in the upper reaches of Manhattan, a medical clinic for the poor.

But to give you have to succeed. Your balance sheets must read well, your employees must do their job, and you must make the right decisions season after season, to expand or contract, to save or to spend, to open a new factory or to fix up the old. The strain of the decisions broke hearts, damaged vessels, brought shoulders into a permanent shrug, made each day a potential disaster, meant you had to be bold or lose everything, you had to be right more often than wrong. It wasn't as easy as it seems to the generations that followed. More than one kind of Cossack can trample you underfoot. It was enterprise not poetry or music or scholarship that roiled in the family DNA.

We came from people who did not wait for time to improve their lot but made the crossing, suffered from dislocation, confusion, fear, lack of secular education, loss of what and who they knew, but still prospered, because

15

prosperity is what America offered even if you had to sell your soul and work on the Sabbath and eat strange foods with customers and your children didn't care or know about the law and all that mattered at the end of the day was the shirts that were left in the inventory and the shirts that were gone, and the sound of the hum of machines in the loft, the cutters closing and opening the blades of their scissors and the sewing treadles moving up and down.

Isaac had died early, suddenly. His two older daughters, Libby and Sylvia, had married well, one an owner of a bank, the other of a paper company that possessed a town in Vermont and acres of timber that stretched across New England, fingers of land reaching out, holding tightly to America. His two sons were in their early twenties and to them he left the business itself. To his wife and his younger daughter Blanche, just twelve, he left all the stock in the company. This is why she was considered an heiress in certain circles. That is why it was an act verging on scandal when she married a man without capital, whose good looks were the only fortune he brought to the wedding canopy.

This is a story of men and women, children who wanted for nothing, who because they were Jews in America survived like fish in a flood the events that carried into oblivion those who had delayed, who were a generation or two generations, a decade, a year, a month late in leaving. If in 1939 my brother had been born in Sulvalki Poland where his grandfather spent the years of his early childhood he would have died before his second birthday along with his sister and all other relatives within reach of the occupying German army. So in a sense he was lucky. But this reasoning is as full of pits as the moon because if he had been born a prince in the fourteenth century in Florence he might have died of the great plague and if he had been born in the Congo, son of a river boater, he might have been bitten by the tsetse fly and turned to dust and bacteria before he crawled. All possibilities are not genuine possibilities. We are what we are, like it or not.

3

a match the matchmaker wouldn't have
made   Due to financial good fortune I came to know my mother gradually, more slowly perhaps than most other children. Our time together was
limited and generally, especially in the earliest years, measured by a daily
quarter of an hour but my eye was always on her, watching, stalking perhaps. Can a child stalk its mother? If a kind of mental hovering, a note taking, a quiet waiting by a chair, by a phone, by a table, outside a closed door,
defines the word, then yes, a child can stalk.

Her favorite brand of cigarettes was Camels but if the pack had been finished, nothing left but the crumpled tin foil liner, she would smoke any
brand that was offered. Often there was a shred of a tobacco leaf stuck on
her lower lip and occasionally a blur of red lipstick on one of her teeth. She
carried white gloves with pearl buttons at the wrist with her everywhere although she was always leaving them in cabs and restaurants and the ladies'
room of The Plaza or The Pierre. In her satin pocketbook she carried a lace
handkerchief with her monogram on it. The handkerchief was usually
stained with powder and smelled of perfume, night cream, and Life Savers.
On her right arm was a bracelet of thick links from which a golden heart

dangled. At the center of the heart a small ruby, a mere blood drop, blinked like a fish eye in the sunlight. On her ring finger was a large square diamond, her engagement ring. She would never take it off. She had a wedding band too. A circle of tiny diamond chips. No matter how hard I begged she would not let me try it on.

Our mother, my brother's and mine, was a small woman, not five feet tall. This is significant because my father who was a little over six feet tall in all sincerity admired very tall women. He found long legs on a woman a particular delight. So why did he marry my mother who was the very opposite of his ideal?

In a more perfect world it would have been because he fell in love with her soul, with that fragile, insecure, curious, sharp, not quite regular, soul that caused her to pull the covers over her head at the sound of a police siren, at every screech of brake to imagine car crashes that mutilated loved ones, to refuse to enter automatic elevators that might go through the roof or plunge into the basement or light gas stoves that might explode or cross bridges that might at any moment fall on their splitting steel pilings. In a more perfect world he would have fallen in love with the way her lipstick smeared across her upper teeth, the way her glasses were always catching in the web of her veils, the way her mascara would run down her cheeks, the way her slightly too large nose with the not quite fortunate bump in the middle was always in need of powder, the way she dropped everything, the way cigarettes burned in ashtrays all around her like votive candles in a church and he would have liked the way she could do the *New York Times* crossword puzzles in fifteen minutes flat, even though she hadn't gone to college. He would have liked the way she devoured mysteries and romance novels. He would have liked the way the powder spilled from her compact and flecked her black pocketbook. He would have liked the smell of her perfume, depilatories, bubble bath, nail polish, beauty creams. He would have admired the way she won at mah-jongg, oklahoma, and canasta. He would have watched her play backgammon (always a Band-Aid over one of the long dark red nails that had broken) and seen that her mind could calculate odds in a flash, card-count with the best of the Las Vegas regulars.

In a more perfect world he would have married her because he wanted to take care of her, cherish her against the wear of time, count the spill of brown freckles on her pale skin, watch her plump thighs move under her lace-trimmed silk slip, but he truly preferred tall women and he married her because she was rich.

He was smooth and dark and trim. His features were perfect. "You should be a movie star," more than one girl had told him. He was straight of spine, washed and shaved, his black hair sleeked down with gel and parted sharply as if by surgeon's knife on the left side. There was something of Rudolph Valentino about him, something of the Riviera jewel thief. He had earned his way through college by working as a lifeguard at a hotel in the Catskills in the summer. Through the long summers women would brush against him, the girls would bring him ice cream. As he sat in his high chair above the pool the rays of the sun would stream toward him and he would stand and flex the muscles in his calves for those he knew were watching.

My mother, when she met him at a fraternity party when he was in his last year at Columbia Law School, feared he would never look at her, a man like that who could have any girl he desired.

His neatness, the olive tone of his skin, the small nose and the slightly hooded almost Tatar eyes, the well-made clothes pressed in perfect vertical creases, made him seem like a royal or a diplomat, one who was so power-ful he didn't need to smile or ingratiate himself with servants. Every night he hung his trousers carefully on a wooden valet. He placed his polished shoes beneath it. His wallet, his keys, his tie were placed just so, left to right, each time. He ate three prunes for breakfast each morning. He suf-fered from migraines. He loathed the greasy smell of Chinese food. He ex-ercised every day. He walked each morning to his downtown law office whose major client was his wife's family shirt business, muscles coiled and springing forward and coiled again. He moved down Park Avenue like a sleek panther pretending to ignore the antelope that might pass by on their way to the watering hole. At a time when virility was marked by conceal-ment, control of emotion, he was, without doubt, a man with a future.

Except sometimes his temper broke through and he would howl and rage. Where was his comb? Who had put his blue socks together with his gray? Sometimes he would grind his teeth and slam doors on his way out of the apartment. He came home very late, after hours at his club which did not allow women past the outer lobby except on Thursday nights, cook's night out, when they were permitted into the dining room. On weekends in the warm seasons my father went to his club in Scarsdale where he would play golf or tennis. He would be gone all day.

He had many political opinions. He read the papers carefully. He would pronounce and he would predict and he would argue loudly with anyone who disagreed with him. He did not debate, he simply called the other person a fool, an idiot, a dummy. He shouted. He suffered from an unabating righteous passion. Other people grew quiet when he began his speeches. He was a Democrat, a Roosevelt fan but he despised the weak just as if he were a Ford or a Mellon. If someone argued back he might punch them in the face. This happened at parties and at restaurants. My embarrassed mother would weep. My father would apologize because society demanded it but there was never any apology in his heart. In his sleep he ground his teeth or clenched them together so tightly that during the day his jaw ached.

My father was also a self-taught swimmer. He had learned in the East River in those hot city summers in the early part of the twentieth century when the boys ran under the Third Avenue El, hitching rides on the back bumpers of the trolley cars that rattled and sparked along the street. He and his friends threw stones at the horses that drew the carts bringing blocks of ice to the laundry-flagged tenements of the East Eighties in New York where the Jewish immigrants from Hungary had gathered, kind seeking kind, paprika in the stores and a language spoken that made them feel if not quite found at least less lost. There the latrines stank in summer and from May to September a child would sleep on a blanket on the fire escape, breathing whatever the air offered.

My father had been brought to these shores at age nine. His father had been a secretary to a mill owner in the low-lying mountains that belonged to Hungary, sometimes to Czechoslovakia and other times to Austria. My father's father had spoken German which marked him as an educated man. He was ambitious for his family and perhaps a dreamer, eventually a chronic gambler. He made sure that his wife and her sister dressed the children every day in starched white shirts, in jackets and small ties and their shoes were shining. They were not riffraff so he said, so he intended. They were not like the poor Jews of the town from which he had fled. He had a round face and a round body and a barrel chest but his wife was built like the Statue of Liberty, long of limb, hair piled high in braids, full breasts, and empty blue eyes. She was nine inches taller than her husband and proud of her height. It was the single asset that marked her out in a crowd. Her height was a comfort to her when nothing else was.

My father would never talk about his childhood. He spoke English only and that perfectly. He claimed he could not understand German. He said he knew no words of Hungarian. He claimed he had never in his life heard any Yiddish. He had erased everything. He was not sentimental about the old world. When pressed he said he couldn't remember the name of the town he had lived in or the nearest city. It was as if he had no childhood but had arrived at adulthood like a Golem, made from dust.

Not a few Jewish families changed their names so they wouldn't be turned down for jobs, schools, or a place to rest their heads while traveling. My father wasn't the only one seeking amnesia.

Their children were certainly not learning Yiddish at local Y's. If they had been despised in the old country for who they were here they could live disguised, without particulars. For the most part they wasted no time on nostalgia. If they went to a Yiddish show on Second Avenue it wasn't because they wanted to remember anything. It was because they wanted to understand the jokes. They were in a hurry to blend, to succeed, to put their feet on someone else's neck. They were forgetting and forgetting as fast as they could. There was no passion in those days for roots. There was in fact an anti-roots mania, and a common assumption among many that America was a land that cleansed of uncomplimentary specifics and would allow a tough boy like my father to become the scriptwriter, the director, the hero of his own movie, a presence without a communal past, without neighborhood, religion, clean of cultural baggage, rather like a wind-driven man riding a horse on the open plain, headed out with the big sky overhead.

So it was my mother who repeated this story which she heard from his sister, Bea, before she stopped inviting her to the house: when the boat landed in Manhattan and my grandfather, not yet thirty, and his wife and his wife's sister and his three children rode the El up Third Avenue, through the canyon of wooden and brick tenements packed with people and smells of all kinds and he looked carefully at the real America where the streets rushed and tumbled, the wheels screeched, whistles blew, he got off at the stop where he was expected at a cousin's apartment and walked his family to the other side of the train tracks and carrying all their worldly goods in suitcases closed by rope led them directly back on the El and returned to the pier. He wanted to go back to Europe, back to Hungary. Once there standing in the heat of a July morning, wearing their winter coats, his family waited outside the ship's office. The father's shoulders slumped and his skin turned gray. The mother's eyes filled with tears. The children were frightened but did not show it. It seemed that they could not go back. So once again they mounted the stairs to the El and in a sense arrived twice. There had not been enough money for the return fare.

What if a merciful stranger had lent it to him? Would that have been an act of kindness or cruelty?

Another story about my father's father. Shortly after arriving he walked the streets looking for an apartment to house his family. He wandered over to Fifth Avenue and saw a For Rent sign and he looked at the grand building and the doorman with gold braid on his jacket and he asked the rent. He was told $250 and he rejoiced. He was right to have come to America. He went back to his cousins and gathered the children and his wife and his wife's sister and walked with them carrying all the suitcases and bundles to Fifth Avenue. Then the doorman, pointing his finger at the greenhorn family, laughed and said, $250 a month. My grandfather had thought the rent had been for the entire year. "Ah," he said to the doorman in his heavily accented English, "it won't suit us after all."

Pride goeth before a fall so they say but pride also is a prod to success, a track to the future. Humiliation of course is a motive too. In the gutters of the streets, on the fire escape ladders, down in the latrines, along the window cracks, stuffed into mattresses, ironed into clothes, hidden in the mops and brooms, folded into the hair with pins, carried under the brims of hats was the ever present shame of those came off the boats, who knew they were not wanted, who knew they did not have the right manners, their accents were wrong, their poverty a stigma, their religion a mistake. For some boys, for some men and women this smack of shame—not to be top but to be bottom—cut to the quick, marked with a slice across the heart, caused grinding of teeth, a narrowing of arteries.

In the old country each man's place was ordained but here your position was your own responsibility. In my father this created an inner geography whose climate was never temperate but either boiled over with flaming lava covering everything in its path or else was transformed into a lock-jawed cold, a blue-white breath holding over an ice-cast tundra, one that permitted no entry, a self all sealed off, nontransversable. This was a climate that spawned pretenders, opportunists, princes without papers.

And so into the crowded tenements came Eugene Frederick Roth another aspirant, another climber, another boy who wanted up and out and onward and who quickly took to carrying a knife to school like the others. He had been called Fritz by his family. Where they had come from that was a good choice, it was the Hapsburgs and their mignons they had intended to please with such a name. But on the eve of the First World War, in the city of New York, Fritz was the enemy, and he had to fight each day, taunted on the winding school staircase. He stole a knife from a table in front of a store. He took the knife to school and cut the forehead of a boy who pushed against him in the yard. He called himself Gene. He no longer listened to his mother. He no longer listened to his aunt who would occasionally try to touch his check or pat his shoulder. He wanted no tenderness. He gave none. He had hooded eyes, snake eyes that gave away nothing, pupils growing small or large depending on the light but never changing, alligator eyes turning round in their sockets searching the reeds for movement.

His father, finally through a relative—everything in the immigrant world was arranged through the bloodlines, marriage lines (pity the orphan, the one who did not have a relative in need of a new employee)—became a salesman for a pharmaceutical company. He traveled to drugstores up and down the east coast. His English improved. His spirits improved. He began to bet on the horses and to play cards for high stakes. He lost as much as he made. Often his family waited for him to come home with the rent money only to have him deny, joke, and flee the apartment once again as soon as possible. His wife grew morose and refused to learn English. She relied for all matters of commerce on her sister, my father's Aunt Minnie, who was the one who signed report cards, talked to the landlord, read the English papers, and fixed supper. My father's mother was one of those who did not jump into the new world, abandoning herself to adventure, pioneering, learning, pushing. Instead she held herself aloof, shy, proud, and sealed off into an ever-hardening shell where the noise of the streets, the sound of the radio with the big bands, the call of the children who sat at her table became ever and ever more remote.

You'd think you might die early if you lived like that but in fact closeted as she was, still dreaming in her native language, afraid of America as she was, she lived into her late eighties, retired in Florida, still trusting only her sister, still in contempt of her daughter-in-law, my mother Blanche, who was, she said in Hungarian to her sister, a midget, a dwarf, hardly a woman at all. Or so my mother told me.

I have a photograph of my parents on their honeymoon in Venice. They are standing on St. Mark's steps with pigeons all around, one lighting near my mother's free hand, the other buried in her muff. They are a handsome couple bundled against the cold. But something in the stiffness of the pose, in the unsmiling gaze they cast at the camera warns us that all is not well. My mother stands before the Gothic arches as if she herself might take flight along with the beady-eyed birds hobbling about on thin crooked legs pecking at the crumbs at her feet. There is a gray cast, a spreading of shadows from the doors of the cathedral as if the stone gargoyles were not as inanimate as they appeared.

My mother told me that on her honeymoon my father would leave her at night and go for long walks along the boulevards of Paris or Rome or Venice, wherever they happened to be. He said he needed exercise. He said she walked too slowly to keep him company. He came back with the odors of perfume and sweat on his clothes. She looked at his perfect face, at his strong back, at the contained movements of his legs, at his shoes perfectly shined and there in the darkness of his narrow eyes, in the hard flat stretch of his body, her desire for him swelled and throbbed. She was afraid of his anger, the turn away of his head, but these also excited her, the faint glimpse of danger at the edge of the bed, the rawness of her ache for his hand on the small of her back, these were confusing but not unpleasant. She considered her bittersweet love a triumph over the more ordinary possibilities she had been offered.

But on the overnight train to Paris she cried because marriage had not transformed her as she had hoped. When she misplaced the first-class tickets for London he said she was clumsy and everyone laughed at her on the dance floor. He called her stupid for the first time when they were buying china on rue de Rivoli and she couldn't remember the exchange rate. He did not like her to wear her glasses but she couldn't see the paintings in the museums without them. She couldn't read the menu in restaurants. He was sick of going to churches. They both wanted to go home. They sailed for

New York from Le Havre with trunks full of linen and dresses purchased from the best houses in Europe but my mother understood on the return trip what had not been less clear as they set out. He would never forgive her for being short.

Whatever was she thinking? Perhaps because her father had begun in life with nothing but his boy's hand on the long arm of the pushcart, she wanted a man who also had nothing, who had the leanness of the hungry, the outsider looking in. Perhaps if her father had not died when she was still a girl she would have not have tried to find him in her mate. Perhaps she felt that this smooth unsmiling man with the Tatar folds at the corner of his eyes would carry her through life lifted high in the wake of his forward motion. Perhaps it was something more subtle than that, an attraction to harm, an itching of an old wound received in the bosom of family life.

Perhaps she accepted his hand in marriage because she wanted a man more beautiful than the receding-chinned, round-faced, sad-eyed, bulbous-bodied but wealthy men who had married her sisters. Perhaps it was simply a childish delight in the surface of things or was it an attempt at flight, at starting over in America without giving up any of the gains?

Sometimes what we call love is just a settling of old scores, or a seeking of forbidden pain, or a circuitous path to the kingdom of cruelty, or she may simply have confused lack of capital with heroism while searching for rescue without knowing from what.

Possibly she turned toward my father believing that she was no more than a paper doll who might be thrown away in a careless moment, torn or discarded at will. She must have believed that this man could fill in her disappearing lines, color her with his cold determination.

Is it really true that he married my mother just because he had been told she was an heiress? Yes and no. He would certainly not have married her if she were of more modest means. But he must have given himself other reasons. He must have said his vows with the common hope for contentment, affection, lifetime partnership, joy, and sexual contentment. He must have convinced himself that his free choice was a choice made out of love however we twist that word and employ it to disguise from ourselves other less seemly motives. Surely at first my mother must have made him feel special, chosen, respected, and held in awe. Her nervous, anxious, fearful need to please must have made his manhood seem more secure, healing deep wounds to his pride that he was unaware were bleeding him dry. Her gratitude for his attentions would in turn have created in him a simple pleasure in being so admired. This could be confused with love or at the very least create an alibi for other less acceptable calculations.

Was this marriage blessed? Could this couple spend the rest of their natural lives together? Did Cupid fall out of the sky laughing?

4

before doctor spock   The baby boy, my brother, and I were
tended round the clock by Greta and on Thursdays and every other Sunday,
her days off, a substitute governess was hired. Sometimes they had names
like Bridget or Mary, but more often they were named Helga or Ursula.
They pinched, they pulled, they shouted in accents, they mumbled in accents, they forgot our names. On the other hand we were neither kid-
napped nor mauled by lions. Many of the women who lived along Park
Avenue took care of their own children on the governess's day off. Our
mother did not. This was not because she was at her office or in her studio
but because she was afraid that her lack of experience might harm us. She
was anxious. She was afraid she might place the baby down the wrong way
in the crib and he would smother. She was afraid that he might be caught
in a draft and catch a cold that could become pneumonia and he would die.
She was afraid of skin rash, perhaps she wouldn't clean him correctly. She
was afraid she was not up to the task of caring for small children. If we cried
she was afraid she could not comfort us. She had not learned how to change
a diaper without risk of the pin stabbing the soft tissue of the hip. She was
afraid she might grow distracted and I would fall out the window or put a

finger in a socket. She was afraid I might not be dressed correctly for the weather.

She simply did not trust herself and so her children were brought in to visit her at the end of the day just before their nighttime bath for a visit that lasted fifteen minutes or so if the telephone did not ring or she did not need to get dressed herself for her evening out. This was the finest hour of the experts, the day of the right way and the wrong way to do things, and my mother, who walked this earth as if at any moment the ground would give way, thought it better to hire someone with good references, someone with real experience, backed by a licensed agency, trained in child care, a professional rather than an amateur.

It is also true that the arrival at seven in the morning (just as Greta would leave to spend her day off with her sister in the Bronx) of the substitute nanny allowed my mother to sleep as usual until well after ten. It permitted her to maintain her daily routine, take her long bath, and have breakfast in bed brought in by the maid on a special tray with a fresh rose in a small vase to the right of the napkin. Don't think she was lazy. Don't think she was disinterested in her children. She was neither. She was merely out of joint with herself. It was a chronic condition. She was timid where it would have been better to be brave. The apartment was furnished by the decorator of the moment, the one her sister used, a decorator fond of art deco vases placed on eighteenth century French gold-leaf cabinets. Sometimes with friends our mother and father dined out at one of New York's restaurants like the Little Club, the Stork Club, the 21, or the Oak Room at the Plaza. Every night we ate dinner with Greta served by the maid on a tray in my brother's bedroom.

Our mother was afraid if she bought a dress it was the wrong color, the wrong style. She would take it back and buy another. She knew with a terrible certainty that she was too pale, too spotted, too small, eyelids swollen from tears, eyebrows painted on crooked. She was quite sure that she herself was unqualified for whatever might be expected. On her bed she spread out her cards and played solitaire in the evening while waiting for her husband to come home from his club where he lingered after work for a squash game, a massage, a sauna. Sometimes her brother visited. Her scotch glass sat on the French provincial night table with a gold-leaf border beside the china shepherdess and her two china goats. The cards were slapped down, then moved as fast as an eye could blink. She was very good with cards. This was the only thing she did with professional confidence.

She did not bake birthday cakes. She did not put away the silver or fold the napkins. She did not polish or sweep or hold the head of a vomiting child. She did not cut the stems off the spinach leaves or scrub at the stain in the pot. She did not search for the teething ring that had fallen under the couch or pour the medicine from the dropper into the infected ear, or place the hairbrush back on its shelf. If you don't have at least that, the building of the fire, the gathering of the plants, the plucking of the feathers, then your bad dreams can haunt you all day long and you may become exhausted by all the vapors and uncomfortable thoughts and dissatisfactions that unchecked float like pollens in the air.

My mother never endured the spine-stiffening discipline of have to and ought to. From the time she woke and rang the bell by her bed signaling the maid to bring breakfast past the five o'clock cocktail hour, past the time for dressing for dinner, going to theater, until she again fell asleep pulling the soft quilt over her body, she felt anxious and fearful. She thought perhaps she was invisible because she could see no trace of herself in the world around.

So it was that my brother lay in his bassinet tended by Greta, closely observed from the door's threshold where she had been told to stay by his older sister who was not allowed to enter the room or to hold him for fear of germ contamination, even though she had washed her hands, holding them under the running water till the skin wrinkled on her small fingers, the same fingers Greta pointed out she all too often stuck in her mouth.

Greta sleeps in my room. She has promised me that she will always sleep in my room. She will take care of the baby and get up in the middle of the night to feed him but she will always sleep with me. Her bed is over by the window. At night if I wake I can see her form under the blankets. It is a large room with a window on Park Avenue. There are drapes. One panel of the drapes looks like a giant's arm dangling down. It is not a giant I am almost certain. The baby sleeps in his own room. There is a connecting bathroom. There is or is not something dangerous in the closet. I prefer the closet door shut. I will no longer play with dolls, they sit on my shelf untouched. Dolls are for girls. I do not plan on being a girl forever. Also I am not altogether fond of babies. I am also not fond of storks. I wake one morning while the sky is bleached pale and the soon-to-rise sun hovers timidly behind the Ruppert Breweries over on Second Avenue. It is light enough for me to tell that the giant's arm is only a drape and I know that a drape cannot reach out and imprison me in a giant palm crushing my small bones. The elevator man sleeps slumped over on the cab's bench. The night doorman is still on duty, his name is likely Paddy or Kevin. He forces himself to stay awake eager now for his replacement to arrive. Why did the Irish start life in America as doormen and the Jews start as pedlars and the Chinese as waiters?

I look over at Greta's bed. It is still made, smoothed bedspread over the pillow, just as it had been the night before when I went to sleep. How is this possible? I cannot understand it. Then I hear water running in the bathroom. I am sly. I am cunning. I lie down on my side with my eyes partially closed and wait. Greta enters the room. She is not dressed in her bathrobe. She has on her uniform. She walks over to her bed and pulls back the spread and pounds the pillow with her hand and pulls back the sheets. Now the bed looks as if it had been slept in. I close my eyes. What is this, have I been alone all through the night? I hear the baby cry. I hear Greta take the baby into the kitchen where the cook who lives in one of the small rooms with bare light bulbs on a green wall behind the pantry will be padding about in her slippers. I go into my brother's room. There where I thought there was only a couch, I see a bed, unmade. I see Greta's bathrobe at the foot of the bed.

She spent the night with him and not me: a betrayal I remember for more than half a century. I learned that the night is negotiable alone. I learned that it is better not to trust in others to protect you from darkness. The night my first husband left a party with another woman I dreamed of Greta and the unslept-in bed. Generously, without a word, I conceded Greta to my brother. I no longer wanted her.

We go to Central Park. German governesses believe in fresh air. If it is cold, if the wind roars, if cheeks turn red and fingers freeze in mittens so much the better. Each day the baby is bundled in the large shining black carriage and I am wrapped in leather leggings, several sweaters, a tweed coat with a black velvet collar from London, hat with earmuffs and we set off for the park. Once there Greta will sit on a bench with other governesses. They will talk German. There are Irish accents in the kitchen, there is a laundress named Willow whose skin is smooth as cocoa who comes from Alabama, there is a Polish shoemaker on Lexington Avenue, there is an Italian tailor who comes to the house to shorten our mother's dresses but German is the sound of women talking of home, uncles, aunts, news. German is the language in which they discuss our bad habits, our failures to eat everything on our plate.

In the warm weather I am dressed in a freshly ironed frock with embroidered smocking crisscrossing my chest. My white socks are folded perfectly at the ankle bone and match the dress in color and design. I am not permitted to get down from the park bench and play in the sandbox. I am not allowed to sit down on the grass or sit on the swing until Greta has wiped it with a towel. Greta washes my clothes and irons them with pleats and starch. She brings a bag with a damp towel to the park so she can wipe my hands if I touch something dirty. The other children too are told to sit and keep their hands in their laps. We are beautiful with satin bows or barrettes in our carefully washed hair. There are red Scotties and blue deer embroidered on our sweaters and pearl buttons down our backs. The boys wear knickers and striped play shirts. They are allowed to bounce balls but not to chase them under the benches or up on the grass. We stare at each other and listen as the almost-understood German floats above our heads. We are the scrubbed legion of the governess-tended.

I am bored. I walk away. Will they miss me? I walk on the cement around the ring of benches. I pass a dog. I want to pet the dog but I am not allowed. Dogs are dirty. I walk. Suddenly I look up. I am lost. Where is Greta? I do not see her. I know what to do. I will not be frightened. I find a little boy about my age. He is wearing a sailor suit and holds a large red ball. "I am lost," I say. I put out my hand. "Can you help me find Greta?" He takes me to his governess who brings me to mine, in fact I was only a few benches away from her all the time. The grownups tell this story to me again and again. "How sweet, how like a little girl." My mother loves this story. I hear her tell her sister. I hear her tell the cook. How did I know that if you are lost you should ask a boy to help you find your way? This is not knowledge one is born with. But this is 1940 and I was nobody's fool.

Sometimes when he has come home before I am asleep my father enters my room. I am always bathed and in my pajamas, my hair brushed one last time. There he is strong and tall, looking at me. He brings me lawyers' legal paper, long yellow sheets. He brings me a pencil with his name on it, Eugene Frederick Roth, Esquire. I hide it under my pillow. I begin to talk, to hold him there. I tell him the name of my stuffed animals, the numbers of times I have caught a ball. The progress I am making on my skates. I stroke his hand. I lean my head against his shoulder. All too quickly he is through with the visit. I feel his eyes leaving me, looking for the door. He promises another visit, the night after or the one after that. I kiss him on the nose, I pet his perfect hair. I look deep into his eyes. I don't see my reflection but I am sure it is there, somewhere. My love for him rattles like a wild animal in the cage of my chest. After he leaves his presence, a weight, a smell, the indented place where he sat on the end of my bed, remains. I begin to long for him to return. I lie down on the carpet with my slippers on. Greta does not allow bare feet even in the bedroom, even on the soft carpet. I think about how it was when he was in the room. I repeat all the words he said to me. I look at the yellow sheets of legal paper. I hold the pencil in my hand.

This visit: a sudden glimpse of bird wing after a long afternoon of rain, it is a father. It is my father. He bends his face close to mine. When the Sun King appears he leaves in his wake adoration, earned or unearned.

Later when my brother is a boy not a baby and I am a girl not a little child I stand by the door of my brother's room. He is in bed, the steam kettle is whistling on a stool by his side. A tent has been improvised with a sheet placed over the bedposts. From the doorway I can hear his wheezing. The deep breaths, the scratching sound of air not reaching far enough. I can see his pale face. I can see his hand holding on to the bed cover. His lips are slightly blue. Again. Greta is by his side. She is sweating from the steam. I see the drops on her forehead. She has a washcloth in hand. She is putting water on my brother's face. He doesn't want her to do that. She does it anyway. He cannot speak. He breathes but not easily. I can see his small chest heaving under his train pajamas. I watch it move in and out and listen to the sound of the air pulled into the passages, blocked, returning outward through his mouth. His fever rises. I overhear Greta tell the cook. The doctor is coming. Again.

Our mother has gone out. She is afraid of illness. She leaves the boy to the care of Greta who knows what to do.

I had walked her to the door. She was wearing a black suit with gold buttons, a hat with rhinestone sequins in the veil. She was wearing Cuban heels that tapped with each step on the marble floor. I breathe in and out.

How easy it is for me. I never cough. I never choke. I don't have lungs that suddenly close their passages. I am robust, round even. My legs are sturdy. His are frail. I wait for Dr. Schloss patiently. I know from experience he will be here. I know that he is the only Jewish pediatrician on the hospital staff of New York Hospital. This is because he is brilliant as well as extremely tall. We are very lucky that he is our doctor because he is a famous doctor. The doctor has no antibiotics to give. They exist. They have been discovered but they are not yet in public distribution. What little there is has been garnered for the soldiers away at war. The doctor enters the apartment, the maid takes his coat. Greta whispers in his ear. Is my brother afraid he will die during an asthma attack? I never ask him. The sheet tent over his bed makes him look like an Arab child in the desert. I wonder if he would be allergic if we lived in the desert. On a shelf in his room sits his medicine, blue bottles, green bottles, an eye dropper, an anal thermometer, an enema bag. I lie on my mother's bed and breathe in and out until the maid comes and chases me back to my room.

My brother is often sick. He has allergies and gets rashes that drive him crazy with a need to itch. He gets impetigo and sores that don't heal. He is covered with creams that smell of sulfur. "You stink like a rotten egg," I tell him. He turns his head away from me. Worst of all he gets asthma from dust so the curtains are removed in his room and mine. He gets asthma from fibers in the rugs so the rugs are removed. He gets asthma from the outdoors so when the fruit trees in the park blossom we stay indoors. He is allergic to sweets like chocolate and fruits like strawberries. He sneezes and wheezes from pitch pollen and from pine needles, from goldenrod and roses. The list of his allergies grows and grows. If I have a cold I am banished to my room so I won't give it to him. He gets it anyway and he begins to run a fever, to gasp for breath. The shades are drawn so the light won't bother his eyes.

Under the sheet draped over the bed's four posters, beside the steam kettle humming on a small stool by his side, he sits bolt upright pulling with all his might to get air into his lungs. His mother is out playing cards. His father will never come into the room. The maid who has brought him toast and tea has placed the small tray on a bureau behind his bed. Greta sits on a couch on the other side of the room. She is waiting for the time to give him his medicine, the red syrup for his chest, the small pills for his headache. The radio brings news of soldiers advancing and retreating, of crops burning and crosses in a field, many crosses in the fields far away. Was my brother seeing in his mind's eye each cramp of his bronchi, each vessel in a tight spasm, withholding oxygen, refusing to release carbon monoxide, did he notice that the white skin on his hands seemed almost translucent? Was he thinking that he might not have a life, not a long life, not a life in which a woman would open the door and come to his bed and stroke his head and play a game or bring him a book or a record? Was he thinking that he had been left alone except for Greta under his canopy and abandoned to the indifferent march of germ and decay?

I know that for me the rooms of our apartment seemed barren, empty of the basic necessities. I waited for my mother. He waited for no one. What could that have been like under the tent where the steam made the air thick and heavy and the fog covered the pattern on the sheets and small chest that was his heaved in and out without pause, like the mechanical pumps on a respirator, like the steel corkscrew on a digging well grinding, down and ever down? Where was the person who should have been holding him in her arms, who should have been wiping his forehead, where was the force that would bring him back his breath, release the pressure that hugged his breastbone? I was not allowed close. I might bring him more germs. I waved from the doorway. Alone in my room I could hear the steam kettle whistling. In the bathroom waiting for the laundress was a pile of his sheets drenched with perspiration, smelling of medicine. No man is an island says the poem. But poetry lies, even good poetry.

5

maine: the home front   My mother, my brother, Greta, and I go to Maine for the summer, the war has started, our father is in Washington, D.C., working for the Justice Department prosecuting people who send anti-American propaganda through the mails. He brings home a pamphlet that says the Jews are killing American boys overseas. The print is red, the color of blood. I find it on the satin couch in the hall on top of his brown briefcase with his name embossed in gold on the flap. He is going to put the people who wrote the pamphlet in jail. My father wanted to be in the army, in the navy, he wanted to be a hero but he is too old. He wanted to kill a German. He wanted to see their guts fall out of their stomachs, their skulls split open, their slimy brains spill on the ground. He said that often. Did Greta hear him?

We are at a family camp called Songowood. It has bungalows and a communal dining room. The governesses eat with the children at the first setting. Later the grownups, mostly women whose men commute to the camp for a long weekend once or twice a summer, have their own meal. We have hayrides and play hide and seek around the bungalows. At dinner each night we sing a song, "Oh Songowood Oh Songowood, we sing aling aling

35

and ding aling aling to you." Then we rattle the silverware as loudly as possible.

I love Songowood. Here the German nannies allow us to play out of their sight. We are soldiers in the war. I am a nurse and I bandage everyone with leaves. We pick blueberries, we sing songs by a campfire. Greta, sitting in a chair at the lake front, knits a blanket for Johnny. There is a huge pile in the closet of sweaters and mittens and hats that Greta has knitted for her family back home. It is wartime, packages are not getting through. Letters are not getting through. We are cut off from the farm in Bavaria. Greta says that they are suffering in Bavaria because all the butter and eggs are going to the soldiers at the front.

In Maine in August in the dark, under the stars the northern lights can be seen. I see them out my cabin window shooting up into the sky. I think my father is wrong. There must be a God. One night when my brother wakes me with his crying I try to lift him up to the window so he can see the stars. He calls for Greta who is in the bungalow's kitchen making him warm milk. She doesn't want him to leave his bed. A draft may blow on him from the leaky windows, which will bring on his asthma. I am sent back to my bed.

My brother screams when he is bathed. He has a strange rash from the water. Greta covers the rash with gentian violet; this is a purple liquid that stains his skin. He stays close to the cabin. He sits and pokes at bugs. Most often his eyes are swollen shut from an allergy. He holds his body rigid if I come close to him. He screams if I sit on the bed with him. I try to tell him a story. He bangs on his toy so he will not hear me. At night he wakes with nightmares, sobbing and sobbing.

My father is making his summer visit. I want him to see me swim. I show him I can float on my back. I can put my head under the water and blow bubbles. He is pleased. Then he takes me out to the edge of the dock. "Jump," he says. "I will catch you." The water is over my head. I am afraid. I see the dark water but cannot see the bottom. He calls to me, "Jump." I want him to catch me in his arms. I want him to know that I am not afraid, that I will always do what he tells me, that even if I drown I will try for him. I smile at him but I hesitate. "Hurry up," he calls. I can feel my legs trembling. I jump. He catches me. But as I rise from the water vomit appears in my throat and some falls, like a stain into the water. I am ashamed. But he doesn't notice. He holds me close to his chest. I can see the damp black hairs on either side of his nipples. I put my arms around his neck. I wrap my legs around his waist. I am not like my mother who sits on a chair in the shade. I am close to him, my heart beating next to his heart. There is no love like the first love. Everything after is a mere ripple, wider than the initial act, but ever lessening in intensity.

Someone has told me that when you have asthma you feel as if you are drowning. I hold my head underwater as long as I can. Is that what happens when my brother's lungs are cramped and the air passages closed? I dream of the steam kettle and its whistle. Maine is cold in the early morning but warm at noon. There is a bird's nest in the beams that support the back roof of our cabin. Standing on a chair I can see three small blue eggs. I bring my friends Davy and Michael to look at the eggs and Davy picks one up and dashes it against the wooden side of the building. I see the yolk against the wall, the broken shell lying in the dirt, the pieces of blue shell look like torn paper. Davy Litwin loves me. This I know. But I do not know why he took the egg in his hand and with a smile on his face threw it as hard as he could the way one might a pebble, a twig, a marble.

No mother will settle her wings over this small bird, no worms will find their way down its upturned beak, no blue sky will invite it upward, no sound of wind in the leaves will enter its ear. It will not need shelter against the storm. It will not see pink dawn or corn in the field, or snow on the ground. It will build no nest of its own. Now I understand about war. I will not play that game again. I refuse to speak to Davy. I refuse to forgive him. I am implacable. "You are a bad girl to be so angry at a boy who has said he was sorry, who grieves because you will not play with him," so my mother said when Davy's mother complained to her. Nevertheless I turned my head away as Davy approached. I got up from a table if he sat down. His governess talked to Greta who made me pretend to like him again.

Childhood sorrows are of course all out of proportion, but a half-century later when Songowood has long closed down and its property now likely used by a gaggle of Buddhists as a summer retreat and parents now take trips with their young children without nannies along, and in Maine only ghosts are playing mah-jongg while inhaling through long black cigarette holders while their feet with painted toenails and Cuban heels push down into the dust through the slow summer afternoons of adult camp, still I can see clearly from that war summer when my father was mostly away in Washington: a blueberry pancake breakfast, a rowboat ride with Greta at the oars and again the three blue eggs in a matted irregular nest on the supported beam of the back porch within a child's reach and the two remaining eggs in the tilted nest and the thick yellow stains oozing down the wall. I still remember a bird's egg with its blue shell sitting in the boy's hand the instant before he threw it.

Blue is the color for boys. Is it possible that it was my own vile wish to smash the baby brother egg that so galvanized my sense of right and wrong in the summer of 1942? Did I protest too much? Or is it true that little girls are sugar and spice and little boys take aim and fire? Oh little moralist that I was, oh self-righteous defender of the weak: in such a season of killing what was so terrible in Davy's egg toss? One bird more or less would not have made the slightest dent in history's back. Also every morning in the main dining room I sat at a table with Greta and ate my scrambled egg without protest. Hypocrite child.

The rain pounds on the cabin roof. My mother has been out at the main house playing cards. She comes in. Her dress is wet. I see her from my bed. She puts on her nightgown and sits on the chair. Her dress on the floor oozes and a dark puddle forms at its edges. She turns the radio on softly so she won't wake us. "Mares eat oats and does eat oats, and little lambs eat ivy," a jingle has swept the country and plays from every jukebox from coast to coast while the boys are standing, row after row of them, in troop ships and far from the nurseries of their childhood, bracing for the landing at Normandy. Greta too is asleep in the room with Johnny. My mother takes out a cigarette and lights it up. She looks for the ashtray. Now she is wearing pink slippers with feathered pom-poms over the toes.

Suddenly there is a flash of lightning and a clap of thunder follows. It is not loud, like the sounds of cannons in a distant battle. But the light by the bedstand flickers and goes off. The lights always go off at Songowood when there is a storm. But my mother rushes to her bed and pulls the cover over her body. She picks up a flashlight and turning it on sees me on the threshold and motions for me to join her in bed. I feel her warm body under the silk of her nightgown. I feel her holding me in her arms and I feel her arms shaking and her legs trembling. "It's only a storm," she says to me. But with the next slam of the clouds I see tears in her eyes and the mascara on her face begins to run down her cheeks. "Don't worry," I say to her, "it's just a thunderstorm and it will be over soon." She kisses me and there is a lipstick mark on my face. She tries to rub it off with her hand. There is a flash of lightning that makes the whole room glisten in an unholy dead light for a second and then a terrible banging that seems to be coming closer. My mother holds me so tightly that her long nails cut into my shoulder. I pat her on the arm. The radio is now all static. The flashlight is under the covers with us. My mother says, "Count, count with me, after the lightning we count till we hear the thunder, that will tell us how many miles away the storm is and if it is going in another direction or coming closer to us." We count the seconds between flash and clap and we know that the storm is near us and getting nearer still. "What if it hits the cabin, what if we burn in the lightning?" my mother asks me. Now my mother is crying. "It's all right," I say. I have never heard of anyone at Camp Songowood burning up in their cabin. I feel certain that if this were a real danger I would have heard about it. Greta is up now. My brother cries. My mother holds me tight. She smells of powder and perfume and sweat. "Oh God, oh God," she keeps saying. She lights another cigarette although there is one still burning in the ashtray. I put the first cigarette out.

Finally the numbers reverse themselves. The storm is receding. My mother closes her eyes and falls asleep. I keep patting her shoulder for a while, listening to the sound of rain on the roof and against the window-pane, a soothing sound, then a new wind in the pine needles adds a whis-tle, out there in the dark in the Maine woods there are rivulets and streams and brown mud and I am not afraid.

This is my memory, but perhaps I was also afraid but did not want to ad-mit it, not then not now. How could a child not be afraid if a mother is trem-bling so? But the fact is that all my life I have loved storms, loud nasty summer storms that crash in the heavens and make the lights go out. Each time one begins I feel a pounding in my chest accompanied by excitement, eruptions of joy, as if I were in the first blush of love, something enormous happening to the soul.

Maine is not good for children with asthma; we go back to the city on the long overnight train. In the corridor outside our compartment soldiers and sailors lean out open windows. Greta will not let me talk to them. My mother stays on at Camp Songowood for another month until the heat is gone from New York, until the new fall clothes are in the stores.

the park: the home front (cont.)   We eat our dinner on trays in my brother's room. We have our baths together, scrubbed in every private part by Greta or her substitute. We are allowed into our mother's bedroom in the early evening if she is home. My brother often chooses not to go. He plays games by himself. He and Greta are reading a book. He and Greta are doing a puzzle. Greta kept careful charts on his bowel movements, urinary flow, wheezing times. His ribs showed. I could count them in the bath. His legs were like those of a sparrow. He collected postage stamps and pasted them in a book. I played jacks on the closet floor. I learned how to toss a tennis ball up to the ceiling, not so far that it would hit and leave a telltale mark, but just below, just right.

He is bored by my mother's bedroom. I am interested in every bottle of perfume, every piece of jewelry. I am interested in all her phone conversations. I sit quietly so she won't send me out of the room. I am a girl and he is a boy. Also I am certain that our mother is the center of the house. He is certain that Greta is the center of the house. His center takes us to school, to birthday parties, to buy shoes, to have a haircut, to a friend's house, to the doctor. My center is available only for a brief while before bathtime, before dinnertime. My center steams and storms, weeps on frequent occasions, drinks straight scotch with one ice cube before dinner, wants to be admired, wants to be loved, but is not, not yet. His center is calm, clean, seems to need nothing for herself, except order, except routine, except more yarn to knit our mittens, to complete the sweater she is making for my brother.

I am in the darkened hall outside my parents' bedroom. In the hall is the china closet. From top to bottom it is filled with blue and red dishes covered with flowers and vines. The dishes come from the grandmother, my mother's mother who died of bone cancer several months before my birth. My mother tells me that my grandmother went to the hospital and the doctors tried a new treatment to save her. They used radiation and the rays from the machine instead of burning out the cancer set fire to her bones so that they smouldered on and on until her death. She burned up from the inside out.

In the last months of my grandmother's life, my mother went to a healer who had a suite in the Plaza Hotel and my mother gave the healer all her jewelry in return for a formula to make a tea that would cure her mother. It didn't work. But, said my mother, perhaps I misunderstood and wrote down the wrong ingredients. The healer was a woman from Budapest who wore a long black velvet gown. She had pulled the curtains closed and held in her hands a silk handkerchief that had belonged to my grandmother so she could design the curative drink. There was a picture of my grandmother in a jade frame on my mother's bureau and every year my mother put a candle in a glass in front of the picture and the candle burned until, like my grandmother, it burned out. I am named Anne after my grandmother who died a few months before my birth. In the hall is also the linen closet filled with lace and silk, with embroidered pillowslips and monogrammed towels. In the hall it is dark and quiet. I sit with my legs curled under me. I lean carefully back. I don't want to make the wall dirty. I lie flat on my stomach so I can see through the crack at the bottom of the door. I can see the light white curtains lifting and swaying with a breeze. I can see the legs of my mother's black desk. I cannot see her sleeping on the bed. When she wakes, she will ring for the maid who will bring her breakfast on a tray and then I will enter the room.

The substitute governess has not arrived, has disappointed. Their voices are loud. My mother says, "You must take them to the park. A father must show interest in his children." My father says, "I have a game, a game at the club. I can't take them to the park. I won't take them." My mother cries. I hear the sound of her sobs. My father screams, "You're always at me, you always want me to do something for you. Take them yourself. That's what mothers do." "I can't," she says, "I have a lunch. I promised." We hear more. Much more. It is not pretty. At last my father throws open the door. The cook puts on our hats and coats and we go to the park with my father. He does not talk to us. He pulls us along. My brother does not smile. He will not look up. I tell my father how much I like his hat. I tell my father that I want to go climbing with him on the rocks. My father likes to walk fast and to leap from perch to perch. I know he likes it that I am brave. I know he doesn't like it that my brother is timid. I have a photograph of us in the park right by the entrance to the reservoir at 92nd Street. By my side is a shaggy blond pony. My brother wears a cap with earflaps tied under his chin. He looks out at the camera bitterly, his lower lip pulled in. His dark eyes flash. He is not amused. I am smiling at the camera. I pick up the ends of my coat and curtsy as I've been taught. I tilt my head to one side. I am Shirley Temple. I hope. My father was not the photographer. The owner of the pony has charged for the photo. It is proof my father says to me, proof in a court of law, that he spends time with his children.

We climb on the rocks in the park. I leap like a goat after my long-legged tennis-playing father. I will not look down. I will not hesitate to go where he tells me. When I reach the highest rock I can see the buildings on both the west and east sides of the park. The glass windows shine like so many approving eyes. The trees are beginning to bud, new leaves curl outwards. The cherry blossoms float in a pink haze behind the museum. I am at the center of the city. Below me the governesses and their black carriages line the walks, the carousel is invisible farther downtown but I think I hear the music playing. My legs are shaking and I cannot keep them still. If my father sees this he will think I am afraid. But my father is not looking at me. He is staring out over the meadow that lies just below the fake castle his mouth in a tight line. What he is thinking he does not say. I lean against his soft blue vicuna coat my cheek against the pocket. My brother refuses to climb. He sits far away at the base of the rocks and waits. He does not like risk. He sees no point in behaving like a goat. Like my mother he mistrusts the stability of the physical world. He is bored by balls tossed and retrieved. He is uninterested in racquets or hoops. Whatever he would like to do with his father this Sunday afternoon he does not say. He is not asked. I am brave like a boy. He is fearful like a girl. This is the victory of my life.

I am pink with triumph. He is pale with boredom. My father tries to goad him into climbing and he shouts down to his son, urging him to come up. My brother turns his head away. He says he wants to go home. He says he doesn't feel well. Perhaps he has a fever. Our father is willing if not eager to take us home. As we cross Fifth Avenue on the way back from the park my father stops at a phone booth. We wait outside the closed glass door. My father puts nickel after nickel into the phone. We cannot hear what he is saying. I put my ear to the crack in the door. He is asking someone named

Dolores to lend him some money. From inside the booth comes a slam as my father hits the glass near my ear. I move away. When he is finished he grabs our hands and pulls us along. Now he is in a great hurry because he has someplace to go. Our afternoon in the park is over.

I knew what was wrong. I knew Cinderella and Sleeping Beauty. I knew Snow White and the Seven Dwarfs. Of course I didn't know Henry James and I wasn't yet a fan of Dorothy Parker but I knew because I heard my mother on the telephone talking to her sister, because it was clear from the way my mother rattled the ice cubes in her scotch glass that Blanche Roth would have liked to have been kissed on the lips when her husband came home late for dinner as usual and Gene Roth would like not to have come home at all and this was the problem that seemed to provoke certain allergies in my brother and created in my mind a long-lasting confusion between the war in Europe and the war at home.

bravery: the home front (cont.)   For a long time his passion was his electric Lionel train that ran around the floor of his room with signal lights, a station house with a little man that jumped out as the train approached and waved a miniature lantern. There were little houses that stood on tiny fake grass hills and a white church with a high steeple by a river over which a lattice-work bridge carried the train tracks toward the next town. The train followed the loops and figure eights of the tracks through a tunnel that went under a mountain on which a herd of sheep grazed. There was a black engine, a red caboose, and a yellow car that carried logs from the northern timber country. There was a coal car with little pieces of black stone in a bin. There was a blue milk car that held tiny bottles of milk in little orange crates. There was a school house with a real bell on its roof. The train went round and around as the tracks looped back and forth across the floor. My brother would sit there on the side with the box of controls in his hand and make the train go backward and forward, the whistle blow, the horn sound, the red and white gates to block traffic went down or up as he decided. He would not let me run his train. When I approached he screamed, he spit. He was smaller than I but determined. I could not, not ever touch his trains. Except in my dreams where I was the engineer of the Topeka, the Washington and the Santa Fe and I roamed across the country, past cornfields and granaries, and through the stockyards of Chicago, through the high Rockies all the way to San Francisco.

Sometimes my brother was very brave. Braver than me. When he was around six and I was around nine one Sunday night while the Allies were advancing, each day a few miles closer to Berlin, we had air raid drills just in case the fortunes of war reversed and we pulled down our shades and turned off our lights so the enemy would not see us. We would go into our hall and wait for an all-clear signal. Walter Winchell was on the radio.

Our radio is in the living room. It is a large shining polished maple wood arched box, arched like a church window with big knobs and a wire mesh screen cut in the center. My mother is listening. "Good Evening Mr. and Mrs. North America and all the ships at sea." We are in our beds in our rooms. Above my bed there is a shelf on which I keep my collection of tiny glass and china animals. Little ceramic dogs with curly tails, an elephant with a glass trunk, a four-inch porcelain tiger with pink painted stripes. Everything that could bite or trample, rip or claw was reduced in size, held in my palm transparent, my treasures. Each birthday a new piece would be added. Now I have a glass carousel with a little glass flag flying from the top. I have a gold charm bracelet I keep on the shelf. Along the chain is a drum, a baby carriage, a small piano, a tiny gold slipper, a little gold flower in a little gold pot.

In my bed I wait for sleep like the beggars crouched by the gates of Jerusalem asking passersby for alms. Above all else I want to put my thumb in my mouth where according to me thumbs belong and according to Greta thumbs do not, that a child who persists, who sucks in secret when the lights were out, a child whose habit survives metal gloves and foul-tasting ointments applied to the fingers could be plucked by the devil and made to eat hot coals till her mouth is no more than a pus-filled blister. I wait for sleep like a foundling placed in the empty basket in the creche in the courtyard at the Catholic orphanage on Madison Avenue. Inside the creche is a bell and poor sinful mothers can ring the bell and run away and the nuns wait a discrete time and then rescue the baby.

From my real bed on real Park Avenue I hear a loud signal, a klaxon alarm. My brother and I come out of our beds and into the hall. The cook and the maid and Greta join us. My father tells my mother to turn off the radio. My mother says that the radio cannot be heard by the enemy planes and anyway it's only a practice drill. She says she wants to listen to the program. My father says something in a voice that is not raised but is not friendly. Greta and the cook go back into the kitchen. They sit in the kitchen in the dark. My mother complains, "You are always telling me what to do." He says, "You are an idiot." She says, "I am not." He says, "You and your entire family have the brains of one pigeon." She begins to cry. He shouts at her. She sobs and says, "You don't know anything about air raids because you aren't in the army." This I know is a very bad thing for her to say. It isn't true. He isn't a coward. It isn't his fault they wouldn't have him because he is too old. Now he has to pay her back. I know that. Why hasn't she been more careful? He shouts again. I am frozen in place. I feel the familiar cramping in my stomach that these fights always bring. I try to think of something to say, something that will interrupt, turn attention, create a new direction for their words to fly. I consider vomiting on the floor but that's harder to do than you might think. My father's arms are coiled and his legs are stiff. His face is cold and his lips are pressed together. The sounds from his throat are alternately loud and grating or low and hissing. My mother's hair is becoming disarranged. My father is clean and cool. His shirt is sparkling white. His blue tie is held to his chest with a gold clip.

"Your legs are flabby," he says. "You disgust me with all that flesh on your tiny spine. You're nothing but a dumb broad," he says, "and you stink like a bitch. You should try soap and water."

I say nothing. My mother's mascara is running. Her glasses have slipped from the top of her head. They were on the black lacquered hall table beside her. She is squinting at him. She hardly sees anything without her glasses but she had told me that men don't make passes at girls who wear glasses which was what Dorothy Parker had said and so she tries not to wear her glasses at least not around her husband but sometimes she does. Now her long nails are scratching at her own face.

My brother is at his doorway and suddenly he hurls himself forward and with his fists flailing strikes at my father's legs, strikes at his stomach. "Leave her alone," my brother calls out. There he is, a small child, a little boy with a habit of wheezing and sneezing, of running fevers, unarmored, without fallback position, without weapon, with only the intensity of the moment to propel him forward, with only the power of the just, David to

45

Goliath: "Stop yelling," he himself yells. His pajamas are slipping down around his slim hips, a fuzzy blue slipper falls off his left foot.

This was bravery. This was courage. I don't care if it was Oedipus that prompted him or it was not. His small arms, his unsturdy legs were moving with honor, in moral fury, heedless of self, they jerked and pushed out of love, out of a search for order and quiet. My brother begins to wheeze. My father pushes him away, hissing at him, "You sissy, you pansy, you fag." My brother is crying, not from the insults which neither of us understood but from the anger, the sound of it, from the fact that my father was standing there undented, unrepentant, his hands curled into fists. My mother rushes to her room. The all-clear sounds. The practice air raid is over.

My father stands for a moment in the hall. His lips are white. I see him there in need of comfort. He too is hurt. He too is lonely. I know he is lonely from the way he opens and closes his fists as if they belong to someone else. I know he is sad because he said things he shouldn't have. I know that after a fight a person feels afraid that all is lost. I go to his side. I put my hand in his hand. I smile up at him. He touches my hair. He puts on his coat and his brown hat with the little red feather in the brim. "Can I come with you?" I ask. He doesn't bother to answer. I know he's still angry and has only angry words in his throat. And I am in my pajamas and slippers and quilted robe and he cannot wait for me to change and it is past my bedtime, late at night when children do not go out on the street.

I know she is lying there with ice cubes in a towel over her eyes in an attempt to prevent the inevitable swelling that follows her just as inevitable frequent grief. My father slams the front door as he leaves, a cold hard slam, like the lid of a trunk of a man that would leave forever, like the slam of a dungeon door on condemned prisoners. This is a sound that prevents any further conversation including the sort that might lead to reconciliation. But of course he comes back later, he always comes back later. I think of him walking as fast as he could down Park Avenue, past my Aunt Sylvia's apartment building and my Aunt Libby's on the other side of the street, down toward Grand Central Station. I think of the lights changing from green to red. He won't wait at the curb. He'll charge ahead. I think of the trains rumbling under Park Avenue, the tracks like a steel spine down the center of the street. I know he won't catch the eye of the doormen who might be rushing out to get someone a taxi. If he sees someone he knows he won't wave or smile. I know that the motion itself, the fast pull of the muscles in his calves will finally by the time he has gone thirty or forty blocks soothe him and the demons in his chest will gradually return to their lair and wait for another day. There is nothing for me to do. No way for me to help him. My Love is striding down Park Avenue without me.

Later I am in my bed still waiting for sleep. I think of the great planes overhead ready to drop deadly bombs on us even though I know that the Japanese Zeros, the Wehrmacht bombers do not have enough fuel to reach the shores of New York. Even though I know that we are winning the war. I admit to myself that if I were tested, if I had to be brave, I most likely would fail. My brother on the other hand could be, already was, a hero.

I know this happened in the same way that more than a half-century later I remember our phone number at 1185 Park Avenue, Sacramento 2-5893.

After my brother charged forward to protect his mother there was a bond between us, I an older Gretel, he a younger Hansel, a dangerous wood, a long night ahead and we are short of bread crumbs. His hand in mine. I saw it that way. He of course had other stories in his head. I may not even have been present in his versions of the tale. Also, although I know it seems like sitting on both sides of the fence, I believed that my father needed me. Why after all wouldn't he? I was equally certain that he didn't need my brother: a fact which at the time seemed both reasonable and agreeable.

6

battle lines   In school I have knit a square that will be connected to the squares the other girls in my class have knitted and our scarf will be sent to a soldier overseas. I have collected the aluminum from the inside of my mother's cigarette packages and rolled it into a ball. I have taken the aluminum ball to school to be made into bullets or tanks for the army. I have a book with a flag on the cover in which I have pasted stamps purchased from my allowance in the blank squares. Someday I will have a war bond of my own. My mother has joined the war effort. She is taking a class that will teach her how to give emergency first aid in case we are invaded. She comes home from the first class with boxes of gauze and rolls of adhesive tape. She is learning how to bandage the wounded. My brother will not allow her to practice on him but I am happy to lie on the floor while she wraps each of my limbs in gauze and then secures the gauze with tape. She is clumsy. It takes a long time. I am not allowed to move. She makes a sling for my arm and bandages both legs up to my thighs. She wraps a bandage around my head. She puts gauze on my eyes and seals them shut. The phone rings. She goes to talk to her sister. Lying on her rug, bound in bandages I consider the war and flying pieces of cement, iron grates that might pierce my heart, ceilings that would tumble on my head and I think of the soldiers waiting evacuation at Dunkirk and I think of blood, mine running out into the carpet. I wait for my mother to return and pull off the adhesive. Finally the maid comes and rips off the bandages, each one tearing at my skin.

My mother goes to work at a thrift shop that is raising money for the USO so that soldiers can be given hot coffee and doughnuts before they get on the troop ships that will carry them off to the battlefield. The first morning on the job my mother is told to sit at the cash register. She is told how to open the draw with the money in order to make change. She sits on a stool behind a high desk on which the cash register with its brass levers and fat number buttons rests. A customer gives her a ten dollar bill. She presses the button to open the drawer and it shoots out and hits her in the stomach and she falls backward off the stool and bangs her head. She shows me the big bump which I feel very gently moving my fingers across its dimensions under her hair. She never went back to the thrift shop. She tells me that most accidents happen in the home, one has to be careful of electric shock from light bulbs and toasters. She tells me that the war effort does not need her in the thrift shop.

When I am in my mother's room with my mother she is usually in bed. She is very tired at the end of the afternoon and needs to rest. She lies on her bed and smokes with a detective novel by her side. She has a pad and paper for telephone messages on the little table. We play hangman. I guess letters for the blank spaces of her words. For each wrong guess she draws another body part, a head, a foot, a nose, until I am hanging from a rope she draws with so many dashes down the page. Then it's my turn. Sometimes she writes down a phrase and together we find little words you can make out of the larger words by changing the letters. *In God We Trust* contains *dog, wed, true, gust,* and *rust* among others. Happy amazing game, this demonstrates over and over that everything is unfolding from something else, that we are all connected and the alphabet is the spring, the box, the source. On my mother's bed, torn from the day's newspaper lies the crossword puzzle. She can do it in pen, in no time at all. There are lipstick stains on her paper and she grins at me as she gets a difficult answer. She calls her broker for the day's results. She plays the market, up and down and keeps the figures in her head and giggles as she issues her instructions, "Darling Max," she says, "buy me 200 shares. I know you don't like it but I have a hunch." "Ah sweetie," she says, "you're so smart that's why you're my broker." But Max is replaced by Harry and followed by Sheldon and through it all she is doing fine. I know because she tells me so. "Wish me luck," she says. "Blow a kiss to U.S. Steel." I listen to her on the phone. I wait for her attention to return to me, to our game. There is no other word you can make out of *love* except *vole* which is a tiny disgusting ratlike creature, she explains to me. Love is really a thing all alone, outside everything else. I understand that.

It is Saturday and I am not going to school. Greta and Johnny have gone to visit a friend of hers who works as a governess for a family that has twin boys my brother's age. My brother seems slow in making friends. Greta is trying to help. I am sitting in my parents' bathroom on a pink shag carpet watching my mother in the bath. She is lying in the soapy water and I see her breasts with the dark nipples appearing and disappearing as the water rises with her sighs and splashing hand gestures. The bathroom smells of powder, of nail polish, of cinnamon soap, of perfume. It is not exactly a good smell, something medicinal, something harsh, something of the toilet, some kind of cleanser used on the floor. My mother's hair is in a plastic cap. She doesn't want to spoil her set. Twice a week she goes to the hairdresser who washes, puts her hair into curlers and pins, and then she sits under the dryer for almost an hour and then the hairdresser combs out her hair and she looks at herself in the mirror and reapplies her eye makeup and her lipstick, always dark red, a slash of it on her white gloves, on the collar of her new suit.

My mother tells me about the hairdresser who has a boyfriend who steals her money. Now she tells me that a rich woman on Long Island has shot her husband thinking he was a burglar or was she having an affair? She tells me that Frank Sinatra is getting divorced again. She tells me that her second cousin died of breast cancer because her first husband punched her in the breast. She tells me that her sister Sylvia is cold as ice and probably never loved her husband Charlie because she could never love anybody but herself. She tells me she thinks that my Uncle Sy's wife doesn't like her. She tells me that her friend Helen had burned a black hole with her cigarette stub in our new dining table because she was jealous of my mother's dining room furniture. Now my mother tucks a stray lock of hair back under the cap. Her eyes are almost closed because the lids have swollen again. I am watching, I am still, I am patient. I reach out and pat my mother's pale freckled arm. I am happy to be in the room with her. I am happy to sit with her while she bathes. Years later I read of Swann's obsession with Odette and I thought of myself on the bathroom floor. A child too can love with the ferocity of quicksand closing over its victim. A child too can seek ways to hold on to the tilting planet by placing someone else in charge of gravity.

My mother and father sleep in twin beds pushed up against one another, covered by separate pink monogrammed spreads. The line in the middle of the two beds serves as a constant reminder that the San Andreas fault was real, that the earth could split along a crack.

This morning my mother surprises me. She asks me to light her cigarette. I do. Her ashtray is perched on the rim of the tub. It is already filled with lipstick-stained butts, black ash, and a cotton pad that she had used to wipe off last night's wrinkle-preventing cream. After I have lit the cigarette with her gold lighter, pulling the smoke into my lungs the way she showed me, she turns her blue nearsighted eyes to me and says, "I think I should get a divorce. Do you think I should get a divorce?" They say that children have a sense of adventure, approach the future with interest and anticipation, and are ready for challenge and change. I must have been a conservative child. I preferred the status quo. I greatly preferred my unsteady perch on the limb to free fall. I have an opinion. It is the wrong opinion.

She tells me about Virginie. Virginie is a French teacher who gives private lessons. She has recently arrived in New York from Toulouse. A visa was obtained just in time from a relative who sold insurance to my Aunt Libby which is how Virginie knew my mother. Virginie had a charming lisp. Virginie had a small red painted mouth and white teeth and big black eyes. She wears a blue beret on her cropped head. She has a tiny waist. The other night I overheard my father say that he could put his hands around her waist and his fingers would touch. I heard my mother say that Virginie was looking for a husband. All over New York there were women with accents, thick R's, th's that sounded like d's and d's that sounded like t's. These were women with unpronounceable names, who were seamstresses and experts in hat making or cooking or party giving. It was easy to find a woman of former status who would shop for you in case you had other things to do. The phone was always ringing with the name of a woman selling pearl pins or silk stockings from a leather suitcase and would make a house call up and down Park Avenue at your convenience. All those women my mother said had lost their homes because of the war and they were lucky that they were here. My mother helped them whenever she could.

My mother started French lessons with Virginie but soon gave them up. Virginie wears a gold bracelet given her by a lover in Paris who has gone to fight in the Resistance. Virginie is tall. My mother hears that a hotel room had been taken under the name of Mr. and Mrs. Liberty. According to my Aunt Libby who did her duty and told my mother those late nights at the City Athletic Club were not just nights at the club.

Whatever exactly my father was doing with Virginie in the hotel room has I understand nothing to do with the stork. My mother allows me to rub her back with the washcloth. "I am so alone," she says. "I'm here," I say. "I hate French accents," I add. "So do I," she says. My mother drags her fingers through the soapy water. "It's not just Virginie," says my mother. "Who else?" I ask. She shrugs. That's not the point. I know the names and the numbers don't matter. I am a wise child.

If I had my choice I would stay by my mother's side forever. I wouldn't go to school or the park. I would learn to sit with my legs crossed and smoke cigarettes and play cards. I would never have drinks in the Biltmore Hotel where other people could catch sight of me with someone else. I bring my mother a towel. I would bring her flowers but I have none. There is nothing new under the sun but I don't yet know that and I stroke my mother's arm but I wonder does my father also prefer Virginie to me. I know he does. I know it like I know the shape of my thumb as it fits into my mouth. In my parents' bedroom the curtains move slowly with a breeze that blows along Park Avenue, an ill wind that promises rain. My mother struggles to get into her girdle. It is very tight and her full hips keep escaping its form. She pulls up her stockings. She lets me pick a dress from the closet. She lets me adjust the hat on her head. She lets me place the fox with his little paws around her shoulder. I always kiss the fox on his long-dead button nose in case he can feel, in case he remembers running in the woods, with the shadows of the leaves moving across his back. The fox has a full tail that drifts down my mother's arm. I hold the tail for a moment. Then she is gone and I sit in the hall of the apartment my back pressed against the velvet-flocked wallpaper. I consider it. Virginie and my father had been seen together at the Biltmore and my Aunt Libby's friend Helen had told my aunt who had told my mother which made my mother angry at Helen as well as at her own sister who should not have told her but did so because she was her sister. *Virginie* (*vine,* like in the jungle).

Later I try to tell my brother what I had learned. He pays no attention. "It doesn't matter," he says. "I don't care," he adds. I should not have told him.

Throughout our childhood I often tried and tried as hard as I could to take from him his small portion in order to increase mine. Not Greta, Greta I left for him. He was her favorite and I didn't care. My brother went to church on Sunday mornings with Greta, sitting beside her during the morning mass among the Germans in Yorkville. What did he think of the stained-glass windows, of the heavy gray stone, of the dark wooden pews that smelled of polish and detergent and what did he think of the candles at the shrine of St. Agnes which sat at the left side of the nave and always there were candles in little glass containers flickering on and on? What did he think of the resurrection and the birth and the holy mother of whom there was a statue with a chipped blue mantle and wide gold halo at the front of the church? He never told me.

december 25, my birthday   I did know that he did not like Christmas. This was a day that Greta always took off and went to her sister's. This day also happened to be my birthday. My mother had her sisters and their husbands and children to lunch for a celebration for me or partly for me. We had a Christmas tree and presents. My brother did not want presents. He stayed in his room. He would not come out when the guests came. He didn't like it that I had extra presents because it was not only Christmas it was also my birthday. My mother loved the tree. When she was a child living on West End Avenue in December she would walk along peering into the windows of apartments on the lower floors and staring at their glistening Christmas trees. The Christmas tree was an American symbol of happiness she said and we should have one too. "Was it a holy day?" "It's about being merry," she said, "Merry Christmas," she added. So when I was about six years old we got our first tree. It sat in the foyer on a large white sheet. My mother was careful about money and never permitted Greta to spend an adequate amount on the tree. But despite the fact that it was never round and perfect the way it should have been, but always skinny in spots, leaning to the left or the right, broken limbed in the back I was impressed. Why not? It had magic little lights, it gave off a sweet smell of pine. The ornaments and the shining tinsel promised everything but delivered only the expected.

Every year on Christmas Eve my parents screamed at each other, not about the tree but about the fact that my father did not come home to decorate it in time and when he arrived he said something disparaging about what my mother was wearing or the color of her hair or her sister Libby's taste and he brought exactly the wrong present for my mother, something she had explicitly said she didn't like. One year he brought her a gardenia with a pin to wear on her dress. It let off a heavy sweet smell, reminding of urgent need, a smell of pressing emotion.

My mother says the scent of gardenias makes her nauseous. My mother likes violets and pink roses and she had said so often. She knows that the gift of the pure white gardenia is a mockery of her wishes. She says so. It begins. He says, "Whatever I do, you don't like it." She says, "You had your secretary buy the gardenia. You didn't do it yourself." He says, "I don't have time. I'm always on the phone with your brother." She says, "You have time to go to your club and sit in the steam room for hours." He says, "I thought you liked gardenias." She says, "Your secretary thought I liked gardenias and I don't." Their voices get louder. I stare at the miniature village with a tiny ice skater on a small mirror pond that sits at the base of the tree. Greta has bought that with her own money. It's true that his secretary always picks the wrong thing. Leather gloves that are out of fashion, a negligee that might fit a rhinoceros, a poodle pin my mother never wore. And for me the secretary buys dolls. I don't play with dolls. She buys clothes that might become a girl several years younger than I am. My mother will return everything.

Every year on Christmas Eve after my brother and I go to bed Greta goes out to midnight mass. Then in the foyer we hear not the sound of twelve tiny reindeer, not Santa with his finger on the side of his nose but a familiar rumble that has nothing to do with peace on earth and goodwill to man.

My father takes the large lamp that sits on the French commode in the hallway and throws it to the floor. We hear the pieces scatter across the black and white marble squares. My mother, red eyed from weeping, red nosed from weeping, hair damp against her forehead, mascara running down her cheeks, a lipstick stain on her white blouse, comes to my bedside. I pretend to be sleeping. She shakes me. "Wear your slippers when you go see the Christmas tree. There are sharp splinters everywhere and the maid has already gone to bed."

The church a few blocks away rings its Christmas bell. The radio plays carols all night long. The sky, the portion between the east and the west side of Park Avenue that I can see from my bedroom window, is clear and there are stars, not of wonder, not burning bright, but stars of gas and chemical, far away, moving in loops across a globe that seems not so much redeemed as empty.

yearning and envy   Soon I was old enough to have friends from school and camp who wanted me to go over to their apartments to play on a Saturday afternoon. They wanted me to go to the Translux on 85th Street with them to see the morning cartoons. I did not want to go. Instead I waited for my mother to wake up. I would pass the time in thought, like a child on a hot day by a riverbank, dangling feet in the rushing water. I would lie still like a cat in suspension between jumps. Years later I would wait for a boy to call, for a man to return home, for the sound of steps or elevator doors opening. I learned patience. I learned that counting backward helped pass the time, that rehearsing stories that I would tell her when she woke helped pass the time, I learned that time itself could be frozen and one's mind could occupy itself in a state that was near sleep, a hypnosis of waiting. I would wait for her to ring the bell and then the maid would come and at last I would be let into the room and could sit beside her while she dressed for the day.

My brother learned how to play chess. He was six and a half and I was nine. This was a game he was willing to play with me because he kept winning more and more easily. How was this possible? I am so much older. Finally I ask. He tells me. "You have to think a few moves ahead. You never do. You fall into every trap I set." I do. I never think ahead. I can't. He can. "I don't want to play with you anymore," I say. I try in my own room to see if I can teach myself to imagine the board and how it would look if I moved my knight here and he moved his queen there. The pieces won't stay in place in my head. I am confused about where they had been and where they were supposed to be going. They tumble and fall and my imaginary board is impatiently swept away. I can't plan in my head and I know he's right, that has to be why he wins. "Teach me how to do it," I ask him. He won't. I do not love him more deeply because he is smarter than I am. And then there is the piano.

The teacher arrived and I learned how to do the scales. But I couldn't keep a tune. I couldn't tell what was up or what was down, what was low or what was high. I seemed to have a profound deafness when it came to music. I didn't like it. I liked words and plot. I liked suspense and resolution. I liked stories about horses and Indians and mysteries about crooks and stories about lost children and how they were found. I wanted stories about pioneers and brave girls and best of all I wanted to read about fathers, especially fathers who were lost at sea and then after a long time when the daughter had almost given up hope, returned. My pleasure was in words.

I stopped taking piano lessons. But my brother had perfect pitch. He practiced at the piano all the time. He listened on the Victrola in his room to Mozart and Beethoven and Bach. When I would come home from school, careful not to put my books down on the upholstered furniture, careful not to lie down on the freshly made bed, careful to wash my hands so that the germs of the day would not stay in the house, I would hear his Victrola and the sounds of an orchestra, or a violin. I would open the door to his room. He would wave me away. He was listening. Sometimes he was sitting cross-legged on his bed following the score with his eyes and conducting with his hands. I knew that his soul had chambers in it that mine did not. I was flat and dull where he was rich with sound and emotion, with pattern and theme, with knowledge of something that I could not crack. I knew that his music was not a distraction like my jacks game which was excellent or my jump rope skills which were among the best. I knew that in the music there was an answer to some question that I couldn't even frame. His slight body, his fingers now always practicing scales, the sound in his head created for him a kind of magic carpet, a way of being satisfied that was outside my possibilities, better than anything I would ever know. I scuffed my shoes against table legs. I could not catch a theme or its variation. I did not hear it go and I did not hear it come. He was like the Houyhnhnms, the wise white horses in Gulliver's travels, and I was like the Yahoos, the beasts that were nasty and cruel, savage and small of head. I was filled with greed and jealousy, which stopped my ears so the music could not enter, and he was man in God's image. At the very least he understood the angel voices while I was deaf, dull, always checking the time to see if soon my mother would come home or soon she would open her door. And although this is a child's judgment there was much in it that was right.

The piano was my brother's passage to a better place. If I tried to sit next to him on the black stool while he practiced he would insist I leave. If I tried to open the door to his room so that I could try to find something of interest, of profundity in the sounds of violin and cello that came from his Victrola he would close the door. It didn't matter. I would not have heard anything, had I stayed at his side like a siamese twin. My ears were defective. His were perfect.

He took lessons from a real musician not just a refugee lady who needed the money but someone who had been trained at a musicians' academy in Vienna. My mother was proud that he played so well. My father was not interested. My father never listened to music. Neither did I. Neither in truth did my mother but she knew culture when it approached and she arranged for Greta to bundle him against the cold, to make sure that he had his asthma medicine with him and she or Greta would take him to the Philharmonic concerts. What did he hear at those concerts?

Once lying on my stomach and staring through the bottom crack of the door I saw him while he was listening to music. His eyes were alert. His body still. He did not move with rhythms. But his shoulders were tense and his fingers would sometimes move as if he had his own piano.

For these special occasions on which Greta took Johnny to the Philharmonic she wore a black silk dress and her good shoes and he wore a small blue jacket and a tie. "Stay out of my room," he would say to me as he left. I would enter and sit on his bed.

Of course I had my own special outings. I went to the Plaza for tea with my mother and my Aunt Libby. I ordered hot chocolate that arrived in a silver pot. I had pastry with whipped cream and raspberries. My Aunt Libby had satin dresses and suits with low-cut necklines. She smiled and smiled. She had a silver-handled mirror that she used to check the back of her hair style. She had silk underwear with lace trim. She was interested in parties, who went to them, what they were wearing, what they said about each other. She was far more cheerful than my mother but she was occupied by many small questions, which nail polish to wear to the opera, would people notice that her shoes had silver buckles. She was determined to have a good time. She never could understand my mother's more nervous and morose disposition. "Laugh," she would tell her. "Shut your eyes if a man touches you. Turn out the light and let them do what they want to." "Who cares about those dopes?" she said when my mother was weepy. "Just ignore them, go buy yourself something expensive." Libby had a pearl bracelet with emeralds and a diamond pin in the shape of a swan.

She had a bedroom facing Park Avenue on the ninth floor. My aunt's bedroom had green walls and a dark velvet bedspread. She had a dressing table with a green velvet-draped skirt and there on its mirrored top rested perfume bottles, tweezers, ropes of costume jewelry satin boxes, and a set of brushes for painting eyebrows. Her hall closets held china rimmed in gold with red lions, purple fish, platters with green leaves heavy with grape clusters as well as cups and saucers with blue and white portraits of shepherds and their sheep. The windows were covered in pink taffeta fabric with scalloped edges. My aunt had lipsticks in every shade. She let me try on her pearls, her fake emeralds, the gold rings with snake tails and diamond chips.

My aunt loved parties and had many friends with whom she went to the theater and to concerts. She seemed to know everyone on Park Avenue. Her servants were Irish or Slovak. Her hair was done three times a week. She laughed into the phone and she smiled at everyone. She believed in society. She did not think it was a game. She thought that pleasing people was as necessary to survival as eating and eliminating. She had a long neck and a long nose and she refused to think unhappy thoughts, she refused to know more than was necessary, and she intended to find the small satisfactions sufficient. She refused to look in dark corners. A crying child was hurried off to the servants.

She cared for herself above all and was always careful not to offend a friend, not to alienate a person on a club committee. She didn't believe in mentioning painful matters. She devoutly believed that she was put on the earth to enjoy the softness of table linens, the cut of a new dress, the company of friends at a concert. My mother's older sister was an intelligent woman who had understood early the perimeters of her world. She crossed no lines. She played within the rules. She made of the small things a pleasure. She disliked troublemakers, questioners, all politics. She did not believe that the inner life was good for you. She had a wide smile but a hard shell.

I drank my hot chocolate at the Plaza wearing my maryjanes and my best velvet dress listening to the conversation between the sisters. I wished I had a sister.

7

the help: helping   After the end of the war while my father
continued as the lawyer for my mother's and uncle's shirt company and
we had a new turquoise living room with a large Chinese screen in gold
and pink across one wall, Hedwig became our maid. She had hair that
stuck up at strange angles under her cap. She had black eyes that stared
at me and made me uneasy. She was a good cleaner Greta said but she
spilled disinfectant on my rug and there was something about her long
face and the irregular teeth that worried me. She too was Catholic and
she put up a large crucifix in her room and it reflected in the mirror that
hung over the green wooden bureau and in the dim light I worried about the
nails that pierced Christ's hands. On Hedwig's day out I would sneak into
her room to touch the crucifix. The impulse was not religious. It was done
more the way a certain kind of boy would light a firecracker. After some
months Hedwig told my mother that she had become pregnant with the
back elevator man. My mother didn't believe it because Emma had told her
that the back elevator man was planning on marrying the young Irish maid
in the apartment above us. Then Hedwig said that she was in fact pregnant
by her priest. My mother didn't believe it. Then Hedwig said that she was

pregnant by my uncle who was always very kind to her but not that kind. On a weekend when my father was away (where was my father?) my mother decided to fire Hedwig and Hedwig refused to leave. She said my mother was a witch. She said she would do us all harm. She locked her door and wouldn't come out. My mother took all the knives out of the kitchen and she took an umbrella into her bedroom. She took my brother and me too and Greta and Emma and we all spent the night in her bedroom with a chest barricaded against the door. My mother slept on the bed with all the carving knives and my brother and I slept in my father's bed and Greta and Emma spent the night in the chairs. In the morning the police came and took Hedwig away to a hospital.

Then the postcards began to arrive from the hospital which was on an island in the middle of the East River. The postcards said that Eugene Roth was the father of her child and if he didn't come and get her out of the hospital she would kill us all. Then after a while we got a postcard that claimed that a Doctor Muldowney had stolen her baby. This was followed by a postcard that said that I was her baby, stolen at birth by the Jews. My father paid no attention to the postcards. My mother said that Hedwig had gone mad from wanting a child and had made up all the fathers and had never ever been pregnant because no one had ever wanted her which was the greatest sadness of all. I resolved to stay sane no matter what, no matter if no one desired me, if I never got pregnant, no matter if I had no husband or china closet of my own. I wasn't sure if a person could will themselves sane but I intended to try with all my might. I could see that the division between the sane and the insane was the one border one never wanted to cross.

Our cook Emma liked music, popular music, and listened on the radio in her room. If my brother heard her radio he would put his hands over his ears. "That's not music," he would scream. The cook would laugh and turn up her radio louder, "Says who?" she would say.

Emma lived in one of the two backrooms in our apartment. She came from Wilkes-Barre, Pennsylvania, from a mining family. She was white and puffy, heavy and flat faced with pale blue eyes that spoke of prairies and plains and an empty sky. She wore her hair in a long braid coiled about her head. She cooked plain American food, mashed potatoes, roast beef, spinach. She made chocolate pudding and tuna casseroles and for my mother's dinner parties she made tomato aspic in molds and apples stained in a crimson berry sauce. She would go to Radio City Music Hall on her day off and she kept all the programs in a box which she once showed Greta who told me.

Emma was not fond of us. She would not allow us in the kitchen when she was cooking or when she was eating or when she was sitting at the table cutting out pictures from old magazines for a scrapbook she was keeping. She would not let me read to her. I tried. She would not let me listen with her to her favorite programs on the radio. She said I did not belong in the kitchen. I was not allowed to open the icebox door myself or to get myself a glass of water from the tap. I had to ask Greta who would get it for me. As I got older I had other images of kitchens in my head. I read about families in which the mother cooked and the daughters baked cookies and after school the children had milk at the kitchen table. I yearned for such a place with a stove and a bread box where I was permitted even welcomed.

Emma's brothers and sisters had married and they had children. Not for Emma that kind of life. I worried about her. What must it be like to be alone in the tiny room with a sink in the corner and a shower stall that you shared with the maid and no one to love you and no one to talk to and no expectation of change? I wanted Emma to meet someone at a dance, at church, in the park. She met no one. How is it possible that someone's life goes by with no wants, no possessions, no aspirations, day after day, weeks into years, making other people's dinners, watching other people's children? How is this a life? In a country where all people are created equal this should not be. But it was. It definitely was. I understood that equal was opportunity not result but where was Emma's opportunity? She was older than the doormen and the elevator men and they were Irish and she was not and anyone could see that Emma in her cook's uniform with its starched apron and blue and white striped dress, with her hair in braids around her head and her heavy upper arms with their flabby flesh exposed and thick legs encased in support stockings, was a lifer in our apartment. Greta I did not worry about. She had her unmarried sister who lived in the Bronx and was a saleswoman at Macy's. She had my brother. She said her reward was in the world to come and she didn't seem to mind waiting.

But it happened that someone from Greta's church had a brother who was alone and wanted to meet a woman and it was arranged that Greta would go out to dinner with him. Greta dressed carefully for the occasion.

She wore a small amount of pink lipstick. She combed her hair and pinned down a wet curl at the side. The curl when dry was perfect. She wore a black dress with matching shoes, the one she saved for holidays. She had a plain wool brown coat but she put a rose pin on the lapel. I went to bed hoping that the date would lead to love, would lead to marriage. There was a softness in Greta's face as she left that night, a kind of shine that I had not seen before. There was a flutter in the voice and a shy duck of the chin as she spoke of the meeting that opened up to me the hours without, the untouched hours that Greta had spent, washing and cleaning, following other people's children around, making sure that shoes were polished and dresses ironed. I was old enough to understand that the body needs to be touched, the hand needs to be held, that God is not a substitute for a mate and that it might not have been the right choice for Greta to have come to America to become a governess. She too deserved a room of her own, dishes of her own, an icebox and a bathroom that were all hers that she didn't have to share with Johnny and me. But she returned late that night and took off her good dress and hung it in the closet in my brother's room and never mentioned the man again.

Something had gone wrong. Perhaps he was ugly. Perhaps he found her ugly. Perhaps they had nothing to say to each other. She never said what was wrong but after that she seemed older, an unpicked fruit. Later when it became politically incorrect to refer to women as old maids, when the game itself was removed from the shelves, when no one said don't take the last piece of cake or else you'll become an old maid, I still carried the sorrow of it. Whatever the politics may be it is not right for a woman to be in bed alone night after night and to possess only the temporary love of children on provisional loan.

miami   We went on a vacation to Florida, Greta, Johnny and I, and my mother. We took a train. We slept on the train. All through the night I heard the whistle blowing. All day I kept my face pressed to the window. We passed through Baltimore and Washington and small towns with churches nestled in low-lying hills. Their white steeples rose up toward the mountains beyond. I saw a boy by the railroad tracks carrying a bucket. In a brief instant he caught my eye and waved. All the way down to Miami Beach, all through our two-week stay at the Roney Plaza Hotel each night I dreamed about the boy. In the bucket he was carrying were fish or frogs or rocks covered in velvet green moss or snails or peanut butter sandwiches. Once I dreamed he was carrying children's arms that had been cut off at the elbow and there was blood in his bucket.

At the Roney Plaza we spent the day at the beach under the striped umbrellas with Greta who wore her uniform even on the sand. My mother played cards on the veranda and went shopping with her sister at the stores where she bought me white pinafores and sandals. We had dinner in the children's dining room with Greta who ordered for us. Through a glass partition I could see my mother sipping drinks on a patio with her sister and leaning forward to dip her hand with its long red fingernails into a silver dish of peanuts on the other side of the table. I watched her and I watched her hoping she would turn to see me. She did not.

The last night of our stay I am allowed to go with my mother and aunt to the night's entertainment. Dunninger a hypnotist has come to entertain the guests. Greta gives my thick hair a hundred strokes with the brush and dresses me in a white pinafore decorated with little blue gingerbread men embroidered around the hem. I wear a blue barrette in my hair and sit at my mother's side at a table in the warm air. She fills the ashtray with burning ash and lipstick-stained Camel ends. Around the patio waiters circle with drinks, orange and red lights blink in the palm trees. There is a bandstand with musicians. Dunninger is announced with a huge drumroll. He is wearing a white tuxedo. He announces to the guests that he can cure anybody who wishes it of the desire to smoke. "Don't volunteer, Blanche," says my Aunt Libby laying a tanned arm on my mother's shoulder in an attempt to restrain her. But my mother sees opportunity and jumps to her feet. "Please," she says, "try me." I sit on my aunt's lap and watch as Dunninger brings my mother up to the bandstand and says to her, "You will fall asleep and when you wake you will light a cigarette and when you take the first puff and you inhale the smoke into your lungs you will get sick to your stomach, sicker than you have ever been in your life before, you will run to the ladies' room and you will think you are dying and you will finally pick up your head and say to yourself 'I will never have another cigarette again as long as I live.'" He snaps his fingers. The lights behind the band dim and rise and the musicians begin to play and my mother comes back to our table and in a few moments she takes a cigarette out of her purse and she lights and draws in her breath. I see her go pale, green around the upper lip, and her hands tremble. She smashes out the cigarette and she screams that she needs the bathroom. People at the tables around are pointing and laughing. She takes my hand and drags me with her and running on her high heels as fast as she can she pulled me through the marble lobby with fake coconuts hanging from artificial palm trees into the ladies' room. I wait. I can hear the sounds of choking—vomit rising and stomach in spasm. I can hear her scream, "Oh my God, oh my God, I've been poisoned. I'm dying." I put my head down on the floor and called up to her through the closed door, "It's all right. It's just what Dunninger said you would do. You're not going to die." At last she comes out the door. She's white as milk. She stands at the sink and stares at her reflection in the mirror. "I was so sick," she said. "Now," I say, "you'll never have another cigarette." We go back to the table. Everyone is staring at us. I smile at all the people hoping they would see that my mother was fine. We are fine. Then while Dunninger is telling another lady that she will kiss the first man with a blue tie she sees after he woke her my mother lights another cigarette. She says, " I don't feel well. I think I might be sick to my stomach again." My aunt and I watch her carefully. She inhales once and then twice and then again. A wave of nausea comes over her but it passes. She inhales her cigarette. She blows a smoke ring for me to catch and put my finger through. "It's all right," she says.

By the next day the effects of Dunninger's suggestion are all washed away in the sunshine. In the late afternoon I have my last slice of coconut and we get on the train to return to New York.

poor daddy   It didn't happen just once. It happened once every six weeks or so. I would come home from school and find the door to my parents' bedroom shut. The curtains would have been pulled tight. My father was in his bed and in the hallway outside the room I could hear him moaning, a terrible deep howl moan. My mother would knock on the door. No answer. She would open the door very slowly. She would put her head in the room but keep her feet on the threshold. I would stand behind her.

My father would have tossed the pillows on the floor, rolled the blankets up, and I would see him in his maroon silk pajamas rocking back and forth, a green cast to his face, his teeth clenched, his hands balled up into fists, and his eyes red and running. He had seemed trapped, like an animal that was about to gnaw off its own leg to gain its freedom. A migraine had arrived. My mother would ask him if he wanted anything, a glass of water perhaps? He wouldn't answer. She would go over to the bed and put one of her hands on his arm. He would scream, "Don't touch me, don't touch me. I don't want you in here. Get out." She would stand up as if to go. Sometimes she would say something. He would bang his hands against the wall, "Get out, get out." He would shout and his voice was deep and terrible. It was as if we were in an earthquake, in a bombing, as if the room were splitting apart. Through the crack in the window curtain I could see the sunlight reflecting from the roof of the building across Park Avenue. Inside the room I could see sweat on my father's forehead. "But," my mother would say, "should I call the Mazurs and cancel the theater tonight?" and he would howl in fury. "What the hell do you think?" I wouldn't say it but I agreed with my father. He was sick and she was talking about going to the theater. He was in pain and she couldn't comfort him. Standing behind her, watching him as his head was pressed in an invisible vise I was convinced that I would be able to soothe the pain, I would run my magic fingers across his brow and smooth away the ache. I was convinced that there was a path through the fury and I could find it and he would not scream at me but grow quiet like a tame lion who needed only the firm hand of one who cared for him to set-tle down to a peaceful nap.

I believed that my mother's ineptness stemmed from the fact that she showed that she was afraid and everyone knew you must show no fear in sit-uations like this but instead walk calmly. I thought of my father's migraines which would last for twenty-four hours or more like volcanoes erupting, ter-rible acts of God, beautiful in their ferocity and not really dangerous if you knew when to pack up and leave. That was something my mother did not know. She would send the maid in with tea and toast and he would howl louder. She would try to bring him the *Herald Tribune* when it arrived around five o'clock in the afternoon. He would tear it to pieces and leave the crumpled paper balled up in her bed.

When it was over he would emerge from the room, showered, perfectly dressed, the handkerchief folded in his pocket, his conservative silk tie matching his suit, smelling of after-shave. Only a strange paleness of face, a certain fleeting muscle spasm in the corner of his mouth would tell you that anything had been amiss. He would come home later than usual that night, needing a sauna, needing a massage, needing something at the club that was not in his house. Poor Daddy, I thought, so lonely. Poor Daddy, I thought, will he die? It was my medical opinion that his bad temper sometimes got backed up, the way the drain in the sink in Emma's room did, and when it was clogged, the temper rose into his brain and having no target outside his body caused spasms of pain inside his head.

I see my father running along the streets of Hungarian Yorkville chasing a trolley car in order to jump on its back bumper and hitch a ride. I see him among the ice trucks and the horses still pulling heavy carts and the tumble of vendors and laundry and names called and sneers and boasts and shoving that make a boys' world, one in which you cannot show weakness or the pack is down on your head. I see him in the forbidding red brick building that was Bellevue Hospital lying on a bed at the age of ten alone without his mother or his father or his aunt, waiting for the orderly to take him to the operating room where they will cut into the bone behind his ear and drain the massive infection that threatens his brain. I see him with fever reddening his eyes and the thin striped hospital pajamas clinging tight to his sweating body. I know that he doesn't understand clearly what the doctors will do and I know that the adults in the beds around him are recovering from amputations, from hallucinations, from the errors of surgery as well as its miracles. I know there are no pictures on the wall for a boy to look at, no flowers on a bureau, only a long time to wait. I know my father showed no fear, told no one what he feared. He did tell my mother who told me that the night after his own operation was over and he was lying in his hospital bed with a bandage over his ear a man in the bed next to his pulled himself to his feet and said, "Kid, I'm going, now. Tell my wife Sadie, I left some money rolled up in my socks." The man then went to the window and opened it wide and in his hospital gown, flapping behind him like an extra skin, he jumped and my father, leaning out the window, saw his body on the ground below. The next day they sent my father home and he never did tell Sadie about the money.

I know that one summer he was challenged by some of the boys he hung out with along the East River's edge to swim out to Hellgate Bridge where the currents were dangerous and the big freighters loaded with coal floated down to the harbor pushed by small tugs. My father jumped in the water and wearing only his underpants swam out into the current and all the way to the iron cross bars of the railroad bridge and he fought hard to get there and harder to get back and his arms were trembling when he pulled himself out of the water and he probably was afraid but he didn't tell the boys that. I wasn't there but I know it.

One day I am given three single dollar bills to pay for art supplies at school. I forget to give the money to the teacher. The bills are left in an envelope in my cubby at the end of the day. The next morning I remember that I must give the money to the teacher whose name is on the envelope. I put my hand into my cubby but my cubby is empty. The teacher tells me to bring another three dollars. She is not mad at me but when my father overhears at the breakfast table my request to Greta to give me a second three dollars in a second envelope he jumps up and grabs me by the arm. He brings his face close to mine. "You lost the money," he says in cold fury. "You just left it there for some cleaning woman to take, you careless, stupid, little girl." He shakes me. "You don't care about money. You treat it as if it grew on trees." He laughs bitterly. My arm hurts where he is holding on. "You wasteful child," he grits his teeth. He looks at me as if I am the most loathsome soul on earth. He pushes me away. "Get out of my sight," he says. "Take her away," he waves to Greta. After that I began to lose things, socks, books, mittens, pencils, hats. If something weren't tied on to me I dropped it and forgot it. I no longer put my allowance that Greta gave me every Sunday before she went off to church in my piggy bank. I couldn't remember where I had put my piggy bank.

After that each time I heard him coil for the attack. I heard the low hiss of the words forming at the back of his throat or the loud banging of his voice suddenly springing forward I grew calm, quiet, hidden inside an empty landscape where I would wait patiently for it to be over. I was still as a rabbit in the glare. I was playing dead. I was dead. I felt nothing. I understood everything. I knew it would be over soon enough and in the meanwhile time hung suspended about me like Dalí's dripping watches over the sand. I wasn't angry or sad or afraid. Because I could do this I could run to the door at night if my father came home before my bedtime and throw my arms over his knees. I could pat his face and bring him his drink and his slippers and carry his soft leather briefcase to its resting place in the closet. I could let my love of him pace around in my heart without hindrance, without qualm or hesitation.

8

eating   It was a while before Johnny told me. He would sit at the small table in his room where we ate our meals and he would keep his hands folded in his lap. When Greta brought in the plates he would quickly switch them so I had his and he had mine. Greta would switch them back. She didn't like his exchanging the plates. She had given him a little extra of this or of that. It was a principle. You ate what was on your plate. You didn't leave anything. You didn't switch plates with anyone. It didn't matter they were the same. I told him so.

He would watch me eat while he ate nothing at all. He would not drink his milk. He would watch me. I ate fast. I guzzled and gulped and swallowed. He watched. I wiped my mouth, I scraped the plate. I ate broccoli, rice, and thick slices of meat loaf. I ate rolls and butter. His plate was full, untouched. He watched my mouth for signs of twitching. He waited for me to clutch the air in a desperate gesture, grab my stomach, and roll on the floor in pain. Finally he told me. He took me into his closet and closed the door. We sat on the floor in the darkness. This was a hiding place away from Greta, away from Emma, away from the maid. No one could hear us while we were talking in the closet. "Mother is trying to poison me," he said.

I was close to ten years old. I knew as surely as I knew all the times tables backward and forward despite having gone to a very progressive school that this was not so. I knew it as I knew that the sun rises and the moon shines over Park Avenue moving across the sky from dusk to dawn, that the war in Europe was going to be won by our side, that boys had a penis and girls something else. I knew it like I knew that horses loved apples and the picture cards were worth more than the numbered cards. I knew it like I knew from summer camp how to play mumbletypeg with a knife that was tossed into the dirt, like I knew how to roller-skate and ride a bike and how to jump rope, with a friend, with five friends, or by myself, like I knew that I breathed in and out, oxygen–carbon monoxide. I also knew I could catch balls and throw them hard. Watched by Jerry our daytime doorman I had practiced long hours on the sidewalk outside our building, bouncing balls inside the cement squares, up against the brass mailbox. I was a fierce player. I was like my father.

Our mother is not trying to poison him. But how to convince him. I try denials. I try emphatic denials. He insists. I tell him that she never goes into the kitchen, when would she be able to put poison in the food and how can he be sure that she isn't trying to poison me instead of him. He admits that perhaps I could get murdered too, an afterthought, a bystander blasted by a bomb meant for someone else. But he has no answer to my reasonable objection that she never goes into the kitchen. I am sure of myself. I am sure she prefers me to him. That I am closer to her. That if she had to save only one of us from the Nazis it would be me. But still I don't think she is planning on poisoning him. And besides she really never goes into the kitchen. "But she could," says my brother. "She could at night when we are asleep. You don't know that she doesn't," he says. This is true. We decide to stay up and see.

On Greta's night out, after the substitute nanny has come to see if we are asleep, after we hear the front door close letting us know that she has gone at last, we each leave our rooms. We wait hidden in the dining room with its long blond wood table until the hall lights are out. Greta is spending the night at her sister's and won't be back until seven the next morning. We wait the two of us behind the portal to the living room through which we can see the dark hallway and the door to the now-dark kitchen. I keep falling asleep at my post. My brother does not sleep. He is waiting. Then suddenly the door to my parents' room down the second hallway opens and our mother in her pink lace nightgown and her mules came down the hall. She turns on the lights as she goes. We pull back into the darkness of the living room but we see the door to the pantry open and the light go on. "I am right," said my brother, not hiding his pleasure at being right but not entirely pleased. " She goes farther into the kitchen itself. "She is putting the poison in the milk or the eggs or the meat right now," he whispers to me. We wait. A few minutes later my mother emerges. She has a plate in her hand with a large pickle on it as well as a rye bread sandwich that seems to be dripping mustard. Some spills on the floor and bending down, with the edge of her nightgown my mother wipes up the spot on the black and white marble floor. The lights in the hall go out. The door to the bedroom opens and closes. "See," says my brother. This is not proof that she is trying to poison him but it is proof that she had the opportunity.

Over the next few months my brother becomes even thinner. I become even rounder because impatiently I would put my fork in his food and quickly while Greta wasn't looking swallow his chocolate pudding, his spinach, his baked potato slathered with butter. He turned his head away as I pour his milk down my throat. I eat his raspberry Jell-O with a banana slice suspended in the center like a drowned body in a still lake. Only a half-hour later, when he can see that I am still among the walking and talking does he gingerly pick at what remains on his plate. Meal after meal, through pancakes and french toast, through scrambled eggs with jelly, through pork chops and baked ham, through wiener schnitzel and red cabbage, through steak and stewed tomatoes, when Greta leaves the room we talk about poison. "Why would she poison you?" I ask again and again. He shakes his head. "You're too trusting," he says. "You'll die before you grow up." "I won't," I say. "I'll outlive you," I say. "Maybe you're in on it," he says and there is a sorrow in his voice that makes my eyes burn. "I'm not, I swear," I say. "No crossies," I add. But he looks at me unconvinced. I am probably not the most truthful and honest of siblings. I am not beyond betrayal but I know right from wrong and reality from dream or so I hope.

I knew how to read. I rushed to the door to be the first to bring in the mail that the elevator man dropped on our welcome mat each day. I read every issue of *Life* magazine. I knew about Siamese twins, about the sailors eaten by sharks, about twisters in Kansas and floods along the Mississippi

banks. I knew about Sister Kenny and her polio treatments and I knew how
fragments of flaming buildings flew above the ground while brave London-
ers clutched each other in basement tunnels. My mother also subscribed to
the *Reader's Digest*. I improved my word power every month by taking the
test. I read the jokes and the stories of men and women who struggled on
despite the loss of limb or eyesight. I also read about Freud. What exactly I
read I'm not clear but I knew that psychoanalysts had come to this country
and could heal the mind with talk therapy, that the mind was a delicate
structure but with the right words could be altered. There was hope,
boundless hope in psychotherapy.

So finally I form a plan.

Greta is in the kitchen attempting to sell Emma a raffle to her annual
church bazaar. Our mother is in the living room playing cards with her
friends. The card table is covered with its usual green felt cloth. There are
ashtrays at each seat and they are filled. When making a difficult card
choice my mother often blows smoke rings, perfect circles of smoke out her
mouth. I had tried to do it but had failed, proof, my mother said, that my
buck teeth with a wide space between the two front ones were in dire need
of orthodonture. (My own fault for thumb sucking.) Smoke rises from the
table and curls around the room drifting up to the ceiling like spirits of the
dead. The gold inlaid table at the end of the turquoise couch holds a plate
of cookies and a silver pot filled with coffee. Near by sit the silver creamer
and sugar bowl each with clusters of tiny silver grapes on the handles. In
the late afternoon the maid will bring in the crystal cut highball glasses and
a bucket of ice and the women will fix themselves bourbon and scotches or
dry martinis from the bar. The maid in her black uniform with its doily-cut
apron will then empty the overflowing ashtrays, the lipstick-stained butts of
cigarettes falling now and then onto the deep blue carpet. Other afternoons
I would be lying behind the heavy drapes listening to the women's conversation, drifting as the sound of ice beating against the crystal glass mingles
with the hiss of shuffling cards, the rise and fall of voices.

But this afternoon after the game has started I take my brother out on to
the street. I smile a warm greeting to Jerry my favorite doorman so he won't
think it strange that we are out without Greta. Carefully I cross the street.
The buildings on the next block over have awnings and underneath the
awnings stand doormen in uniform with hats and brass buttons. On either

side of the awnings in every building there are doors with steps up or down to doctors' offices. There are gold nameplates beside the doors. I ring the first bell. A nurse comes to the door, "What kind of a doctor is Dr. Barnes?" I ask. The nurse tells me. He is the wrong kind. We ring the bells of about six doctors, ear doctors, pediatricians (at that one I hear wailing babies inside the waiting room), orthopedists, a surgeon, and then just a block away, in the lobby of the apartment building of one of my school friends a man comes to the door. "Yes?" he says when he sees us. "What kind of a doctor are you?" I ask. "A psychoanalyst," he says. "That's what I need," I say. My brother squirms. "Lets go," he says. I hold on to his arm. "Come in," says the doctor. "I'm just between patients." It may be his deep reassuring voice, it may be the soft afternoon light that glows on his dark wood desk. It may be the collection of small stone Greek statues that sits on a glass shelf near his couch but my brother tells him that our mother is trying to poison him. The doctor asks our name and telephone number. I give it to him. He promises to help. My brother and I go home.

I did not doubt for a moment that he would do something, that my brother's mind could be cured of its irregularity. About the science of medicine, about the power of the doctor, about the goodness of the doctor who would help because he was asked I had no doubt.

We had found by accident, the good luck of location, the office of a prominent child analyst, Dr. Maurice Friend, who also by luck was between appointments just at the moment we rang his bell. He called my mother and told her of our visit. She went to see him. She came back her eyelids puffed and her nose red. She was not angry with me for taking my brother to the doctor. She went to bed and called her sister and this was the beginning of psychoanalysis in our home.

Now is this story literally true? Do I remember it this way so that I can be a heroine in my own family tale? Did I ring the bells of doctors along Park Avenue or did I just think of doing it and not actually in the real world take a step outside our apartment? I'm not exactly sure. As I tell the tale and I have told it often it rings somewhat untrue. It seems natural that I would have read of psychoanalysis and decided to get help for my brother, but that a doctor would invite us in, not knowing who was going to pay the bill, that sounds extremely unreal. It certainly was an odd referral if it happened this way. Perhaps I simply told my mother that Johnny thought he was being poisoned. If I did that I broke our bond, broke my word, behaved like a company fink under duress (a peculiar image for a child whose bread was buttered by the business not the union, which I knew from listening to conversations between my mother and her brother was the enemy to be kept at bay at all costs).

Johnny was taken for hours of interviews and tests to a famous child psychoanalyst who had studied with Anna Freud in Vienna, a woman named Berta Bornstein whose offices at 1148 Fifth Avenue were considered hallowed space by growing broods of refugee psychoanalysts and their American disciples who were colonizing the Upper East Side.

Dr. Bornstein's first suggestion was that my mother enter treatment herself. She did.

9

neurotics—here there and everywhere   My mother's brother thought she must be nuts to go to a psychiatrist. He thought she should try instead to improve her golf game, get more exercise. My mother's sister Libby thought that psychiatrists were for people who were seeing things, hearing voices, the lunatics screaming in the asylum. She made my mother promise that she would tell no one that she was seeing a psychiatrist. My mother's sister Sylvia decided to take my mother with her on a shopping spree in Brooklyn to cheer her up. I was allowed to go along. Sylvia lived at a few buildings down on Park Avenue in an apartment with dark brown walls and velvet hanging curtains on every window. She had two sons Howard and Christie, who were older than me. She had perfect posture and always stood as straight as a lamppost. There was a tension around her mouth that never went away and she never smeared lipstick on her teeth the way my mother did and the polish on her nails never chipped. Her hair was held in place firmly and she wore a huge ruby ring on the finger of one hand and on the other she wore an emerald surrounded by diamond chips. She had a long neck that was always extended like a swan and around her throat she wore pearls that fastened with rubies.

Was everything my mother told me about my Aunt Sylvia true? There were no independent witnesses, no verifiers. And even if her words weren't true, it doesn't matter. I always believed my mother's words. I never forgot them. My mother told me that when Howard was seven Sylvia and her husband Charlie had gone to Europe to spend two months at a resort on Lake Como. They had left Howard and his little brother up in the company town in Vermont with a governess named Erica in charge. Howard wrote to his mother, "Please, please come home. Erica is mean and I cry for you every day." The letter took two weeks to arrive by ship. Sylvia thought the letter was sweet and never considered changing her travel plans. Another letter and yet another followed. "I am miserable. Erica has hit me. Come home. Erica puts me to bed at five o'clock and I am not allowed to get up. Please come home." Sylvia did not. She went for walks by the lake and bought a gold necklace in Zurich and glass in Venice.

My mother told me the story. She should have come back my mother told me. This was an example of Sylvia's selfishness which is why we never had family dinners with the Gilmans. My mother would make a face if it was Sylvia on the phone. "She bores me," said my mother. But we went to Brooklyn in Sylvia's long black car. "She has a money complex," my mother said.

The chauffeur sat stiffly in the front and I was instructed not to speak to him. We sat on black cushions and my mother smoked so many cigarettes that we had to open the windows and empty the ashes from the silver ashtray as we crossed the bridge.

My mother and her brother and sisters had been raised in a house on Riverside Drive. It was true their father had once had nothing, had once sat on the fire escape of his tenement on Elizabeth Street and wondered how the rent would be paid, but his children had known only comfort, only private schools where little girls had skating parties and went to the ballet and the opera, to tea dances and wore ball gowns. Sylvia was of the generation that had only second-hand experience with deprivation and so why was she so afraid of the imaginary place she called the poorhouse? The fear of being without was deep and vast and her heart was full of holes, like a sieve, so there was no comforting her. This was not avarice or greed although it appeared so, it was something closer to terror and very communicable. My

mother told me that money was a symbol for feces and Sylvia was consti-
pated.

In Brooklyn we went to a big hardware store, rows and rows of plumbing
parts, toilet seats, rubber items, steel springs. My aunt and my mother and
I left the car waiting at the curb. Inside my aunt made her purchase and a
man carried it to the car. What we had was twenty dozen light bulbs purchased at five cents cheaper apiece than could be had in Manhattan. We
had gotten the bulbs wholesale. The trunk, the back seat, the space next to
the chauffeur was now filled with inexpensive light bulbs. "Money is
money," said Sylvia. "We've saved money," she said but did not seem satisfied. For the return trip I sat on the floor because the seat was filled with
boxes of bulbs. When we returned to Park Avenue, the chauffeur unloaded
the bulbs into the marble lobby of 1095 Park Avenue and I was given a bulb
for the lamp in my room as a souvenir of the trip.

"No one believes that the money they have will last them forever," explains my mother. "Sylvia is not a secure woman," says my mother. "She's
not very smart," adds my mother.

But the Gilman family had begun to buy paintings by someone named
Picasso and someone named Braque and the paintings were bought as tax
deductions. Sylvia knew where you could buy everything cheaper, including
cheap little art galleries in Paris. She was an encyclopedia of wholesale op-
portunities.

"Does Sylvia love her husband Charlie?" I ask my mother. My mother
says, "You can't ask that question about someone like Sylvia."

I wondered if I would ever know all the things my mother knew. When
we rode together on the bus downtown she would point out to me who on
the bus was Jewish and who was not. How I could not imagine. She whispered in my ear that the woman two seats in front of us was dying of cancer. She could tell from looking.

Nothing changed in our house. Greta picked Johnny up early at school
so he could make his appointments with Dr. Bornstein whose evaluation
seemed to be taking months. Greta would wait for him beside the whirring
fan near the wooden table that held children's books for all ages. In the con-
sulting room he played he told me with Dr. Bornstein.

"She's ugly," he says, "like a witch." "What did she say?" I ask. "Did you tell her about the poison?" I ask. "You are not allowed in my room," he says. "I don't want you in my room." I stand on the marble threshold of the bathroom we share. "Make her close the door," he shouts at Greta. I close the door.

Many evenings my mother would go out to parties. I felt her absence like a held breath. All was still.

Sometimes the parties were at our house. Then Emma would be cooking all day and the crystal and the fine china and the embroidered linens with monogrammed matching napkins from Belgium would be pulled from the closet. Emma made apples dyed in cherry juice and placed each in a small crystal glass dish for the dinner guests. In molds in the shape of fish and fruit she would make red and green aspics and before the party they would be placed on silver platters engraved with nymphs and centaurs decorated with garlands, and fish salads would be piled up on the platters. I was not allowed in the kitchen but as the doors swung open and closed I would get a glimpse of the silver being polished lying high on the counters. There were glass fingerbowls etched with gold vines at each plate. Extra maids arrived and my father would come home early and disappear into the bedroom and appear in a splendid suit with a silk tie in time to mix martinis. I would wear my quilt bathrobe and my maryjanes and sometimes I would walk among the guests helping to pass out the plates of cheeses and deviled eggs. I had instructions. If a Mr. Goldstein was standing alone I was to ask him about his factory in the South and when he was answering me I was to ask him to wait a moment and go get a Mr. Lassinger and introduce the two men and ask Mr. Lassinger his opinion of whatever Mr. Goldstein had just said. When the conversation was started between them I was to leave and attend to another wallflower. My mother explained to me that some men were shy and awkward at parties and needed help. She couldn't be everywhere at once and so I was her assistant. If I had trouble thinking of something to start a conversation I was to ask a political question. "What do you think Harry Truman's chances really are or will there ever be a Jewish state?" It's simple said my mother, the trick of making men like you is to ask the question that begins them talking. Then they feel good and that's what makes them like you.

After dinner there was dancing, records were stacked up near the Victrola that had been pulled into the hall. My father danced with all the women. He was stiff, his back was too straight, he held his partner as if he were afraid she was bearing germs and what he really liked to do was light up a cigar with the men and tell them what he thought about the world. If someone disagreed his voice would rise immediately to a shout and his eyes would narrow and the vibrations of his electric temper would crackle through the apartment. "Rum and Coca Cola" would play on the Victrola. From my room in my bed I could hear the music and the voices.

Once my mother asked to me stay awake and hide among the fur coats piled on her bed. Someone in their crowd was stealing money from the other women's purses. My mother didn't know who. I lay on her bed among the coats drifting in and out of sleep, anxious to do my part in catching the thief. I see Rose Isaacs, dark and skinny Rose Isaacs wife of Dr. Irving Isaacs urologist and champion golfer enter the room. She takes her own bag which has a rhinestone poodle with a fake ruby eye for a handle and goes into the bathroom. I drift back into sleep. Then I hear a door close. I open my eyes in time to see that it is my father's closet door that has closed. I get up and stand outside the closet. My heart pounds. I have always been afraid of closets, witches and demons, rank evil, snakes and skulls, bones of the murdered, murderers with bloody axes lie in wait in the dark recesses of closets. These of course are the fears of a little child. I no longer have them, exactly. I know perfectly well that nothing out of the ordinary, nothing inanimate resides in closets. From a crack under the door I see that the light is on. I hear a rustling. I open the door wide and there is Rose Isaacs with her skirt pulled up to her waist and her leg resting on a low shelf and she is putting money, a lot of money folded up into the top of her stocking. She stares at me with eyes wide. "Don't tell," she says. "Please be a good girl, don't tell." Her breath smells of scotch. But I run out into the party: men and women draped across our furniture, maids clearing dishes, glasses everywhere, cigarette smoke so heavy that my eyes water. I tell.

Later my mother explains to me that Rose has a neurosis. She is a kleptomaniac. She needs help. She is stealing to replace something she thinks she has lost. "What?" I ask. "What has she lost?" "I don't know," my mother answers. Doesn't she know or won't she tell me? Either way I cannot forget Rose Isaacs' wild dark eyes and her pale startled face and her black hair in a gold clip falling forward as she bent down toward her leg. "Everyone is missing something," my mother explains to me. "It's Freudian," she says, "you'll understand when you're older." I beg her. She explains it to me. "There's a hole inside Rose and she's trying to fill it, just the wrong way." I begin to look for holes in people. I find them. How many little words can you make out of *kleptomaniac?* *Mock* for one, *plot* for another, *man* for a third.

My father is an expert on political matters. He reads two newspapers a day. He has opinions on everything. He knows that Yalta was a disaster. He knows that the unions are sabotaging the country. He also personally knows the Tammany Hall club guys. He admires a young Carmine de Sapio. Tough as nails, he says. He knows what contracts are coming down the pike. He knows what city hall intends before it hits the papers because he's heard it from a guy who heard it from a guy. My father believes the Negro has been shafted. He thinks Trotsky was a fraud and Lenin a coward. He thinks Golda Meir is a freak of nature but Ben-Gurion knows what he's doing. He thinks that India deserves independence but Gandhi is Swiss cheese, a dreamer, a dope. He thinks that a teaspoon of honey each day will keep cancer away. He believes that the GI bill of rights was a good thing but that the antitrust laws are the work of communist infiltration. He announces his opinions to anybody who will listen. Sometimes I challenge him.

At first I amuse him and catch his attention. Later as my debating skills improve he reminds me that girls should not argue. His opinions are only constantly wrong when it comes to stock tips he has gleaned from the sauna at his club. He loses money. He loses again and again. He borrows from my mother. She says he has a black thumb for stocks. He says he has a sure thing, Leon heard it from Herb who has a connection to the Chase Bank.

Capitalism, dog eat dog, bigger dog eat littler dog, does not make men confident of their worth. If the American male in the forties looked up at the implacable canopy of the universe he would find no helping hand, no pat on the back for effort. He would not have time for harmonizing, time to dance under raindrops, to take deep Om-like breaths and float off with the white wisps of August's dandelions into the zen of the day. In capitalism the losers are hung out to dry. Their spirits shrink or cringe.

My mother does not attribute my father's peculiarities to capitalism. She thinks he is a garden-variety neurotic and should see an analyst. She points out that he is too clean and orderly. She says his migraines come from inner conflict. She says his bad temper is a symptom. She says that he could be cured. I grow hopeful. Everything would be different if he would only see an analyst. Will he?

My father had a younger sister named Bea. His sister did not go to college and nobody suggested she should. She ran around with a bad crowd as a teenager and when she settled down she married a thin pale meek small-boned jeweler who owned a small store that was forever being robbed in Queens. She was only in our house once or twice. She spoke in a hoarse growl with a street sound, like a cab driver. She was a very big woman, tall and so fat that she needed help getting out of chairs. She smelled of cheap perfume and sweat and chewing gum. She wore low-cut dresses and her enormous breasts always seemed ready to burst out of their lacy confinements. She and her husband went to the Catskill hotels and danced in the contests all year long. She was a rhumba queen and had a shelf of trophies in her apartment in Astoria.

When she visited she taught me the rhumba. She was light on her toes although her belly shook from side to side as she moved. Her hips shifted as if they were meringue on a dessert plate. She wore big earrings and her palms were wet and sweat dripped from her neck. Still, in our living room she danced on just as if she were Salome herself. It was like watching an elephant float in thin air. My mother closed her eyes. My father said, "That's enough Bea." I could have danced the rhumba with her forever.

If my father was a counterfeit not a real prince, here was the proof. What kind of prince would have this kind of sister? My mother looked down on Bea, not simply because of her weight. My father married up. My mother married down. Here lies the dingy underbelly of the wonderful story of immigration. Class lines were permeable in America and that was good but those left on the wrong side were embarrassments. Family unity unraveled because of the individual speed or lack of it in catching on, in moving up. Boys of course were pushed forward, girls were held back at home. Education meant everything. My father at Columbia University was able to date my mother, an heiress more or less, while Bea left among bus drivers and shoe salesmen did as well for herself as she could.

My mother would not forgive the Queens accent. My father who did slip her money from time to time was not proud of her. She was not Park Avenue. She was not acceptable at our table. A child who couldn't pick up the clues and thought that it was a fine thing to win the rhumba contest at Grossingers would certainly have been in bad trouble.

Far from being un-American, snobbery is the apple pie cooking in everyone's oven.

My mother told me that Bea was a neurotic. She ate and ate till she blew up like a Macy's Thanksgiving Day balloon, her face like a watermelon, because she needed love. Her triple chins, the waving flesh of underarm were all symptoms of sorrow. Could psychoanalysis help her? My mother said it could but there was no money for it. The jewelry business was hanging by a thread. She would just have to eat herself into her grave.

No question neurosis can be fatal which worried me because my mother had a few even a child couldn't avoid noticing.

My mother and I are driving out to Deal, New Jersey. We are going to visit my mother's friend Sally who has a summer house by the beach. We enter the Lincoln Tunnel, the long two-mile tunnel that connects the island of Manhattan with the rest of America. The cars are moving very slowly, a funeral procession would have more speed. It is hot in the car and my underpants are sticking to the car seat. My mother sits on a red plump cushion so she can see over the wheel. She wears her dark glasses and her lipstick has smeared on her teeth. She asks me to light a cigarette for her which I do from the lighter in the dashboard. Its little coils are a bright dangerous orange. We enter the tunnel. My mother tells me to keep my eyes on the walls and let her know if I see a leak, a dripping of water. She explains to me: tons of the Hudson River water are sitting on top of the tunnel, surrounding its thick walls. At some point the pressure will be too great for the walls and the water will form a crack and then a bigger split and then suddenly the water will come rushing through and all of us in the tunnel will drown. My mother grips the wheel. "What will you do if I see the water?" I ask my mother, we cannot turn back, we cannot go faster. "We'll know," says, my mother, "that we're going to die and we will have time to say goodbye to each other." I stare at the walls of the tunnel, at the rail on the walk at the sides. Could we outrun the rush of water? I am braced in the car, ready to bolt. I do not intend to sit there and let the water rise over my head. I consider the weight of the water on the walls. At last I see the first rectangles of sunlight against the worn brick and soon the opening that leads out of the tunnel. In my life I will never be afraid of tunnels. Also I will never stop staring at the walls, is that a leak or a stain I see over there?

My mother tells me that her fear of leakage in the tunnel is neurotic but she can't help it. My mother is also afraid of cats. She pulls my arm and changes direction on a street when a small gray kitten emerges from underneath a parked car. The December mail brings a calendar from the hardware store. On the cover is a black cat drinking milk from a saucer. My mother throws the calendar into the waste basket and asks the maid to remove the basket. Black cats are bad luck. She will never go into the cleaners on Madison Avenue because the owner has a calico cat that sits on the counter. She is afraid it will pounce and scratch out her eyes.

One day I come home from school and find my mother is in bed with heart pains. She is very pale and holds on to my hand as if we are going to have to say goodbye. We wait for the doctor to arrive. He comes and I am chased from the room. After a while the door opens. I am waiting outside with my own heart jumping. My mother calls me into the room. It was nothing at all. "Anxiety," said the doctor.

I often went with my mother to a variety of doctors' offices where she was examined for stomach pains that might be cancer, or might be ulcers, headaches that signaled brain tumors or the onset of a stroke, swollen feet that meant the approach of kidney failure or debilitating muscle decay.

One morning as I waited for the elevator man to come to the eighth floor I became convinced that this was the day I would get polio. It wasn't the season but I knew it could happen anyway. I imagined myself in a wheelchair. I imagined myself in a coffin. By the time the elevator arrived I was shaking all over. By the time I got on the school bus I had been distracted from my fright. The next morning while waiting for the elevator I remembered that I had thought I would get polio and I hadn't. Perhaps I figured the reason I hadn't become ill was that I had thought of it before it could happen. So I again thought I might get polio and for good measure I added diabetes. I didn't get either and so began a morning ritual which involved a list of terrible illnesses that might afflict me during the day, all recited in the early morning before the elevator. This ritual I believed was responsible for my continued good health despite the treacherous microscopic life that persisted all around us. My mother said it was neurotic.

What my brother did to protect himself from death I did not know.

After the war some of the downtown buildings install automatic elevators. My mother will not ride in one. She is afraid the elevator will smash through the roof or plummet to the floor. Her dentist is nineteen flights up. She is afraid to be alone in the stairwell so I go with her. She takes off her heels and walks in stocking feet. Her bracelets clang as she moves her arms. She drops a glove or her eyeglass case or a handkerchief or a piece of paper or a magazine and I run down a flight of stairs to retrieve it. She tells me to count the steps as we are going up. She stops every few floors and rests. She takes out a cigarette and lets me light the match. Smoke floats out over the iron railings and disappears in downward drafts.

I sit in the waiting room reading *Life* or the *National Geographic* feeling the animal world near but far, too far away. We walk back down.

My mother is afraid of electricity and will not change a light bulb. She summons the building's superintendent if a lamp won't shine.

I've heard her talk on the phone with my Aunt Libby, the favored sister, with whom my mother also discussed every moment of her life about the strange rash on her back or her suspicion that she had a tumor in her ovary. Is this a neurosis? I think so.

I begin to worry about my mother's mental health. How many neuroses can one person have before they grow totally crazy?

In my fifth-grade class is a tall awkward girl also named Anne who inhabits her body as if it belonged to an unfriendly stranger. She has nothing to say to her classmates who ignore her. She hangs to the side in recess. She has long braids and thick glasses and she chews sores into her fingers which always seem in some stage of infection. She lives at 1185 Park too. She waits for the school bus with me. The doormen don't call her "Annie Lass," which is what they call me. As we wait for the bus I arm-wrestle with a boy. I trade playing cards with reproductions of Rembrandt's *Blue Boy* and the Eiffel Tower for others with pictures of dogs on them. I bounce a ball off the wall near the doctors' offices on the side of the building, sometimes I hit an early morning patient or the ball rolls into the street and the doormen chase it for me. But the other Anne doesn't move, clutching her school bag to her chest as if someone is planning to steal it. She writes. She writes poetry. She writes amazing poetry with large words (some I don't know) and swooping long lines. She writes about dying. She writes about a voice that speaks in her head. I am jealous of her poetry. She is a far better writer than I am. I'm no fool. If in such a small class in one school in all of America someone is better at it than I am, then what can I hope for.?

In the spring she drops out of school. She no longer waits for the bus with me. She disappears. My mother tells me she has had a nervous breakdown and has been taken to a children's hospital in upstate New York for treatment. "Anne has gone mad," says my mother. I am alarmed by her madness. I am pleased that the competition couldn't stay the course. I wish we did not have the same first name. My mother and my brother have visited psychoanalysts and so of course will be cured and will not go mad like Anne. This I believe but not with all my heart.

ballad for americans   My brother and I went to Ethical Culture which was a private school forged in the furnace of John Dewey and the progressive education movement. Ethical Culture under the guidance of Algernon Black, a man who had as sonorous a voice as any minister in America, preached each Sunday calling for universal brotherhood as if all our lives depended on it, which as the pictures of the recently liberated camps in Eastern Europe confirmed, they really did. The congregation and its imposing building connected to the school on 61st Street off Central Park intended to unite white and Negro, Jew and gentile in a moral rational humanistic religion and this religion infused the school with goodness. These were moral enough people who hoped for the best for themselves and usually for others. There was none of the nails-ran-in stuff of the Holy Son and only the most general universal rules of the difficult Father. The school as well as the religion was liberal and sweet. It was the new age creed for that new age.

In the end however, the school and the religion primarily served only Jewish families who had better things to do than be Jewish, more modern things, more profitable things, more prestigious things, more appropriately American, less swamped by the tragedies and claims of the old world. What endangered chameleon doesn't dream of invisibility? But my class at Ethical Culture only had one white Christian child, two Negro children, and one child in a wheelchair. They were all on scholarship meaning that they had to be bribed to go to a school with Jews so eager was the prosperous gentile world for a culture that was nonsectarian, universal, and truly Ethical.

When I graduated from the sixth grade I wore a white dress with a small yellow rose pinned to the waist. The class performed Paul Robeson's "Ballad for Americans." From all parts of the auditorium different kids called out their professions, Engineer, Musician Street Cleaner, Farmer, Bartender. We announced as a class our profound devotion to the American vision of equality for all peoples. We truly were the "Nobodies who were Anybodies who believed it." Together we wrapped ourselves in the flag of a land that never ever existed outside of folksong lyrics written by the blacklisted, the utopians, the wool-over-the-eyes, dreamers and sentimentalists who had nothing in common with the parents of the children singing with all their might on the platform.

We were the much softer, very well-orthodontured second generation living along Central Park West, Park Avenue, Fifth Avenue. We wanted to believe that poverty and prejudice were just so much spoiled milk from the pre–General Electric European kitchen. When we raised our collective voices in the auditorium and belted out "Our Country's strong, our country's young our greatest song is yet unsung," we believed it. Hadn't America won the war because we were good?

One Saturday late afternoon my mother is at the hairdresser and my brother is in his room with the door closed and my father comes in the apartment and immediately walks to the telephone in the living room. I hear him go through the hall and I open my door. I stop on the threshold of the room. I hear him talking. "Judge," he is saying, "I am prepared to offer you the full amount you asked for. Delivery in cash, of course." Yes, Judge, he says. "It's a perfectly fair amount," he adds. "I agree," he says. "This will not be a long trial."

My father hangs up the phone. I come into the room. "What was that?" I say. "Are you going to give the judge money?" My father looks embarrassed. "You were eavesdropping," he says to me. "You have no right." His voice begins to rise in a dangerous way. "But," I say, "what about justice, what about a fair trial?" "We are going to have a fair trial," says my father. "The other side gave the judge money too. This equals it out." He waves me away as he goes to the bar to get his afternoon scotch and ice. I have more to say. I don't say it.

therapy   It is after school, before dinner, I am playing cards with my mother. The scotch glass by her bed is almost empty. She asks me to get her another. She is improving my canasta game. She is telling me about her friend Nina's husband who had stolen money from the company he worked for and had hired a lawyer to defend him. I ask her to explain a Peter Arno cartoon in the *New Yorker*, which has something to do with a nude lady and a martini olive. "Later," she says. "I have something important to tell you. Dr. Bornstein told me that Johnny is in terrible danger. The problem lies deep in his character. Johnny is highly intelligent, gifted but very anxious. His deep fears bring on his asthma."

"Help him," my mother had said to Dr. Bornstein.

Am I as smart as my brother? I am not.

My brother entered treatment. My mother began her own analysis. Now in addition to taking the Fifth Avenue bus downtown and shopping for clothes at Saks and Bonwit Teller's and Bergdorf Goodman's, in addition to canasta and twice-weekly visits to the hairdresser that took a minimum of two hours, in addition to pedicures and chiropodists, internists and dentists, podiatrists and department stores, and then visits to return the clothes that were originally purchased but finally rejected my mother had five weekly sessions with her analyst. Sometimes during school vacations I would wait for her downstairs in the lobby. She wouldn't let me go into the waiting room. She would come downstairs with her eyes red and her makeup askew. She wouldn't tell me what happened. Then we would go downtown on a Fifth Avenue bus to Saks Fifth Avenue so my mother could return or purchase an item and she would tell me the plots of novels she had read or movies she had seen.

Bliss. I remain the favorite child, the best beloved.

Soon my brother stopped thinking that he would be poisoned with each meal. Otherwise everything seemed the same. He was a pale thin child who wheezed when he ran. He had dark circles under his eyes because there were many nights when he didn't sleep at all. What was wrong with him? I knew. I didn't have to ask. In the street I would see a father holding his son's hand and my heart would beat erratically. There it was. I would see a mother bend down to help a child who had fallen learning how to roller-skate and I would stare with wonder. I knew what was wrong. It was in the way my father had told my mother she was a two-bit flea-ridden whore. It was the way he shouted when he told her that he hated the way she wore opened-toed shoes or despised the way nicotine gathered between her two front teeth and the smell of her smoker's breath. She told him that he must never say anything about her breath again and he had, very often.

Of course there were things that were right with my brother too. Sometimes he giggled and smiled, a big toothy wiseacre smile, a rueful, wistful, sweet and not-so-sweet smile that seemed to make his shoulders move, that made his blue nearsighted eyes crinkle up and almost close, a smile that stretched across his face, a hint of cruelty, a dash of amazement, and always a humor, a wit that followed a pun, that followed a joke he had heard or one that he repeated, that followed the Jack Benny wisecrack, that followed a Groucho Marx slap on the side of the head, that followed his mind where the upsidedowness, the insideoutness of anything made him grin. He began to tell jokes in accents, with his eyebrows raised, in whispers, in shouts. He loved jokes. Why did the old truck get off the road? Because it was retired. Why did the potato chip jump off the Empire State Building? Because it wasn't Wise. An old woman with a bag in her arms came rushing downstairs when she heard the garbage truck, "Am I too late?" she asked the driver. "No," he said, "jump on in."

10

rye: a house in the country   My parents bought a
summer and weekend house in Rye, New York. My mother purchased it
with her money and my father was obligated to pay the taxes and the up-
keep. He never did. For both of them this was salt in the wound, continually rubbed in. The house was on the water and from the porch we could
see the tide come up over the rocks and then recede again. We could smell
the seaweed and watch the gulls dip up and down over the occasional sail-
boat that floated farther out.

The house had a dock and in high tide you could jump from the ladder
and the dark deep water would enclose your body. The rocks formed a small
jagged quarry running down to shallow waters where bait fish and algae
gathered, snails and barnacles clung to the mossy black side of stones.
There was a flagpole and an American flag was raised and lowered whenever I remembered to do it. My bedroom had a dressing table with a white
tulle skirt and a mirror with flowers pressed into the frame. My bed was
covered with a white spread with pink stars across it. The wallpaper was
pink with tiny fairies waving gold wands across the walls. The carpet was
white and I had to take my sneakers off before entering. My brother's room

faced the water and had a terrace. Greta slept there with him until she left. My mother did not like the country.

We belonged to a country club with a large swimming pool in which in August my mother was afraid to let me swim because of polio. She would play cards at the poolside with her friends and my brother would stay home with Greta and I would sit on the chaise and watch the passing scene. She did not like tennis or golf. She did a slow careful sidestroke in the club pool wearing a white bathing cap with a strap under the chin. She did not want to get her hair wet. She did not want her eye makeup to run although it always did no matter how careful she was.

As soon as summer was over my mother went back to the city. She did not like bugs. She did not like driving. She would not ride a bike or dig in the garden.

She had a canasta friend named Lilian Birnbaum. The Birnbaums lived in nearby Green Haven and Harry Birnbaum owned an insurance company. The Birnbaums had a teenage daughter who was a tennis star at the club. Lilian Birnbaum also had a midnight black miniature poodle, named Louella in honor of Lilian's favorite columnist, Louella Parsons. Louella was never separated from her owner. While Lilian played cards or sat under the hair dryer the poodle would sit on her lap. In the winter Louella went everywhere in the sleeve of Lilian's mink coat and sometimes Lilian would forget that Louella was sleeping against her elbow and when she took off her coat, Louella would come tumbling out. Lilian would pick the dog up and combing her nails through the pom-pom on the end of the little tail she would whisper in her ear, "Mommy's sorry, so sorry." In the summer Louella was carried about in a handbag and as Lilian approached you could just see the little nose wet and running above the clasp. While my mother played cards I would hold Louella. I examined the tiny legs and the small paws that were as big as dimes. I looked in her soft black eyes and smelled her fur, shampooed each day and towel-dried. Then Louella was pregnant by a miniature champion. Each of the babies was to be worth many hundreds of dollars. Lilian knew I was attached to Louella. She invited me over after the birth. In a small jewelry box on her bed placed on the pink satin coverlet right in the center of her embossed monogram I found five tiny dogs, each the size of a finger, each with perfect face, little curls, one white, the others black like their mother. Louella had trouble nursing and so Lilian would feed the puppies with an eyedropper. She allowed me to help. She had a green marble sink with gold faucets in her green marble bathroom. She invited me into the bathroom with her as she applied her makeup. She took the jewelry box with her and put it on the side of the sink so she could keep one eye on the puppies. She was running hot water to wash her hairbrush. I was standing by the bathtub when she suddenly reached for her powder on a nearby shelf and with a jerk of her arm knocked the box into the sink. The drain was open and she shrieked as one of the puppies slid down the open black hole and then another one. She reached with her hands to save the third but too late as the swirling water covered the waving paws. I grabbed for the fourth as did she and I got it between my thumb and forefinger. I raised the wet puppy up to my chest and felt its small faint heartbeat. Lilian tearing off her blouse took the surviving puppy and stuffed it in the top of her bra hoping her body warmth would restore the dog. She was weeping. I was weeping. I looked down the drain, there was nothing but darkness. On the floor the tiny eyedropper sat. Louella slept undisturbed on a pillow on a flowered chair. It wasn't my fault. No one blamed me. My mother's friendship with Lilian cooled.

But this turned out also not to be my fault. My mother told me that her other friend Marion told my mother, who told me, that Lilian had been boasting about a certain hotel in White Plains where she went with a certain man at least once a week all through the warm summer months. My mother told me that once again my father had not been able to resist temptation. I thought of the miniature poodles swirling downward to certain death in the sewer system. Everywhere there was betrayal of trust. I was neither surprised nor shocked.

She was afraid of the dark water and would not swim except at the pool at the club. My mother did not play tennis or golf. She played cards at the club. My father played tennis all morning and went off to play golf and then to a massage or a drink in the club main house in the afternoon. Sometimes when I would beg him he would play tennis with me for a half-hour. I smashed and ran and chased balls. When he told me what to do, turn my side to the net, follow through, I tried with all my might. When he complimented me I felt my skin grow warm and tight and sometimes I could hear my heart beating in my chest, alive. I was his tennis partner, I was his friend. My brother refused to learn to play. He did not like balls. He said it was a stupid game in which your body moved while your brain slept. By default I would be my father's heir. In the fall goldenrod grew on the sides of the roads. In the spring the dandelions released pollen into the air. My brother did not want to ride a bike with me. He stayed in his room. He wheezed.

When my brother was about eight and I was eleven, in late June when school was out and before camp started, the horseshoe crab birthrate seemed to rise. Down at the base of the rocks there were usually two or three or more large horseshoe crabs with their babies attached to their backs. The crabs are shaped like horseshoes, with beady eyes rising from their brown slime–covered head bodies and a long saw-toothed skinny bone tail that swished in the shallow water behind them. They are not pretty or intelligent creatures, a primitive form reminding of prehistoric origins, of nonverbal urges. If you picked them up by the tail and turned them over you could see their many pincer legs frantically moving in the air and their soft underbellies covered by a membrane of glassy white interrupted by thin brittle bone sections. Their babies cling to the mother's back and receive food from her until they are big enough to swim off by themselves.

One day I call to my brother and show him the baby horseshoe crabs riding on their mothers' backs in the tidal pools. I expect him to admire them with me but with a quick motion he grabs the baby by its small tail and pulls it off the mother's slippery shell. He puts the mother crab back in the water on the other side of the rocks. The baby is destined to die without its mother. The mother begins to rush about frantically, a dim sense, an instinct of species preservation stirring within its small neural system, legs clawing at the mud, searching for the baby, now far away, moving off blindly into the deep toward inevitable extinction. My brother picks up another mother and child crab. I see my brother fling the baby crab out as far as possible, as far away from the mother as the muscles in his small arm will allow.

I step into the muddy pebble-filled dark pools trying to reattach baby with mother. I can find the baby but can't find the mother or the other way around. I try for hours to reunite the pairs and my brother sits on the rocks and watches me with a strange smile on his face. After the first time he does this day after day. I beg him not to do it. I bribe him with anything of mine he wants. I have nothing he wants.

In the morning after breakfast he rushes down and pulls another horseshoe crab away from its mother and then another and another. I go deep into the water cutting my toes on shells, chasing after the crabs.

"I'll tell," I say. I tell. Greta doesn't want my brother to get his feet wet. My mother says, "They're just crabs." I think of the baby starving, of the mother searching and I call my brother a Nazi. He laughs at me. Every morning in June the game that is not a game is repeated until I go off to camp, and in September when I return there are no more crabs carrying babies on their backs, the season is over.

There is one game he will play with me. He is fond of Captain Marvel comics. In these comics a boy named Billy is able to change into a superhero who can fly and has extraordinary muscle power by shouting the word *Shazam*. His arch enemy is a mad scientist named Sylvester who is always planning to poison the water supply. I take the role of Sylvester, who has a high cackling laugh: something like Heh, heh, heh. We play in the basement where it is dark and damp. Greta is knitting in the kitchen. We race around up and down the cellar steps. Usually I allow him to catch me. "Foiled again," I scream and he stands over me triumphant, good has vanquished evil once again. But one day I run up the steps and out the basement door, and I turn the key that was left in the door and lock my brother, a.k.a. Captain Marvel, into the dark basement. (He can't reach the light switch.) He pounds on the door. "Let me out," he calls. "Help," he screams. "Shazam," he shouts, "Shazam." "Shazam," he calls to the heavens waiting for the transformation from Billy to Captain Marvel that never comes. "Heh, heh, heh," I laugh from my side of the door. Greta hears him weeping and lets him out. Wicked I am. Guilty I am. But not sorry. I am not sorry. Did my brother tell on me to Dr. Bornstein. Probably. Did I worry about what Dr. Bornstein thought of me? Yes I did.

sleep-away camp: an experiment that fails

Doctor Bornstein had told my mother that my father should spend more time with my brother but my brother only wanted to practice the piano. At my all-girls camp in Maine I was content. All through the long summer I cared about the welfare of the Tiger team, about hitting the bull's-eye in

archery, about gaining my Red Cross swimming card. I had promised myself
that like my father I would be fast and free. I would run till my breath would
give out. I was always the captain. I believed in winning every game.

Dr. Bornstein thought that camp would be helpful for my brother. He
went to Camp Wigwam which is where the boys of our family went to mingle with others from families just like ours although perhaps from Cincin-
nati or Nashville. In Maine the mornings were crisp, cold and your skin had
goose bumps. In the afternoon the heat rose and dust floated up from the
baseball diamond. In Maine the lake was filled with leeches that sucked at
the skin and underwater hidden weeds that undulated with the wind. In
Maine my brother went on a hike with his cabin and he sat down at the side
of the road and refused to go another step. It seemed without point to him,
this climb through the fields. He did not want to make a birch bark canoe
or to learn the names of plants or bugs. He did not want to improve his
swimming and he was chosen last for every ball game. He did not want to
run or catch or push or pull. He didn't want to lift or carry, carve or whistle.
He did not like camp songs. He would not eat the food in the dining room
where there was noise, shouting, and no one wanted to sit near him. He
sneezed and wheezed and ran a fever. He was allergic to everything in
Maine, the bugs, the pine, the lake water. There was poison ivy growing in
bunches by the side of the road. He got poison ivy and impetigo. The camp
nurse covered his legs with calamine lotion. There was pollen in the air and
his lungs would clutch and he would have to suck hard to draw breath
down.

Pine needles, strawberry bushes, butterfly wings did not amaze him. All
he knew was that outside of his apartment on Park Avenue there were dan-
gers to his lungs, things of the earth, things of the Garden of Eden would
make his airways swell, and his nose leak and his eyes water. Where there
was the humming of insects, the song of birds, the sound of old fallen
leaves gathering around an oar, he saw the enemy: the omnipresent spores
of germinating chlorophyll-seeking, photosynthesis-capable, sun-drenched,
rain-fertilized life.

He knew while he was exiled to camp that everything good for him was
indoors and everything outside a potential danger. He feared that the rain
would give him bronchitis and the dust-filled air would choke him and the

indifferent counselors would leave him for dead on the side of the road, an empty metal canteen attached to his camper's belt.

He came home. He had lasted until the first week of August. He hated every moment. The other boys in his cabin mocked him. The counselors teased him. He would not go in the water. He would not go for hikes. He did not want to play. He would not compete for ribbons or trophies. He sneezed all the time. He lost weight. He did not like the thin mattress on the bed. He did not like the cold water that ran in the shower. He would not pull the scratchy regulation blanket up over his chest. It gave him a rash. Alarmed the head of the camp finally called my mother to pick him up. She sent her sister Sylvia's chauffeur to bring him home. There was no question in my mind. There had been a divine error. He should have been a girl and I should have been a boy. I had the throwing arm for it. He did not.

II

goodbye greta   Then one day after school my mother takes me
to Schrafft's where Irish waitresses in black uniforms with white aprons
serve chocolate syrup–filled sodas and chicken sandwiches with the crusts
cut off. Dr. Bornstein had decided that it was time that Greta leave the
household. It was time that my mother paid full attention to her son. My
mother explains this to me. It isn't good for Johnny to be with a governess.
He needs his mother. It isn't that I can't understand that. It isn't that I
haven't always known that. It was simply that I had hoped, believed, come
to expect that we would continue, my mother and I, as we were, a locked
pair, girlfriends, best friends. I had expected that nothing would change.
My brother would never count. I was wrong or so my mother said that day
at Schrafft's. I am nearly twelve, too old for a public scene but I make one
anyway. I tear my napkin into tiny pieces. I let my tears flow and my sobs
burst forth loudly from my throat and I blow my stuffed-up nose again and
again on the little white napkins the waitress keeps bringing to the table. I
make a public spectacle of myself. I can't help it.

"It's my fault he's so neurotic," my mother says to me. I am not so sure. I
think it is my fault. Under the table I pick at my scabbed knees. This con-

cern for Johnny, although I had sought it, makes my stomach sink. Was I not the more important of her children? Was I not really her child and the other one a mere afterthought, Greta's child? Was I not enough for her? I want her to ignore Johnny. I do want to be good, even in the absolute privacy of my mind I want to love and not hate and I am ashamed of my selfish thoughts but they will not go away.

I knew that my mother's hairdresser's daughter had gotten pregnant before marriage and her entire life was ruined and she had to leave her home and it was the same as if she'd died or maybe worse. My mother told me so. I knew that my mother when she wasn't playing solitaire would sometimes build a house of cards but that it always fell down. I knew that if you had sex before marriage your children might be born with cleft palates. I knew that if you sat down on toilets in public places you could get an infection that would leave you crazy for the rest of your days. I knew that if you saw a nun and didn't spit over your left shoulder you could be a disappointed woman. I knew that if you opened an umbrella inside the house a fatal disease would fall on your head. I wanted my mother to tell me everything she knew so I could know it too. But I didn't want to know that Dr. Bornstein had said that my mother should pay more attention to my brother. I wished she hadn't told me that.

Within a few weeks Greta left the house. I didn't care. She had been nothing but an embarrassment to me, picking me up at friends' houses, appearing at school plays, insisting on rubbers and sweaters and wool hats. She had stayed in our family long after everyone else's governess had gone. There was little affection between us.

What my brother felt he did not tell me. He was now interested in the Civil War and spent hours arranging his lead soldiers on the fields of Gettysburg and Bull Run. Greta was not competent at puzzles and knew little American history. Nevertheless she was his anchor to this earth. She was the one who held his head when he vomited. She made him blue scarves and blue mittens. She watched that his bowel movements were regular and administered enemas if they were not and checked that he brushed his teeth. She woke with him in the middle of the night when he had a nightmare or trouble breathing. He had outgrown her and could dress himself and bathe himself. But still there are some things that no one at any age can ever do for themselves. She did those too.

He may have told this to his analyst or he may not. How does a child say to a therapist, The person who has mothered me is not my mother and the person who is my mother has not mothered me? How does a child say the person who has mothered me will pack her clothes and leave the house and the person who has not mothered me will remain? What does it mean that the nonmother can send the mother packing? What does it mean that the Jesus of the nonmother is not the God of the mother and the language of the house, the food that comes to the table, the clothes on the back, the toy soldiers, the piano lessons, the sheets and the bed, belong to the non-mother woman and nothing at all belongs to the mothering one who will leave, everything she owns in one suitcase, with her brown felt hat on her head and her scrubbed hands in woolen gloves? What does it mean that except for a birthday card and a Christmas card with a picture of the Madonna on it addressed with a childlike European script for Johnny Roth that arrived regularly the original mother has vanished?

I come home from school and find my brother sitting in the chair beside my mother's bed. The room tilts. I say nothing. I am cheerful. My body weighs a thousand tons. Later in my own room I see the lamp light reflected in the windowpane and grow frightened. Where is the lamp really, behind me or in front of me? I am alone and will stay alone forever.

But after a while my brother no longer enters my mother's bedroom at the end of the afternoon. He does not join my mother and me in our conversation. It bores him. Our conversation does not include him. When he gets asthma and lies in bed under a tent made by a white sheet and the steam kettle on a stool beside the bed a substitute governess comes to tend him. We go on as before. I am safe but on guard. He could return.

at last a dog   I had wanted a dog from as long as I could re-member. It began when I was waiting in the hall outside my mother's room for the door to open. I would pretend I had a big dog with soft brown fur that would put his large head in my lap and keep me company. I read all the books by Albert Payson Terhune about collies who found their way home through hurricanes and floods, who back on the farm in Kansas knew through some magic empathy, some animal love that was larger than time or space, that their masters lay in the trenches of Verdun, blood flowing from mortal wounds and howled inconsolably through the night. I read books about boys walking through the woods with their dogs at their heels. I thought about a dog that would sleep at the end of my bed. I wished on every first star that I would get a dog. I wished on all my birthday candles for a dog. I knew that it would take a miracle for my wish to be granted. We did not live on a ranch in Wisconsin or a small town like the characters in the books I was reading. And besides my mother was afraid of dogs and cats. She was so afraid that we would sometimes cross the street to avoid a dog and its owner moving toward us. I on the other hand had no fear. When I saw a dog on the street longing would make me stop and on my knees I would put my face into the dog's fur and my hand would slide up and down the silky legs and I would press with my cheek against the black rough cold nose. When I was bored I would go downstairs and wait for dogs to pass so I could pet them, always asking first as Greta had taught me. Always washing my hands as soon as possible afterward for fear of bacteria, after all a dog's tongue had been in disgusting places. I wasn't really afraid of urine or feces, of dirt on the sidewalk, of food turned rotten, I was afraid of the shadow of a dog that wasn't there.

At last just before my twelfth birthday I began a successful campaign. I would walk through the living room when my mother had her canasta game and I would talk to my imaginary dog. I was too old for this to be more than a sham, a manipulation, a way to shame my mother in front of her friends to give in. "Blanche" one would say, "you really should get that child a dog." "It's not healthy," someone would add, "her talking to an imaginary dog at her age."

Finally, perhaps as the analyst worked on my mother's dog phobia, my mother agreed and the Christmas morning I was thirteen a tiny black dachshund appeared with a red bow under his neck beneath the Christmas tree. It wasn't the dog of my dream. It wasn't the right size or shape or fullness of fur but it was a dog and I knew that compromise was the essence of happiness. Its small size made it possible for my mother to be in the room with the dog and not scream. A few days after Christmas my brother picked up the dog whom I had named Guppy after the tiny black fish and opening the eighth-floor window of our apartment held the dog as far out the window as his arms could reach. The dog was squirming in his hands. The drop below was long and fatal. The buildings on Park Avenue were indifferent. The doorman, even had he seen a child holding a dog perilously above the street, could not have left his post and rushed upstairs. The cook would not come to help me. The maid was out the back door talking with the rear elevator man. My mother was out at the hairdresser, hours left until she might come home. The cold air blew into the apartment from the open window. "I'll drop Guppy, I'll let go, if you don't give me half ownership of the dog," my brother said. Possession, exclusive possession was always the point of having a dog or so I thought. But freezing at the window I knew about Solomon and the baby whom the real mother would not allow to be cut in half, and I knew that half a dog was better than no dog at all and I felt in the pit of my being the way the puppy would feel dropping fast and faster, understanding and not understanding that great pain was coming. I saw the dog smashed into tissue and bone, blood and teeth on the ground just near where the taxis were pulling up to the curb, where the gold embossed mailbox was attached to the gray stone wall of the building, where the doorman's white gloves glistened in the sunlight. There was frost on the dog's small nose and ice chips on his lower lip and his short legs waved in a frantic attempt to find the ground. I gave my brother half ownership of Guppy and he pulled his arms back and I closed the window.

However, shortly afterward Johnny began to wheeze and an asthma attack followed and the governess who was hired to take care of him while he was ill wouldn't allow the dog in his room at all and then the pediatrician said we couldn't have a dog since it was making my brother sick and so Guppy was sent away to a cousin's where I was allowed to visit on Saturdays and did so for over two years.

Now my brother's room looked very different from mine. His lead soldiers in their exact uniforms, miniature insignias, rifles strapped to the side were lined up in battle formation over a table kept in the corner. He kept his allowance in a small safe in his closet. The combination was his secret. I spent my allowance on sodas and movies with friends. Sometimes I would ask him for a loan. He held my pearls hostage till I returned the three dollars I had borrowed. He took my watch with the gold face and the black velvet band and kept it in his safe and refused to return it even when I had managed to save up the price he had demanded for the loan. I gave up on my watch. He collected stamps in a book and he knew each name and each date of issue. I lay on my bed with its pink-flowered bedspread and day-dreamed of owning a horse, of living on a ranch in Montana, of a father returning from a war and reclaiming me as his real daughter and taking me off to the woods of Canada to live with the Mounties. I read my mother's mystery novels and the stories in the *New Yorker* from which I learned that women and men were like parallel lines that would never meet.

Although I was beginning to consider the hurt of the oppressed Negroes and the refugees in camps and the hungry everywhere I paid little attention to the soreness of my brother who lived in the room next door with a bathroom shared between us. So it took a long time for me to understand that Johnny who had lost his Greta could not allow me the sole possession of my beloved dog. It took me a while to understand that something had divided us when we should have been united. In the stories I was reading the siblings reconciled and planned and plotted their adventures together. In real life on Park Avenue we stayed in our separate rooms and opportunity after opportunity was missed. Whatever we needed we were unable to give it to each other.

masochism   Now that Greta no longer was with us we ate with our parents at the dining table except for those nights when my mother was out at the theater or my father stayed late at his club or my mother had a card game or my father went to a political meeting at Tammany Hall. He was hoping for a judgeship but one never came. My mother told me that he was rude to people and so they never even gave him a chance to buy a judgeship, not even one on traffic court.

On the weekends my father went off to his clubs to play tennis or golf or squash or swim. He had massages and saunas and came home late and when he was home he paced in the hall. Night after night he called my mother a dumb broad at least once before dessert. Now something new entered their arguments. It was the mighty question of who had started the fight. The fight whatever its spark soon settled into a shouting match over who had begun the battle. Some moral superiority was accorded the participant who was the victim of the other's bad judgment. The heart of the battle beat loudest when it came to the question of who was to blame that the battle had begun in the first place. The maid kept on serving the dinner, the meat on silver trays, the vegetables served in bowls with silver ladles. I kept on eating. I ate everything in front on me. I stared at the food and at the maid approaching my place with the tray. My fork, my knife, kept moving in a steady path toward my mouth. My mother was certain that there would have been no fight if only my father had not raised his voice, smashed his fist against the table, said something cruel about her brother or sister, or criticized her dress or remarked on the bad choice of upholstery for the hall chairs. My father on the other hand was equally certain that the fight would never have happened if my mother hadn't worn bobby pins in her hair after he had told her a dozen times he found them repulsive, if she hadn't reminded him that he was overdue on the loan she had made him to pay his last quarter's taxes. If she didn't insist that he talk to her stupid friends, if she hadn't complained that he was late again for dinner, if she didn't try to keep him on a leash, if she hadn't asked Emma to cook the roast beef rare which she knew he loathed. At the dinner table my brother would sit and stare out into space and his fingers would move up and down the table edge practicing some piece of music.

As the real sounds would get louder both my mother and father would turn to me and ask, "Well, who started it?" I always knew but I didn't always want to say. Also who started it isn't the most important question moreover who started it tonight isn't always the right way to look at the problem because tonight's provocation could have been caused by last night's and all of them connected in one long joyless conga line that went round and round year after year. But I had to answer the question. They waited for me to answer the question. There was a pause, a silence, a temporary truce in the air.

Judiciously, aware that this was not a time for partisanship, that everything depended on my answer I would choose. "Mother shouldn't have worn the bobby pins you hate but perhaps it wasn't necessary to tell her she looked like a waitress in a truckers' diner," I would say. Then my mother would cry and leave the table and my father would throw down his napkin and leave the house for a long walk no matter the weather, no matter the hour, walking would calm him. Nothing calmed my mother.

I am standing on Madison Avenue downtown waiting for a bus with my mother. We have been to her dressmaker's. It is cold and a rain begins. She is wearing open-toed shoes. I feel the cold inside my gloves. I feel it on the tips of my ears. We press against the side of the building but we are still getting wet. A sharp wind is blowing. The bus is not coming. I say, "Let's take a taxi." My mother says, "Are you crazy? Money should be saved, money doesn't grow on trees. Money can't be spent whenever you like." We wait for the bus. I think perhaps my Uncle Sy will come along in his company chauffeured car and see us and bring us home. He doesn't.

One Christmas after my Aunt Libby and her family had come for brunch and I had a birthday cake with a miniature Santa Claus on top and a red and green candy wreath trimming the sides my mother, father, brother, and I went out for dinner to a Chinese restaurant. There were red and blue bulbs and mistletoe hanging from the dragon decorations along the walls. My mother loved Chinese food. My father hated it. He hated the smell of sesame cooking oil. He hated the smell of odd spices. Because it was Christmas and my birthday we went to the restaurant. I was wearing a black velvet dress with a white lace collar. My brother had on a shirt and a striped tie. He had not wanted to come. He kept his head down and would not look at me.

My mother and father have straight scotches. I have a drink with a red cherry in it. My brother says he is sure the place has cockroaches. My father says he can smell spoiled meat. My mother says the restaurant is one of the best, her friend Fay recommended it. My father says that Fay whose husband was a financial failure and who therefore had to work removing hairs with an electrolysis machine in an office on 57th Street is a dumb broad. My mother says she is not. The food comes and the waiter divides it all equally and places it in front of us. "I am not going to pay for your son's creepy analyst anymore," says my father. "He's not getting any better and I won't pay the bill." "A decent father pays for his son's medical expenses," says my mother. "If you think he needs the head doctor," my father says, "you pay for it." "It's your responsibility," says my mother. My mother turns to me, "You think he should pay for it, don't you." "Yes," I say as mildly as possible. My father turns on me. "You're a fool," he says. "Don't call her that," says my mother. I can see other diners looking at us. My brother keeps his head down. His face is ashen. "Please," I say, "not here, not on my birthday." "You're always on her side," says my father. My mother says, "You still owe me for the last quarter's taxes. You owe me all the money on the investment you made in that stupid shoe stock that is now at 8." "You'll get your goddamn money," says my father. "No," says my mother. "I haven't a chance." My father takes the corner of the tablecloth and pulls it up. The dishes go scattering, noodles and moo shu pancakes, shrimp in a glassy white sauce, bits and pieces of snow peas slide to the floor, mushrooms and rice clumped together on the silver dishes turn over slowly. My maraschino cherry falls on the seat. My mother's drink spills, amber liquid on the red leather seat cushion. My mother howls as if she had been wounded by a cannon ball. The waiters rushed over. My father stalks out of the restaurant into the night. In my mother's lap chicken bits with sesame seeds soak into her skirt. My brother says nothing. There is a dampness in my eyes. I blink it away.

No face can be saved now. My mother's is broken like a chipped plate, my brother's is masked, and mine is discovering that shame can be swallowed and people can stare at you without damaging any vital organs.

Something else. I had wanted to leave the restaurant with my father.

It was around this time that I began to betray my mother at least in imagination. It came to me that I alone, without her, could make him happy. I would not question him or undermine him. I would compliment him and listen to him and ask him questions so he could lecture me with the answers and all would be well between us. It came to me that there was something about my mother, always wanting attention, unwilling to wait calmly for him to turn to her, always demanding he notice that she had a cold or a new dress or had replaced the lamp shades that provoked all the trouble. I would know how to be sweet to him, to leave him in peace, and in return he would always be happy with me. I thought that if I always agreed with him, admired him, smiled at him he would blossom like the paper flowers you drop in a glass of water and their deep-colored petals open and dazzle the eye. I thought my mother lacked tact. She confronted and demanded instead of standing by. If I had been his wife I would never eat at a restaurant he didn't like. I would never wear something he told me he disliked.

Above all else I would instantly give him all my money so he wouldn't feel bad. I knew that money was a salt in the wound. Maybe it was the wound itself. If I were his wife I wouldn't make him feel small or penniless. I thought my mother was at fault. She simply didn't know how to love him. I would. I knew I would. With the stroking palm of my hand I thought I could make his headaches go away.

Ah, now how much I love him in his pain, how I long to release him from the trap of my mother's bed. When he slams the door and goes for his long walks he now sometimes allows me to go with him, my legs aching with the long reach. But I don't complain about the pace. We walk in silence thirty, forty blocks and then turn around. I am a good companion. I don't ask for conversation. I am also a traitor.

"What if no one pays for my analyst?" my brother asks me. "Don't worry," I say. She'll pay. There is more talk of divorce.

My father did not want a divorce. His temper had cost him most of the few clients he had with the exception of the family firm, the Van Heusen Shirt company. He had a very ample retainer to represent the company. This was his major client. If there was a divorce he would surely be fired. He promised to reform. He promised to be faithful. He promised to pay attention to his wife. My Aunt Libby told my mother she was making a fuss about nothing. "Just ignore him," she said. "Enjoy your life. Who cares about him. Men," she said, "don't matter." My mother's analyst definitely did not agree with this position. But my Uncle Sy advised his beloved sister to remain in the marriage. The scandal would be bad for the entire family. She would be a threat to other people's marriages as a divorced woman and would be invited nowhere. She would be a pariah. He cautioned her to remain in the marriage. Divorce at the end of the forties and throughout the fifties was not common and often left a woman without friends. Divorce was an admission of failure not just of your marriage but of your life's purpose, your assumed work, your absolute duty.

My mother, even with the help of her analyst whom she told me understood her better than anyone else in the world (except me), was not yet able to brave the world alone. She needed more time to prepare herself she told me. She decided to give the marriage another chance; she decided this again and again. A loud eruption, a volcanic shouting, a grand weeping would bring her to the brink and then she would pull back. Over the edge lay the unknown.

There would be days, maybe a month, of calm, or order. I could feel the tension in my stomach ease and then it would begin again.

She had grown plump and wore her dark glasses all the time to cover the shadows under her eyes. She had gas in her frequently extended stomach and her gums bled and when she went in the sun her freckles spread and her dyed blonde hair had a greenish hue. " I'm an ugly duckling," she would say. "You're not," I would counter. Her analyst explained to her about masochism. She explained it to me. I understood perfectly. "I must be a masochist," she would say to me and her eyes would fill with tears and I would say, "Promise me you'll stop being a masochist," and she would say, "I will, as soon as I can, I promise."

She tried not wearing her glasses. She kept them on top of her head for emergencies. She couldn't recognize friends on the street until they had bumped into her. She couldn't tell if the light was red or green at the corner. She would wait for someone else to cross. Later when contacts became available she tried but kept dropping them or losing them and they made her eyes sore. Once she went to a party and kept her glasses in her beaded pocketbook. She saw a black ashtray on a coffee table and she smashed the lipstick-stained end of her cigarette down, only to hear gasps from all the people sitting around. She had ground her lit cigarette, ash and butt, into a large dish of black caviar.

12

waterskiing   My tennis game improved. I could smash anything at the net and sometimes my father would agree to play a few games with me, before the adults took the court. I would go with him to Rye and over to the house a few miles away where a refugee sweater manufacturer Gert Siegal and his wife Elisabeth had arrived just after the war and rebuilt his business. The house they lived in was on the water. They had a speedboat and a tennis court and their little girl had a pony. Their young boys tumbled about the long lawn watched by the butler or the Polish nanny. Elisabeth Siegal did not play tennis. She lay in a lounge chair by the side of the courts and watched. She wore short play dresses and her long legs were smooth and tan. She had big wide dark eyes and black hair and was younger by a decade and a half than my mother. She sipped ice tea from tall glasses that were brought down to the courts on a tray by a maid. Gert Siegal did not play a good game of tennis and my father said he was a fat jerk. It was true that his stomach bulged out over his shorts and that he had begun to lose his hair while my father's was still black and silky and perfectly slicked to the scalp. Often Gert Siegal would take me waterskiing with his sons after the tennis game.

My mother wasn't interested or wasn't invited. I watched the men's tennis game. I applauded my father, silently of course. He slammed, he smashed, he raced to the net. He grit his teeth, he tried even for the most difficult balls. I thought he was showing off for me until I realized that the lady of the house whispered into his ear when the games were over, that she made sure that his glass of lemonade was full of ice cubes, that she never looked at any of the other players. Sometimes when one of the partners was unable to come I was allowed to substitute on my father's side. I too could smash a ball, run to the net, and serve an ace. The tennis coach at the country club had suggested to my mother that she should move to California so that I would have a real opportunity to train and compete. My mother did not respond.

When I played with my father across the court I tried for every ball. I hit as hard as I could. I would never admit exhaustion. I stretched my arms and legs out to the sky. I thought he admired his daughter sweating on the other side of the net. Joy circulated through my body, happiness was completely mine. But when I played on his side he would yell at me to get out of the way and he would try to play both his side of the court and mine. If I hit something out or into the net he would scream at me. "Goddamn idiot, keep your side to the net." If I double-faulted he would groan. But I also knew he was pleased that I was such a good player. I was his athlete, almost his son. Sometimes he would put his hand on my shoulder and tell someone that I was a natural. I had strong legs. I was steady. When he did that I felt there was nothing I wouldn't do to please him.

But the lady of the house was always smiling at him and after the game he would have me wait and wait while he sat by her side and they talked in low voices. It seemed she could only understand the newspapers if he explained to her what it all meant. She would smile at him while he talked. "What a brilliant man your father is," she said to me.

I knew that the Siegals' house offered attractions beyond the tennis court.

My mother told me a story about Elisabeth. Is it a true story? I have heard another version from Elisabeth herself and her story has none of the drama, none of the pointedness of my mother's story. So I doubt my mother's story is true in all the details but it may well have the essence, the truth as it reveals itself through fiction. Was my mother lying when she told me the story? I doubt it—perhaps embroidering, binding her tale into history in such a way that I, her audience, could not help but gasp. On the other hand perhaps every single word is true.

My mother told me that Elisabeth was the beautiful daughter of a Jewish sweater manufacturer in Vienna and his Catholic wife. The daughter was raised as a Catholic and when she was twelve was sent to a convent school in the snow-capped mountains above the city. She had never been told that her father was Jewish. Then in 1938 when Hitler marched into Vienna, she was finishing her last year at the convent when word came to the head of the school, a Sister Agnes who had been warning Elisabeth for many years that her body would damn her soul, that Elisabeth's father had been arrested in a roundup of Jewish businessmen and she must go home at once. In Vienna she was told by her weeping mother that if her father was to be rescued from the Nazi jail, she would have to marry immediately into another sweater manufacturer's family, the Siegals. They had received visas to England and would be able to buy Elisabeth's father's release from jail but would do so only if their dateless son were to marry the daughter of the household, uniting the families' destiny. Who could resist such a bargain? What woman would not use her beauty to save her mother, father, and younger brother? That was my mother's version of Elisabeth's story. Later Elisabeth would tell me another version, something about being on a honeymoon in Paris when the Nazis marched into Vienna. I am confused. Is everything a variation on the truth?

From England the family came to Westchester and the sweater business prospered for all the years that Gert Siegal's father ran it, employing the rest of the family. But as the story goes, Elisabeth was not in love with the not so lovely Gert. She bore him children. She went to parties and danced with him but she did not feel like a woman graced with good fortune. She lay on the chaise lounges of her estate and tanned her body in the sun. At night she wore a sleeping mask so her face would not develop lines. In her bedroom she sat at her dressing table and put creams on her forehead and creams on her arms. She believed in resting most of the day to save wear and tear on the body. She dressed in the evening stretching her limbs in front of the mirror. She was smooth and clean and men at the country club, men who came over to play tennis, admired her, stayed to drink a glass of ice tea with her, looked into her dark eyes, and spun for themselves romances that were secretive and pleasing and hardly ruffled the serenity of the spirit that she believed necessary to the preservation of her beauty.

Elisabeth herself told me that when she was a child she would walk into the woods in the parks outside Vienna and she would pretend to find a family of elves and she would play imaginary games with them, feeding them porridge from acorn cups.

Should the atomic bomb have been dropped on Hiroshima? "Yes," shouted my father. Should we have gone after the commies at the end of World War II? "Yes," my father said and agitated by the thought of allowing the Russians to exceed us in any way, he yelled at his tennis partner who thought it was more important to cure cancer than to conquer Russia. Elisabeth smiled at both men. Elisabeth nodded in agreement with everyone. Her eyes were usually covered by dark sunglasses but once when I saw her without them I noticed that she kept her eyes closed most of the time, as if preparing for a long sleep. I thought of her as Heidi living with a frog who did not turn into a prince. Red and blue ribbons tied back her straight soft hair. She told me she always had dogs in Vienna and here in America she had horses and skinny gray whippets whose bones stuck out from their tight skin that slept by her chaise and twitched nervously in response to the rise and fall of the human voice. The gardener had planted purple flowers along the path that led from the Siegal house to the tennis courts. The maid served drinks accompanied by ice in silver buckets. Elisabeth sometimes slept while the men played. Sometimes she would wake and call bravo but no one was quite sure whom she was cheering. All the men would turn to her and nod.

The nuns at the convent had loved her, she said. Sister Marie-Beatrice had given her her own gold cross she said. She didn't know where it was now, she didn't need it she said. She told me I should brush my hair five hundred strokes a day so that it wouldn't be so stiff. She told me to wear powder on my face and keep a hat on my head so the sun wouldn't turn my skin into alligator hide. She wore high-heeled sandals from which her painted toes peeped out as if they held delicious secrets. She had another baby, her fourth child. The nanny kept him out of sight.

One June afternoon after the tennis game Elisabeth and Gert and one of his sons and my father and I went out in the Siegals' boat to water-ski. By then I could ride the waves with one hand holding on and cross the wake back and forth. I would look down at the foaming crest and feel the rise of panic and push the fear out of my body and swoop up and down with the curve of the boat. With the wind on my face and my hair going wild I was like a monkey jumping from tree limb to limb, I was a soul sprung from its body, a fish rising from the depth into the dazzle of salt spray.

My father did not know how to water-ski. He had been talked into the boat by Elisabeth. She sat on the red leather seat in the bow applying lotion to her already glowing skin. After my turn Gert suggested that my father try. He jumped into the water. He got his feet into the skis and called out that he was ready. As he was told he pointed the skis toward the sky but before the motor started he let their points dip downward. The boat jerked forward and should have pulled my father up but instead he went under. The skis were moving forward rapidly but they were pulling him deeper down into the water. My father should have let go of the rope and the bar he was holding in his hand that connected him to the forward force of the boat but he didn't want to admit that he had made a mistake, not in front of Gert, not in front of Elisabeth. He wouldn't give up. He held on. The boat moved forward toward the outer harbor. He did not float to the top. He was down under in the dark green water. I screamed. Elisabeth put her hand on Gert's arms and he turned off the switch. The boat stopped. We waited. At last my father surfaced. He was green around the mouth. Once in the boat he hung his head over the side and vomited. I watched the muscles on his back as he retched again and again. His skin was translucent pale. His hair hung limply, inertly. His legs were shaky. Why didn't you let go of the rope everyone asked him. I knew why. He was grim-lipped on the way back to our house. He told me that waterskiing was a woman's sport. He was only trying it out to be polite.

my father's cronies   On maid's night out, Thursday evening, and then only in the dining room, women were admitted into the City Athletic Club. No matter the day my brother did not want to go with my father, I did. I was allowed to stand only in the vestibule and wait for him to come out. When the door would open I would peer inside and see the burnished wood walls, the coatroom off to the left, and the men, milling back and forth in their dark suits. My father had a friend at the club. Peter Leonard was his name. He and his wife lived a few blocks down on Park Avenue. He had a big belly and a kind laugh. He had dropped out of high school to join his father's hat business. He thought my father was a fount of wisdom and he allowed my father to lecture him hour after hour on the evils of communism, the perfidy of women, the economic big picture, the stock market. "Leonard," my mother said, " is an idiot." And that's why, my mother said, he latched on to my father: because Leonard himself could never complete a sentence. His wife Sandra was nervous and trembled when she held her coffee cup. She wore big diamonds on her fingers and on her wrist she wore a diamond bracelet with rubies. She had long thin legs and she walked as if she was drunk even when she wasn't. A woman had to wear high heels even if she didn't have the balance for it.

Leonard liked to play golf. Sandra liked clown paintings and had a collection in her living room. She also had a complete unopened collection of the *Reader's Digest* condensed classics on a bookshelf. My mother had the same collection but she had read most of them. Leonard had a big voice and a way of commenting loudly on women's body parts. My mother didn't like the way he smelled. My father appeared in contrast to Leonard like the president of a university, like a man of books although he was really only a man of the daily newspapers.

I think Leonard had met Kopatkin on a plane and introduced him to my father. Kopatkin was not a member of the club. He was a small-time, small-fry orchestra conductor, someone on the edges of the music world who sometimes had bookings and sometimes didn't. He bet on the horses. He smoked big cigars and dropped their ashes over the carpets. He told jokes in Yiddish. He would translate them for my father who tried to laugh. He was round and very small and totally bald. Sometimes when a new acquaintance set him up with a wealthy divorcée he would stick his date with the check for an evening at the Carlisle or the Little Club or the Copa. At least that's what my mother told me.

He was permanently unmarried. He admired my handsome father. He arranged for a more distinguished piano teacher for my brother and sometimes on weekends my brother would go the Hotel Volney where Kopatkin kept a suite and play for him. Kopatkin took Johnny out to dinner at Toot's Shor. He urged my father to listen to music. My father ground his teeth when he had to sit still and listen. His hands balled into a fist. But still my father spent more and more of his time with Leonard and Kopatkin. My mother hated Kopatkin and therefore I did too.

The friendship between the three men became part of the chemistry of our household and the piano became a way that my brother whom Kopatkin said had genuine talent could gain some grudging respect if not interest from my father who deeply believed that only perverts would stay inside and practice the piano when they could be out improving their tennis game, getting fresh air into their lungs.

My father had a few strong beliefs about health. Ahead of his time he walked everywhere. Exercise is the key he said. Also he ate no foods with fat. He disliked red meat, butter, and all sauces. He ate simply and every morning he had cereal and prunes. He believed that prunes were nature's anticarcinogens. He believed in bowel regularity. He hated pastrami, fancy French food, and anything that smelled of grease. He hated gravy or sauce. He was thin and perfectly fit. He did not like the foods on his plate to mingle or touch one another. If this happened the maid who was serving dinner would have to remove the plate and bring another.

My mother called Kopatkin and Leonard the Bobbsey Twins. But to my father they must have seemed heaven sent. They listened to him. They respected him. They needed him. They were men. Once I saw my father sitting in a chair in the bedroom in his black stockings held up by braces, his perfectly starched shirt, his pants waiting for him on the wooden valet by his closet and I saw him touch his own freshly shaven face with complete tenderness and I saw in his black eyes such an emptiness, such a hole that needed filling that love surged upward in me and flooded my every nerve, my every muscle, and my head grew light.

My father stays away at his club. A week, two weeks. I don't see him. They are considering divorce. They are having a separation. This is not bad. This is progress. But my mother is in bed most of the day. She dresses only to go out to the analyst. The analyst thinks perhaps she should go into a hospital. A mental hospital. Should she? I am not sure. "I could never stab myself with a knife," she says. "What would you do?" I ask. "Cut my wrists and let the blood run out into the bathtub," she says. "Maybe I could jump out the window," she adds. We are on the eighth floor.

I pretend I am sick. I stay home from school. I don't want her to take a bath without my company. I wake up several times a night and go quietly into her room to make sure she is in bed and that the windows are closed. She seems not to be sleeping. The light is almost always on. The room smells sour, of perspiration, half-eaten sandwiches, stale cigarettes, chewing gum. I call my father at his club. I can hear a loud voice calling his name, again and again over a loudspeaker. Then my father is on the phone. "She misses you," I tell him. "Be a good girl," he says. "Relax," he adds. I call my Aunt Libby. My Aunt Libby comes over. She goes in the bedroom with my mother and closes the door. I wait outside. My Aunt Libby comes out. "Your mother is sleeping. All she needed was a good sleeping pill. Don't worry," says my aunt.

After a month my father returns from his club. His jacket again hangs on the wooden valet. His keys and his wallet are on the tray. He is trying to be kind. He doesn't spend all day Saturday at the club. He takes my mother to a matinee. "Does anybody get better in a mental hospital?" I ask my mother. "Of course," she says. But I can tell she isn't sure.

Distinguished Jews of America (1917), a blue book of successful ex-greenhorns, arrivistes, parvenues, leaders and givers, capitalism's happiest poster boys, daring and bold, a crowd if not "our crowd." Most pre-ivied, pre-professional, post–sweat shops, MBAs granted by the street, wits well greased by need. Here they are patting themselves on the back. If they don't, who will?

DISTINGUISHED JEWS
of AMERICA

A Collection of Biographical Sketches of
Jews who have made their mark in
Business, the Professions,
Politics, Science, Etc.

Edited by
J. PFEFFER

With an Introduction by
ALBERT M. FRIEDENBERG

Volume One

1917

DISTINGUISHED JEWS of AMERICA PUB. CO.
NEW YORK

Moses Phillips, my great grandfather. Here he is a man slapped in the face by the Enlightenment, no longer in the old world, not yet in the new, but still he keeps his hat on his head and his feet on the ground.

Blanche Phillips innocent and round. If only there was a camera that could show anxiety, capture bad dreams, and tell the future.

Isadore and Sophie Roth, my father's parents who came from somewhere on the Hungarian side of the Hapsburg domain. I've heard it said that Hungarian Jews are worse horse thieves than Rumanian Jews, or is it the other way around? I heard that this grandfather was a gambler—better I suppose than being a horse thief although both can find themselves strung up.

The Roth family before departure to America. Isadore, Sophie, Bea and Eugene Roth. This is one of those photos taken in a fake living room by a professional, guaranteed to make any family look as good as gold even if they don't have any.

Edward, Beatrice and my father Gene Roth. One for all and all for one—up to a point. My father will become a lawyer, Edward a heart doctor in Miami and Beatrice, well, she's a girl.

Blanche Phillips on the edge of marriage. A rosebud to be gathered, time is at her back; one wonders if the photographer was thinking about the short span of beauty, the brief virginal sigh—or was he immune to the probabilities so focused was he on the girl sitting stiffly before him, afraid the camera would find her wanting.

Blanche Roth in wedding gown, on the day of—too late. What beautiful silk, what beautiful lace, what stillness of the fingers in the lap. If only I had been there I would have held her hand and kissed her face and calmed her nerves. Is the picture lying? Was she so beautiful a bride or am I a partisan who finds her all-white moment so gorgeous that it verges on the cruel?

Blanche and Gene Roth on their honeymoon in Venice. Perhaps Alfred Hitchcock took his inspiration from this flock of photogenic pigeons. Look at the old stone and the crevices and the arches of the old world and see these newlyweds in the traditional pose—more vampire novel than romantic kitsch—or is it something about the clothes?

Blanche and Gene in
their early days
together—such
sophistication maybe?

Blanche and an unknown man.
Why was this picture found among
my mother's things? Was this man
a passing body or a real friend?
Were there possibilities, arrangements, rendezvous? I don't
think so. But maybe . . .

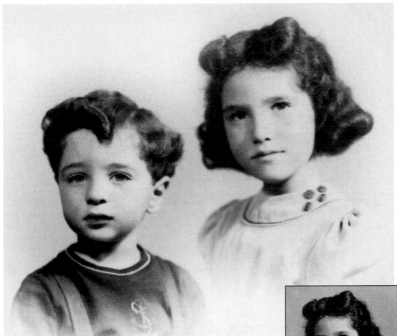

Here we are brushed up for our portraits. All looks well, doesn't it? You can't see how long it took to take the tangles out of my hair, to get the curls just so. That's the way it is with portraits. They tell someone's truth but not necessarily the subject's.

With very best wishes for a Merry Christmas and a Happy New Year

Here it is—a Christmas greeting, no identity politics, no identity conflict, just a wish to join in the general Ho, ho, ho. Who knew back then that if you sat on Santa's lap he'd send you a bill?

Here I am with the pony that waited at 90th Street and Fifth Avenue at the entrance to the park. The photographer hid under a draped cloth. They say that girls ride horses because of sexual connotations, some rhythmic hints, a practice for mastery of the large beasts that await. This particular pony was a prop rather than a promise. But under the right circumstances a girl can touch a prop.

Here I am with a basket. Sweetness and light. I am learning how to be adorable.

Greta has taken me to the park. I am still a good girl or so it seems.

At camp (top left). On a dock (top right). Am I posing for Miss Preteen Swimsuit? Johnny at Camp Wigwam (bottom left). Nothing good is happening, he would tell you. With my father on visiting day at Tripp Lake Camp (bottom right). Somewhat disheveled, yet you can see from my proud stance that I am a girl in love with her father.

Anne by the club pool. I like the club.

Johnny by the club pool. He doesn't.

Here we are on the lawn in Rye. Once he
threw a brick at me and hit me above the eye.
I probably deserved it.

Johnny before religion.

My mother with a man who I think was a captain in the Israeli army come to raise funds for the fledgling state. We had a little brush with history. It was too short to be included here.

My father with a woman. Who?

Blanche with her friends. I remember their names and their fates but that's another story.

My mother and father on a lawn chair in Rye. Now isn't that a pretty picture? I can hardly believe my eyes.

Portrait of me and my brother.

Here I am at the sixth-grade graduation.
The tomboy within is gasping for air.

Here I am at a holiday dinner with my cousins. I remember the dress, it was
taffeta and velvet. Our stories were so short then and lacked narrative. If only
they could have stayed that way.

My high school graduation photo in a ball gown (1953). I thought in order to escape all you had to do was leave home.

My mother with her nephew at a company meeting in Miami in 1955.

My mother dancing with her brother in 1958.

My mother at a dinner table at a wedding in 1958, four years before her death. This is not a woman who deserved a daughter who was convinced that Jean Genet trumped Richard Rodgers when it came to things on the stage.

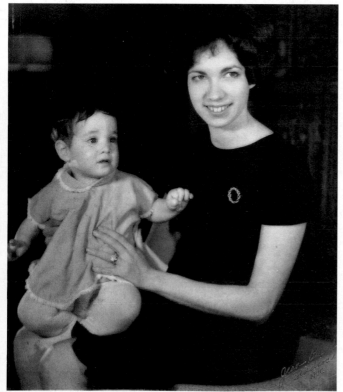

I am a married woman with a baby. My mother wants my picture taken. I pose like a proper lady. I know I'm in hot water.

My brother, a grown man, tells a joke. He likes the joke. In his mind electricity crackles, wit and fury meld. A smile comes unbidden, not quite permitted. The old world hangs on his shoulders. Bach is in his ears. He doesn't go into the sun. Another joke is waiting at the tip of his tongue.

The two of us, my brother and me, he is ill and I am anxious. Our story nearly done.

13

breaking the fast with roy cohn   On the high hol-
idays my mother went to synagogue all dressed up in a new suit. She wore
a black hat with a veil and soft leather gloves that kept falling off her lap
each time she rose as the ark was opened. She sat next to her sister and I on
her other side dazzled by the sounds of Hebrew rising and falling, signifying
a controlling hand, a very personal judgment of my evil heart, a heaven
above and an earth below and a place in the universe for each voice, sup-
plicating, rocking back and forth. I listened to the Hebrew words, repeated
down through the years, exactly the way I was hearing them, a plaint, a
melody, a song that carried a message to the heavens above, to heal, to protect. The song expressed utmost humility, complete abasement before the
great unknowns; it intended to ward off the bad, to bring on the good. The
sound of the Hebrew was like the sound of a baby cooing in its bassinet at
the sun, like the sound of the river flowing over the stones and the fallen
logs and the clutter of leaves, rising and falling with the currents and the
rain, down to the sea. The melodies carried the mourning soul on its way
toward worse sorrows. The melodies contained reproach and complaint. In

their repeated caressing of the words there was no way to escape. The whole of the people of Israel were transported to the sanctuary of the temple where the goats were selected by lot and one goat sacrificed on the altar, his blood touching the white tent above, and the other goat sent out into the forests with the sins of the people on its head. It was impossible not to imagine the gathered multitudes, the priest in white robes entering the holy place where Aaron's sons had been killed for trespassing on the sacred, where the hot Jerusalem sun beat down on the stone steps and the families on the hillside sat together year after year until the more powerful armies came and drove them out, oh beloved, beloved Jerusalem.

My mother did not understand a word of Hebrew because she was never taught but she knew by rote some of the passages. It was clear to me that through the Hebrew melody we were climbing up toward God, heaving and panting, weary but exalted, dizzy and drained, on and on we were going. Standing up, sitting down, every line repeated over and over, the ark opened and closed, time was frozen, boredom and sleepiness came over me. My mother and her sister Libby whispered to each other in a steady drone. I was wondering if God had forgiven me, my mother and my aunt had more immediate concerns. At last my mother would squeeze my shoulder and we would push our way to the aisle so we could leave the synagogue and stand on the front steps. My mother would pick up her veil, the one with rhinestone sequins scattered in the black netting that was attached to her stylish hat, and light up her cigarette and blow smoke rings out over the coming and going congregants. Happy New Year everyone said and I was kissed and kissed by women and men. Behind each Happy New Year I heard an anxious ringing, don't get sick, don't let the enemy win the war, don't let the stock market fall, don't let my business fail, don't let this be the year my spouse is run over by a truck, killed in a train accident. Happy New Year, let only good things, honey and apples, sweetness and love befall you, all the rest is there, biding its time, not now, not this happy new year.

My father won't go to synagogue with us. It's ridiculous. Superstitious. Mumbo jumbo, boo-hoo ladies' stuff. On the holidays he goes for long walks in the park. He goes out to his club with Leonard or Kopatkin. My mother begs him to come just for the Kol Nidre, just for twenty minutes. "It looks bad," she said. "You should come." "You and your sister," he says in a tone that doesn't require that the sentence be completed. He says that he can live without God. My mother does not exactly believe in God either. She does believe in fortune-tellers and at least once she went to a seance to contact her dead mother. She did not believe in the old laws, in the separation of milk and meat, of Sabbath observance, of study of Talmud and Torah. She did believe in doctors. Her phone book had three pages of doctors' names with their specialties listed. Inside the synagogue she nervously chipped at her fingernail polish, smudged her lipstick, and wiped it off and tried again. Standing by her side in front of the open ark I tried to pray directly to God, though of course my mind wandered and I saw at the bottom of the blue and green abstract mosaic written in gold script the names of Pearl and Sidney Weinberg who had donated the stained glass window directly over my head. In *Weinberg* you find, *grin, wine, renew, ire, web, rein, wire, binge. Pear, leap,* and *reap* come from *Pearl.*

On the steps of the synagogue a man comes up to my mother. He leans toward her, a little closer than seems usual. He lights her cigarette. She lifts her face up toward him. I watch. He lets his arm, encased in a dark blue jacket, brush against her shoulder. I hold my breath. My mother's face has turned red. Her throat and neck are red too. "Who's that?" I say when he moves away. "Never mind," she says.

Romance, the word rises and rattles in my mind. It brings with it the clear ring of a new hope. She should. She should, even if she has to go to a mental hospital first. I find the man in the crowd. I stand next to him. He has a scar on the back of his neck. That might be a good sign. He's already been nicked. Does he have a wife. Does he have a daughter? Can my mother steal him away? I am not confident of her capacity. She is not ruthless. She is always uncertain. She will worry about what other people are thinking but I have hope. The man catches my eye and winks.

My question—If God was a presence in the synagogue, if God was a force in the universe, if my father striding quickly in long steps down Fifth Avenue with his strong back straight as a plumb line dropped from the noon sun, with his camel's hair coat, with his monogrammed handkerchief exposed the exact quarter-inch above his breast pocket, was unaware of God and his demands and his book in which it was written who would live and who would die, would something dreadful befall us? Not in America of that

I was reasonably sure. The thing of the spirit, the pious urge, the turning of the eye upward, the bending of the knee that years later I would see in paintings on museum walls, the streak of light illuminating the face, the hands clasped in humility, these remained to me a mystery. The supplicant pose, the God-inspired radiant shine, the God love that I would read about in St. Augustine, Aquinas, and Benedict, in Simone Weil and the Bal Shem Tov, the spirit of God abroad in the land, the opium of the people, did not penetrate my shallow, material, callow soul although I very much hoped that it might and that the creator of all things might find me worthy.

At the same time I admired my father who shook his fist at the sky, who would give ground to no one not even the deity, not even the creator of thunder and lightning, snow and flood, plague and the Malach Hamavet, the angel of death. My father was not a throwback, not a coward, not a man to beg for a toehold on earth, he was a fast walker, a strong swimmer. He did not need the rabbi to shake his hand. He didn't give a good goddamn about God or his rules and all he wanted was to get away from the crowd, from the women, to get some exercise, to breathe freely. I understood him. If only he wanted my company on his flight. He did not.

I was left walking up the synagogue steps with my mother in the last hot days of Indian summer as the high holidays passed through us, leaving tremors of how it must have been in other times, of Abraham taking Isaac by the hand and leading him to the place of his sacrifice.

My brother wore a blue suit and a tie. He wheezed from the perfume that floated in the air as a crowd of boys his age were running up and down the steps and dashing through the poles that held up the awning in front of the synagogue. He did not join them. His fingers waved slightly at his sides. He was drumming at the air. Actually he was practicing, a sonata of Chopin perhaps, the clear crisp melody that he could hear in his head free of the weeping that undulated through the morning's prayers, though not the sorrow, not the lyric yearning. His Chopin was controlled, intelligent, formal, and subtle, unlike the heavy repeated notes of the cantor's hypnotic, heart-pounding sounds. His Chopin hinted at geometry and what tragedy it spoke of was delicate and graceful. He stood alone, fierce and pale, his faded blue eyes, just like my mother's, distanced behind thick glasses, a child whom childhood seems to have passed by, at least the running and jumping, the chasing and being chased part, the mindless sense of body tumble and ball bouncing part. On the steps of the synagogue amid the sheltered by geography Jews of Park Avenue in their suits and their furs, in their hats and their gold rings, he seemed like a ghost child, a stern reminder that nothing is quite what it seems.

As we walked to my Aunt Libby's house to break the fast with her family, my brother told me a joke. A quarter and a dime are sitting on top of the Empire State Building and the dime jumps off. Why didn't the quarter? It had more sense (cents). He laughed.

There the family would have gathered. My aunt's three boys, older than I, my sad-eyed round uncle who was the only one who knew how to read Hebrew, his sister Dora Cohn who was married to an appeals court judge, Al Cohn, a very important man, and their son, a sallow, taciturn figure with strange slightly crossed eyes that seemed to look at no one and appeared to be blue glass, possibly weapons as well as organs of sight. His name was Roy.

Dora was the ugliest woman I had ever seen, her face pushed in and her lip too close to her nose and her small eyes beady and her skin was gray and mottled and she seemed slightly humped and her voice cackled and cracked. Her teeth were dark and when she smiled I shivered. But my mother said she was better looking now than she had been as a young girl.

My mother told me the story of how Dora had met and married her husband. Her father gained a reputation on the Lower East Side as a man trustworthy and wise about money. He kept his neighbors' savings in a safe in the back of his tailor shop. In a few years he had built a big and prosperous bank and the family lived in the Bronx in a large house and the man my Aunt Libby married was the son and future president of the bank. One day a young lawyer, a recent graduate of City College, had come to the bank to ask for a loan to set up his own office. The young lawyer was interviewed by the bank president himself and was found to be intelligent, passionate about the American Constitution, and determined that one day he would become a judge. He came from poor immigrant people. His father was a working man. He lacked the funds as well as the connections to the right people to fulfill his dreams. At that time a judgeship could be had from Tammany Hall for about $50,000, a sum way beyond the young man's expectations.

The banker invited the young lawyer home for dinner where he met the daughter, the so ugly as to be unmarriageable daughter, and within a reasonable time after a short courtship he asked her father for her hand. Despite the lack of assets that the young man was bringing to the marriage he was accepted immediately.

The young couple lived in the Bronx and the young lawyer received business from the bank and after a small but almost suitable number of years had passed he became a judge, to whom he owed what and how the judgeship was arranged was something my mother refused to say. She said that the only important fact remained that Al Cohn who wanted to serve his country was widely respected as a decent and fair judge who knew the law and was considerate and balanced in his decisions.

Al and Dora Cohn had only one child. The boy Roy became the sole focus of his mother's life. The parents never went out without him. Bridge-playing friends, business acquaintances, dinner invitations were all turned down unless Roy was included, and he was included, never treated as a mere child and relegated to nursery companionship. He grew into an odd boy with a precociously mature manner and an unholy interest in the internal power mechanisms of the courts, the city government. He was aware of the political implications of every case before the courts. Before he was five he could recite the Preamble to the Constitution and before he was ten he knew the names of all the important lawyers in the city and their individual specialties. It was hard to believe he had ever been an innocent baby with a soft spot at the front of his skull. He personally knew all the columnists in New York and he carried their telephone numbers in his hip pocket in case he wanted to call them. He knew who had a lot of money and who was just pretending. He kept a list of New York's twenty wealthiest men. He too believed in democracy but not exactly the same version as his father's. He was driven to school in a chauffeured car because his mother did not want him traveling on the subways. He did not waste his time with parties or girls. He entered Columbia a year earlier than his classmates and graduated in record time. He did not go to dances or football games. He did not so much study as he surveyed. To whatever and whomever was useful he held on. The rest he looked through, ignored or discarded.

As the family gathered at the end of the fast on the holiest day of the Jewish calendar a table in the living room would fill with appetizers, caviar on toast, egg salad, cucumbers and beets, chopped liver, and breadsticks. Roy Cohn would rush to the table and fill his plate and gobble everything down without ceding his place to another. I come up on his left side and put my hand on a deviled egg with red spots of paprika across the top. Roy grabs my wrist and shoves his hip into my side. I retreat. Behind us aunts and uncles and cousins are waiting. Roy sweeps whole platters onto his plate and still stands in front of the table. When he is done there are no more deviled eggs. I look at the empty platters with parsley on the edges, cracker crumbs but no crackers. When he is done the table looks as if vultures have picked at a carcass in the fields.

Roy was at Columbia Law School. Then he was at the DA's office. My mother told me that he was going to be the first Jewish president of the United States. "He's planning on it," she said.

Sometimes Al Cohn had to make decisions that had been suggested by somebody back at the clubhouse. But Dora Cohn always referred to him as "The Judge," as in, "The Judge takes two lumps of sugar in his coffee." As the years passed he became more and more of a shadow, a man who loved America and knew the Constitution but who inside his own house was treated by his wife and his son as an old somewhat ragged tablecloth on which the family ate its noncompany meals. He was a husband who had been bought and he was a judge who had bought his judgeship. When I was a child and I saw him sitting in a chair I would avoid him. His shoulders were always hunched and defeat was in his posture, in the slight tremble of his hands, in the shuffle of his walk. In court they say he was someone else but at home he did exactly as he was told.

My mother told me something else about Roy Cohn. When he was twelve he contracted the mumps. He was very ill and Dora nearly went mad, screaming at the doctors, until the crisis had passed. When it was over the family moved to Park Avenue a few blocks away from us. The judge wanted to stay in the Bronx. But his wife denied him. Roy's testicles had not descended. They were ruined by the mumps and he could never have children. He was sterile. Like the Golem he could not reproduce himself. Dora told her sister-in-law Libby who told my mother who told me that Dora wasn't sorry about what the mumps had done to Roy's sperm. Now he would not marry and would always stay with her.

My mother said poor Roy, he's not quite right. He needs a psychoanalyst. His laugh is flat, not spontaneous at all. He's the kind of boy who might keep a snake said my mother and enjoy feeding it live mice. I don't care if he does become the first Jewish president said my mother, he isn't altogether human. My mother said poor Roy does not have real friends. His mother will never let him go. She wants to be first lady when he becomes president. At family gatherings I stared at Roy Cohn the way one watches a freight train bearing coal or steel rushing through the landscape.

Despite the fact that I was very clear that people went to psychoanalysts because they needed to talk over their problems not because they were crazy I remained obsessed with sanity. I defined it to myself over and over. What I wanted to be when I grew up was sane. I was frightened that one day I might wake from a nightmare and not wake. I was afraid that I might hear voices in my head. I was determined that I would always check on the real world, make sure I knew what was actual and what was not. I worried about my mother. Would she cross some invisible line between nervous and mad? I worried about my brother. Would he be cured before he went mad? I thought of the dark halls of insane asylums and the shrieking voices and the padded walls and the pain of electric shock treatment. (My mother had told me that a friend's brother had become permanently incontinent like a baby because of shock treatments received in one of our more renowned mental hospitals.)

I ask my mother, "Are you still a masochist?" She says, "Real change takes a long time."

jewish history could drive you neurotic   We attended Sunday school. In America, Hebrew School, *cheder,* had changed to Sunday School so we would be more like other Americans. Each week a magazine would be handed out called *The World Over* and it told in simple terms about Jews in other places. It described holidays. It had a cartoon or two. In Sunday school we learned about Jewish history which merges into

Jewish religion in a marriage of fact with fantasy, mysticism with realism. History for Jews has an end in messianic appearance; it also leaves actual footprints on the actual ground. History for American Jews in the forties was less dreamy than in other centuries and more involved with body counts. Nevertheless we had Purim parties at which like all the other little girls I dressed as Queen Esther, let me be the savior of my people because of my beauty and charms. Let the evil Haman hang. We twirl a noisemaker in the face of the wicked prime minister and his even more wicked recent imitators. The moral of the Purim story is that sex is mightier than the sword. A woman's wiles can influence matters of state. In the end looks are everything.

Jewish history was not dull. It turned limp the perils of the Hardy Boys, the heroics of Superman, the rescues of the Lone Ranger. At least every few hundred years a major calamity occurred. There was exodus and exile, slavery and pogrom, there was exclusion and expulsion and through it all there was a determination, a sense of purpose, a heroics that stirred the soul. Yes it was told in simplistic terms, good versus evil, enemy versus friend, all the complexities of politics and power reduced to tribal struggles, to building of temples and waging of wars, of hiding in cellars, of counting the dead and moving on to begin again somewhere else. In my head were pictures of babies dashed against the walls of houses in shtetls of the Ukraine in the pogroms of 1903. In my head were pictures of Jews burning in the fires of the inquisition in the fourteenth century or fleeing in the middle of the night chased by Syrians, Romans, English lords, and crowds of Poles who thought Passover celebrants had drunk the blood of little Christian boys. I saw the Jews on flimsy boats with their gathered possessions huddling together against the sea winds in the harbors of Barcelona, Lisbon, and Liverpool. I knew that the Jews were forbidden to own property, to till the land, to go to school, to do anything but carry merchandise from town to town. In plague years they were accused of bringing the plague, in wartime they were accused of spying, in peacetime they were accused of stealing. I knew about Dreyfus and Leo Frank, about murderous mobs and Crusaders riding to holy Jerusalem cutting out the tongues of Jews along the way. In every country in every century the despised were noble and the nobility murdered with impunity.

Later I would hear this pile-up of catastrophes ridiculed as the lachrymose history of the Jews as if there was a better spin that could be put on the facts. The holocaust was not mentioned, or if so only indirectly, by comparison. That wound was too new, still open, too terrifying. Nevertheless all the earlier treacheries, the slaughters that left dead in the streets seemed like fragments of the broken mirror. If we put them together we would see our reflections in Auschwitz. The pictures were coming out in *Life* magazine. We knew what had happened. It was just easier to talk about the exile from Spain or the two-time destruction of the temple. We talked aloud about the heroics of Masada and silently one by one considered the Warsaw ghetto, burning in the night while outside the carousel with its jingling melody went turning round and round. We tithed our allowances and bought trees to be planted in the deserts of Palestine. On the English side of the prayer book I read that we ask God to forgive us for stretching our necks out in pride but it took brain-wrenching somersaults not to see that a covenant was an agreement entered into by two parties who must both keep up their sides of the deal. Otherwise what was the point?

It took me many years to understand that catastrophe was the common human portion not something particular to Jews, not unique to the way in which the thread of history pulled Jews from one epoch to the next and at the same time singular to Jews, unique: a paradox.

My brother kept all his copies of *The World Over* in neat order on a shelf in his room. Mine spilled everywhere and were thrown out by the maid.

a whirlwind without a voice, a bush with nothing to say, godless on park avenue   For many years Mara (nicknamed Hardy—I was Rothie) Lowenstein was my friend. We were at Tripp Lake Camp together. She was a tomboy like me. She was a natural athlete and in addition she had a cool intelligence that surveyed, considered, was less prone to tears and visions than I was. She liked facts. I liked stories. She could be cutting or cold. She could let me know that she had been to lunch at someone's house and I had not been invited. Friendship for little girls is a shadow play of the Grand Guignol to come. She was direct, clear, and determined. She had the reins in her hands, a leader, I was a follower, a hanger on, grateful for the rays of sun that came my way. On weekends we would open our horse books and draw pictures of horses, of Flicka and National Velvet and other unnamed tall fearsome beasts. We would imagine ourselves riding in the wild bareback on the sweating flanks of a nostril flaring, high stepping, ready to jump, heart of gold, smelling of sweat and manure, horse, but more than horse, eater of lumps of sugar, accepter of gifts of carrots, soft of nose, wild brown eyes that reflected thunder clouds in the sky, large muscles quivering, horse of the dream, Freud would say the shadow of sex rode with us, perhaps, but in addition the horse was the ticket to freedom, the way out of the corsets and garter belts, the counting of spoons that lay ahead.

Hardy lived at 1192 Park Avenue. And our actual riding experience was limited to a few turns around the ring at camp and weekly lessons at an indoor ring down near the brewery near Second Avenue. We were not Connecticut horse girls with black velvet hats and boxes of ribbons in our closets. We were wannabees, hopefuls, granddaughters of people who thought animals belonged to peasants who mucked in their waste instead of reading or trading which was the proper business of two-legged animals.

We played a wonderful game. We would fold paper into a cone shape with a covered top, an art class at Hardy's school was responsible for this skill, and we would fill our cone with water, and then we would open the window on Park Avenue and leaning way out to see the railroad pass uptown and Grand Central Station downtown, staring at the street until we saw a passerby and then we would drop our cones and quickly withdraw behind the curtains. There we were, the mad bombers. We would duck down under the window sash so that when the hopefully drenched person on the street looked up they wouldn't see the floor of origin or the two heads of delinquent girls. It was hard to hit anyone from the seventh floor but we tried again and again. Sometimes we argued: I wanted to aim for governesses pushing carriages and she wanted to aim for ladies wearing hats.

Then her father died. He was a big man with a wide chest (or so I think I remember), an orthopedist who gave his time freely to clinics in Harlem. He helped his daughter keep a scrapbook with pictures of dogs and horses cut from magazines. He hugged her when he came home from work and he gave her an allowance with money he took out of his own pocket. He took her to the movies on Sunday afternoons. Sometimes he took me too. Perhaps I idealize him. Once I heard him scold his daughter. I was jealous. He had noticed something she had done he did not like. I wanted to change places with Hardy. I wanted to be scolded too. He died suddenly of a heart attack. The news came to me along with the pictures of Auschwitz. The news came to me as a slap in the face of just rewards, of goodness and mercy following you all the days of your life.

If God knew what he was doing he would not have taken my friend's father, a man of use to his family and his community. He might have taken instead my father who had no interest in charity.

At the same time I had that unfilial thought I also considered that if my mother and father left each other then I could live with my father and teach him how to scold me if I needed it, how to walk with me instead of ahead of me. I told my mother that divorce would be a good step forward. She agreed but not yet, she couldn't, not yet.

The year I was twelve I refused to attend high holiday services. If Hardy's father could not attend services because he was dead then I would not go either. I did not believe that I should beg God for forgiveness. I thought perhaps it should be the other way around. My mother begged me to put on my new suit and new shoes and accompany her and my brother to the door of the synagogue. She was hoping I would change my mind. I walked on the opposite side of the street. My mother was walking with my brother by her side. Even the sight of them together did not change my mind. I watched them turn toward the crowd of worshippers on the steps and I walked home past the doormen, past the other worshippers all dressed up, moving in family groups along Park Avenue. I was alone.

Delusion, illusion, magic rites, I would have no more of it. I didn't mind that the sky above my head was empty. I was persuaded even impressed by my argument against the existence of God, with its coda against the goodness of God. Still on the way home, in the warm air, with the heat of the day making my legs prickle in the beige stockings I was wearing, attached to a tight girdle that pinched my middle and left indentations in my skin, I found myself with tears on my face.

I was angry at somebody, was it the God I no longer believed in or the Jews who were gathering in the synagogue without me? Was my heart already hardened against God by my father or was I by nature a skeptic, a child of the enlightenment, or was I simply angry at fathers including God the———?

waiting in the lobby   Dr. Lily Bussel was now my brother's psychiatrist. Her office was in an apartment building in the east eighties off Madison Avenue. Sometimes I would go pick him up and walk back to our apartment with him. As I waited for him I stared at the oriental carpets, at the dogs that were being walked by their owners, at the ornate mirrors that hung over gold-embossed tables. I counted the squares in the marble floors. I asked my brother what he talked about with Dr. Bussel. He gave me an unfriendly look.

My mother had changed analysts. The new one had an office on Fifth Avenue and when I waited downstairs the doorman there sometimes let me help sort the mail. Fifty minutes is a long time when you're just passing the time. I was patient. At last the elevator door would open and my mother would appear. Her eyes hidden behind dark glasses. Her hair no matter how recently set in the beauty parlor was now unkempt as if the woe that she had revisited had leaked out her skull and sent the waves in her hair off at odd angles. In her hands she held crumpled tissues. I would wait for her to recover. Slowly she would walk through the lobby, re-powder her nose at the door. She would sigh. Sometimes she would let fresh tears flow.

Divorce: vice, void, ire, dive, rid, voice. Was it coming nearing?

somebody else wants our shirt business   I wanted to move to a farm. I wanted to milk cows. I wanted to go to Palestine and plant tomatoes. I went on the Madison Avenue bus with my mother to Saks Fifth Avenue to buy dresses. I went with my mother to Lord & Taylor to buy shoes. I went to Tiffany's to pick out a pin for a special dress my mother intended to wear to my cousin's wedding. On the bus my mother and I talked. I told my mother I wanted to move to a farm. I wanted to wake in the morning and run into the barn with chores to do, a smell of animal and hay, the first ray of light slipping under the dark slats around my foal. I wanted to help my father save the crop from locusts by digging ditches or lighting fires. On the bus my mother told me that there was going to be a proxy fight. A stranger was trying to buy up the stock of the family shirt business. My mother would never let that happen. She and my uncle were going to fight. They were going to buy up stock themselves. Why? The business belongs to our family, said my mother. "Could you lose this fight?" I asked my mother. "Only if I die of a heart attack," she said, "and I have pains in my chest right now."

On the bus my mother told me that sexual illnesses that made your vagina rot came from sitting on dirty toilet seats. She told me that her friend Beatrice had not been able to conceive a child and had prayed to God to give her a baby and she had said to God that if he granted her prayer she would never ask him anything again. Then she got pregnant and had a healthy baby whom she loved greatly but she couldn't help it, the desire for another was so strong that again she asked God to make her fertile and once more she got pregnant but this time the baby was born with a flat face and a strange nose and could hardly sit and would never speak. This baby was named Hope and placed in an institution and Beatrice visited the baby every week until sometime in the fifth year of its life it caught pneumonia and died. The baby's terrible retardation my mother said must have been a punishment from God for breaking the promise. Or said my mother maybe it was just an accident. My mother's analyst thought it was an accident, bad luck.

On the bus my mother whispers in my ear so the people sitting behind us can't hear. Before she was married Beatrice had been pregnant. She had been having an affair with a married man. She had an abortion when she was nineteen and that's why she had such trouble conceiving. This fact added significant weight to the punishing God argument. "Stay a virgin until your wedding night," my mother pleads with me. My mother asks me what I think: accident or God's justice? I don't want to think about retarded children. I can't think about anything else for weeks.

. I wanted to move to the suburbs and ride my bicycle to school. In my mind I turned geography around and around like a dog pawing a cushion looking for the right way to lie down. There was somewhere else I wanted to be, someone else that I could be. I knew there were other buses to ride.

But Saturday after Saturday after my mother had her late breakfast in bed, after she had her bath, and after her telephone call to her sister, we would go downtown on the Fifth Avenue double-decker bus. We would stop at her favorite drugstore counter and I would have a chicken sandwich with the crusts cut off and a Broadway soda, chocolate syrup and coffee ice cream. My mother told me about her friend Fay's struggles with her husband who had grown depressed and about her friend Ceil's middle son, who was afraid to go to the bathroom outside his house and therefore couldn't go to school. She told me how much of the stock remained in family hands. We needed only 51 percent. The man who was trying to take over now had over 45 percent. Certain cousins, and second cousins, had sold out to him, others threatened and demanded to be paid off. Who was faithful to the company, to the family? Who would remain so as the offer to sell to the invader became more and more irresistible. My uncle and my mother talked about it every day. My mother told me that her analyst had not been able to understand why keeping the shirt business in the family mattered so much to her. She grabbed my hand. "You understand don't you?" she said. I nodded.

My uncle had hired a lawyer other than my father to help with the takeover problem. My father yelled at my uncle once too often. My uncle has a heart condition. You shouldn't yell at a man with a bad heart. The takeover looms over us. Every afternoon I pick up the paper at the front door and I sit by my mother's bed and read her the worth of the stock. It is going up and up. This makes it harder for her to buy more. She is determined. We make a list of family traitors. Together we set the list on fire using her gold cigarette lighter. We flush the flaming paper down the toilet. My uncle has a son who will one day become president of the company so that's one good job my brother will never have. I don't imagine he wants it.

Once more my father moves into his club and this time my mother lets me spend the night in his bed right next to her. I hear her come in after I'm asleep and I hear the soft rustle of her silk nightgown. I smell the cream she puts on her face. When she turns on the light in the bathroom I see the brown freckles on her arms. But then my father moves back into the apartment. I do not know one single person whose parents are divorced. Could everybody else be living in a happy home? If that is so why is the *New Yorker* magazine so full of sad stories? I finally understand what's funny about most of the cartoons, sometimes I even laugh. I especially like the Charles Addams cartoon of a skier with a pole around each side of a tree. My mother says that Charles Addams sends that cartoon into the *New Yorker* whenever he is losing his mind again and needs to go to a hospital. Is he suicidal?

My mother loves the shirt business because she loved her father who built the shirt business and saved the family from poverty. He did this my mother explains to me by employing uncles and cousins and second cousins and in-laws and their cousins. Now a trusted executive sells out to the enemy who is getting closer to the 51 percent he needs. Betrayal, my mother explains to me. Never-ever-to-be-forgiven, betrayal. She talks to her brother in the late afternoon. They banish me from the room. Will I ever love anything the way my mother loves the shirt business?

14

rent a dad   My brother's analyst had a suggestion. My mother followed up on it immediately. She hired a Columbia graduate student to be a male role model for my brother, to play ball with him, to keep him company, to be his friend. His name was Neil and he came to live with us in our country house in Rye the summer I was thirteen. He came from Yugoslavia and he was blond with a long skinny neck and a huge Adam's apple. His ears stuck out from the side of his closely cropped head. This had to be the best summer job in the world. He was there simply to be himself and keep the little boy company.

It might have worked out if I had not wanted Neil to be my friend as well, not really as well, but perhaps instead. It might have worked out if I hadn't wanted Neil to hold my hand and tell me interesting facts about his home. It might have worked out if I had not been on the cusp of desire and if the presence in the house of a boy with hair on his legs and blue eyes and an accent that spoke of far-off places, mountains and rivers that flowed to the sea, and wildflowers that grew in crevices in the rocks beyond his house hadn't given me dreams that while unsettling were not unpleasant.

Neil would go out into the front lawn of our house in Rye and take a baseball to throw it with Johnny. Johnny was not interested in balls. Within moments Neil and I would be playing. I would jump and run and slide in the grass to make impossible catches. Johnny would go back into the house and in the hot morning sun I would feel joy because Neil thought I was a good ball player, because Neil who smiled easily smiled often at me. Neil would suggest a bike ride. My brother wouldn't learn to ride his two-wheeler. It was just the sort of activity he thought stupid, worthless. I would ride my bike down the road and take my hands off the bars and steer with a list to the left or the right. Neil would bike with me. We would take a picnic lunch and eat on the public beaches a few miles away. Was I in love with Neil or did I just want to prevent my brother from finding brotherhood? Neil gave me Hemingway to read. Neil gave me the poetry of Emily Dickinson. Neil told me that he was happy to be in America and I too was happy he was in America.

I talked about politics with Neil. At the dinners we ate together I interrupted my brother and began conversations about things I knew my brother knew nothing about. Neil admired me. I thought he did. I made sure he did. Soon my brother began to dislike Neil. He refused to go for a walk with him and I would go instead. He wouldn't go in the car with Neil or swimming with him in the dark waters of the sound that lay just outside our house. I wanted to swim to the outer rocks which were visible in low tide out beyond the peninsula of our cove. Neil swam with me. I had unruly hair that I hardly ever combed. I had teeth that still required the thick bands of silver and rubber bands were always popping from my mouth and surely I was not a Lolita child. But I succeeded in sabotaging the analyst's plan. Neil could not serve as my brother's role model or masculine companion when he was my crush, my practice male, my seesaw between the freedom of childhood and the warm oozy mysteries that lay ahead.

I went off to camp that summer sad to leave Neil behind with my brother but I needn't have worried. Before I returned Neil had been fired. I wrote his name in ink on my inner arm. I wrote him a long letter at the address he had left. He never wrote me back. My brother never in our lives mentioned him again. I suppose that in the same way that a prostitute in the bed may provide release but does not answer your deepest needs so you cannot rent a father to play ball with your child.

friendship for sale   When my brother was in sixth grade he had one friend and one friend only. This was a diminutive boy by the name of Eric who had dark eyes that flashed with expectations. He had a wide smile and big teeth that protruded forward, not yet touched by orthodonture. He played chess with my brother although he always lost. He was a child to whom losing had become natural. He collected marbles and carried them in his pockets. His father was a big successful man who understood the ways of the world. Eric wanted to be liked. Eric wanted to be liked not just by my brother but by the popular boys in the class, the good athletes, the ones the girls were beginning to invite to parties where they played post office and spin the bottle. He didn't have a chance. He was a shrimp with tiny bones in tiny wrists. He was a child with an air of uncertainty. He was too eager. He, like my brother, seemed doomed to stand at the fringe, to pretend not to hear the whispering behind his back, to avoid tables at the lunchroom. But one day Eric told his father about his social woe.

Eric's father purchased six hockey tickets to Madison Square Garden's biggest game and he told Eric to invite the four boys he wanted to befriend. Eric told him the boys wouldn't come. They didn't like him. His father told him they would come. No boy would turn down this invitation. Eric's father was right.

Before the game he took the group to a special club inside Madison Square Garden where season ticket holders could have supper. He ordered them steaks and Cokes and despite the fact that the boys talked mostly to each other and ignored Eric the evening was a success. Two weeks later the invitation was repeated, followed by an invitation to watch the players warm up a few hours ahead of the game. Johnny was worried. Would Eric remain his friend? It seemed to him that Eric was avoiding him in school. They were no longer walking together to gym, to shop. Each walked alone. I told my brother that he had nothing to worry about. You can't buy friendship I assured him. The boys wouldn't be Eric's friend just for the price of a ticket or a few tickets.

The campaign continued: ball games and Broadway musicals and a weekend on a yacht.

It took a few months but I was proved wrong, very wrong. It turned out that when the boys got to spend more time with Eric they liked him, or they got used to him, or they just stopped thinking of him as an outsider, an odd one. He no longer talked to my brother at all. He avoided his eyes. He sat as far away from him as he could. My brother said he didn't care but I knew he did. "It's not real friendship he has now," I said. "You don't know anything," said my brother and he was clearly right. I had overestimated the power of moral truth and underestimated the power of money to purchase even the cheesy moon.

And what about his sister? Should I have been able to comfort him in the night when he woke with bad dreams? Was I so afraid of his stealing a drop of my mother's time that I couldn't allow him into my circle? Was I hoping he would disappear into a vapor, drift off like the steam from the kettle that stayed by his bed during his asthma attacks? When I listened from behind the bathroom door to the footsteps of the doctor coming and going and the sound of Greta's washing the thermometer in the bathroom sink, did I wish my brother speedy recovery or was I waiting like a carrion bird circling above the possum lying on the road, blood and matted fur?

Sometimes if my mother was out or sleeping behind a closed door I would go into his room and try to amuse him, to befriend him, to tell him a secret. Sometimes I would see him on his floor arranging his toy soldiers or lying on his bed staring at the ceiling and I would feel a yearning for him, a desire to stroke his arm, to fold the blanket over his feet. Sometimes I thought of ways to save him from the high seas. I imagined heavy winds blowing and setting out in a small dingy from shore leaning into the perilous dark waters and heaving his frail body onto the rim of the boat and rowing with all my might back to shore. He wasn't fooled. He saw right through me: a sometimes friend. He must have known that occasionally when I heard his voice in the hall or listened to him practicing the piano, fingers moving up and down on the keys, I thought of ways to drown him.

So I am not an innocent and I would have done anything at all to make him happy except welcome him into my mother's bedroom with me.

I didn't reveal to him that the chair by her bedside was the nave of the house, her bed the altar where our sacrifices should be placed. I didn't help him find ways to talk to her that would interest her and force attention to turn from me to him. I learned how to speak to our mother so her interest would hold. I didn't teach him my method. I didn't tell him when the door was opened and I didn't tell him he should sit with me and listen to her

phone conversations so he could learn what interested her. I didn't tell him
to wait with me outside her closed door or to sit still while she read the paper. I didn't teach him to watch her cigarette ash burn down and then
quickly offer another cigarette from the pack on the night table. I didn't explain to him that if he, listening as she talked to her sister on the phone,
brought her the afternoon's scotch and soda he would find her essential to
his day and she would soon find him equally necessary. I never explained to
him how her wistful voice was a holy thing and like all things holy required
close observation.

This you might say is normal between siblings. We're like pups in a litter
pushing and shoving, writhing around the heaving nipples, a scrambling
that grows fiercer if the milk is thin. Nature grants the runt no special
rights. But in the end we are not brute beasts devoid of conscience and responsibility for one another. Was I not my brother's keeper?

the scales tip in my brother's favor I remem-
ber clearly that we were at my Aunt Libby's at 944 Park Avenue when I first
heard about the Hebrew lessons.

I was sitting on her bed braiding the gold tassels on the brocade spread
listening to the sisters talk when I heard that the Hebrew teacher, the same
one who had taught my cousins, was to arrive later that afternoon to begin
lessons with my brother. I had already decided that I didn't believe in God. I
had already walked out on Sunday school. But I wanted to learn Hebrew too.
We were beginning to hear of the newly founded state of Israel where they
were speaking Hebrew. I knew about the bar mitzvah that lay at the end of
these lessons. I knew he would receive public recognition and gifts. I knew
there was to be a party in his honor. None of this filled my heart with joy. "Let
me take lessons too," I said. My aunt said, "What for? A girl doesn't need to
bother about Hebrew." "But I do." I said. "I do." My mother said, "You can
marry a man who can read Hebrew." "No," I kept on trying, "let me take
lessons." "Don't be silly," said my mother. The tutor came and my brother
disappeared into a room with him. The tutor was a young man from the
Bronx who was earning his way through rabbinical school by tutoring the
boys of families that held bar mitzvahs for their sons, in a cultural nod to

their grandparents, in a gesture of group solidarity at a time when the group still held together because most other Americans wouldn't let them into their clubs or businesses. The bar mitzvah was to be a joyous celebration of young manhood and then it was to be forgotten, a passage meant to leave the past on the other shore. The tutor of course did not think of it that way. For him, with his small tufts of beard and his serious eyes, which seemed like wells in which some mysterious algae was growing, it was something else and when I saw the thin frail back of the tutor disappear into my brother's room, I wanted him to turn around and look at me. He didn't.

My brother received a book with Hebrew letters and a workbook for him to practice copying the strange shapes. I tried to borrow his book. I tried to learn on my own. I tried to get my brother to teach me what he was learning. He wouldn't let me have the book. He hid it somewhere in his room. The Hebrew teacher came to the house twice a week. The piano teacher came once a week.

I took a dance class with a Martha Graham teacher. We wore pale blue leotards and went barefoot on the wooden floor. While I was good with a hockey stick and fine with a basketball dancing was not where my gifts lay and I had trouble following the steps. I also had no desire to watch myself in the mirror or to wave my arms as if I were a cloud. Soon I stopped going to dance class. My brother meanwhile persisted in learning Hebrew.

My brother working with his tutor in his room, door closed, on Park Avenue in 1951, soon knew the Hebrew letters, the sounds they made, the meaning of the words that went backward across the page. And what he saw, what he said as his lips formed the unfamiliar sounds formed the rope that lifted him up, that allowed him to soar higher toward the heavens, that allowed him to join with his people who had been left behind in the little villages of Poland, tucked into the rolling hills of the fertile Pale. He learned to rock back and forth on his heels as the melodies of the ancient prayers sank into his bloodstream, shaping him with the sound of human need, human passion, hope perhaps. *Sh'ma Yisroel, Adonai Eloheinu, Adonai Echad.* Hear O Israel, the Lord is our God, the Lord is One. The black swirls of the consonants, the dots of the vowels, the grammar that slowly revealed its rules to the initiate, all of that he followed into the sweet imploring, the promising, the praising, the pleading, the racing of the hare and the land of milk and honey, the march around the walls of Jericho, the selling of Joseph into slavery, the wandering of nomads in their deserts and the battles of the Maccabees and the miracle of burning oil and over it all came the whispers of love for a God who might be induced to return that love, who had certainly chosen, marked, asked for this child who was learning the language that would reach backward in time to the prophets thundering at the gates of Jerusalem, backward to the rabbis who gathered in discussion in exile in Babylon, to the prayers of a people caught in history's ebb tide, stranded without land, trusting in God, crossing parted seas, pursued by the pharaoh's chariots, burned at the stake by the inquisitors of Spain and reviled in Portugal, exiled from England, hunted across the Urals, all the while the winding melody continued, whispering of the seasons in the language of the other place, of the sanctuary that no longer existed, not even as rubble, not even as gray stones with weeds struggling to grow in the cracks between fallen boulders.

Also my brother's tutor told him jokes.

Chaim, Beryl, and Feibel were three young men who planned to leave New York and go to Texas to start a business. They spoke to their rabbi who said to them, In Texas you will need new names. Chaim you will become Chuck, Beryl you will become Buck. Feibel interrupted, I don't think I'm going to Texas. My brother told me the joke and he giggled his joke giggle. His shoulders went up and down. He smiled at me, a swift quick smile. His face was light, impish, and his eyes flashed (headlights on the nighttime road) with triumph. I wanted to remember the joke to tell my friends, but I forgot the joke. My brother told me another. Soon he had a brainful of jokes that he could call up for any occasion. Sometimes I didn't understand the punch line. I laughed anyway. I always loved my brother's jokes. I loved my joking brother.

My brother was playing Brahms and Beethoven on the piano. He had perfect pitch and a sense of music that seemed to come out of some ancestral deep: was it David and his harp? He also had an ear for the sounds of language and he learned Hebrew quickly and soon could read the prayer book and his portion for the bar mitzvah but he wanted to go on and learn more and he read Hebrew poetry and Psalms. I saw the Hebrew books piling up at the table at the end of his bed. My father said it was stupid to learn Hebrew. No American needed Hebrew. My father bought three new suits from a tailor in London who sent a representative to New York for special clients and then he did not have the money to pay the bill. He told my mother she had to pay. She said a grown man should pay for his own suits. He said her analyst was costing too much and it wasn't doing her any good anyway. She said he had a black thumb when it came to investing. It was perfectly clear to me that she should not have said he had a black thumb. I told my father he was handsome. I told my father that I liked to walk with him as he strode downtown at a pace that made my heart beat and my face grow red. I told my father that if I ever had any money I would just give it all to him. My mother said I must learn how to be popular with boys because everything that would happen to me in this world depended on it.

My brother was growing increasingly unfriendly to me. "Get out of my room," he would shout, if I appeared on the doorsill. "Who cares?" he would say if I asked him a question. At dinner he would sit there without a word, a dark sullen curl to his lips. If I started to tell him something, perhaps I had learned about the Chinese who had built the railroad line from Chicago to San Francisco, he would take off his glasses so my face would become a blur. "You're not a real Jew," he would say. "You can't read or speak Hebrew." "So what," I said. "Who cares?" I added. "Yeah," he said. "There's no hope for you. You'll never know anything important." "What do you talk about with Dr. Bussel?" I asked my brother. "Not you," said my brother. "But what?" I persisted. He didn't answer. He never would.

looking for decent employment   My mother told me exactly what she talked about with her analyst. It was about her childhood when she had been excluded from her older siblings' conversations. It was about how she had no confidence in herself, it was about learning to express your anger directly instead of getting heart palpitations.

I tried to imagine what the analyst looked like. "He has an accent," she told me, "from Austria." "Does he have a beard?" I asked. "No," she said. "Let me meet him," I begged. "I can't," she said. "It isn't done that way." "Will I ever meet him?" I asked, "Maybe," she said, "someday." He was, she told me, the most important man in her life, the love of her life. He understood everything. He told her they were making progress and she told me.

She took flower-arranging lessons. The class met once a week in different people's houses. Once I came home and there were five women in the dining room, snapdragons, peonies, roses, and baby's breath all over the table and each woman had a vase and the teacher was showing them how to cut the flowers. All the vases but my mother's soon filled with white and pink, with tall and short, with narrow and wide flowers. My mother couldn't make up her mind which flowers to use, how long the stems should be. Her glasses were fogged over with perspiration. She pricked her finger with a thorn.

"Do something else," she told me the analyst had said. It's not necessary to arrange flowers, she told me. She took a cooking class. She didn't like it. She took French lessons but didn't like the monsieur who came to the house to teach her.

Meantime her eyes were still always swollen from crying. The fights went on. I began to track the days that they didn't fight, maybe ten six or twelve in a month. Her ever-patient analyst was losing his patience she told me. One afternoon I came home from school and found her in bed with her legs ready for the lady who came to do the waxing, Mrs. Hummel. Mrs. Hummel was a widowed refugee whose father had been a doctor and whose late husband had died in the Resistance outside Arles. Mrs. Hummel who also did my mother's friend Helen's legs arrived at the apartment, changed into a white nurse's uniform, plugged a small burner she carried with her in a black bag into a socket under my mother's dressing table. The burner would sit in front of the mirror and its coils would turn bright red and then Mrs. Hummel would take out a small pot and into it she placed six-inch yellow sheets of hard wax which soon melted in the heat and bubbled up with small popping noises. The smell from the wax pot, a sort of sour sulfurous smell, would float through the room. Mrs. Hummel spread the hot wax on my mother's pale freckled legs with a wooden tongue depressor and then when the wax had hardened she would rip off the piece and with it would come my mother's leg hair, leaving a red bare spot on my mother's leg. My mother would bite her lip while the ripping took place. It hurt. It hurt a good deal. My mother would grasp my hand for support and between patches of hot wax would smoke a cigarette to calm the trembling in her calves. Mrs. Hummel worked for as long as it took, sometimes an hour and a half. "Be brave my darling," Mrs. Hummel would encourage her. "Just a few more minutes and you will be beautiful, perfectly beautiful."

It was during one of the sessions that my mother told me that her analyst had helped her to discover that she must find something useful to do with herself. "What?"she had asked. He said she said, "It's not my job to find your job, that's your job." "Why doesn't he just tell you what he thinks you should do?" I asked. "They're not allowed," she answered.

Then my mother became a Big Sister. This was a program run by the Jewish Board of Guardians in which women were assigned troubled girls who needed a special friend for support. My mother was assigned a girl named Bella Moscovitz whose father had died and whose diabetic mother lay on her bed in the small apartment in Washington Heights and would not get up and could not care for her daughter who at the age of eleven had begun seeing her father's shoes under her bed and knew that they were following her about. So frightened was the child of the apparition of her father's shoes that she was unable to pay attention at school or make a friend. Her mother had appealed for help and the Big Sister program was enlisted so that Bella could be brought on the subway to the midtown offices of the Jewish Board of Guardians where she could have weekly therapy with a clinical social worker.

My mother told me this and I began to think of Bella Moscovitz waking in her bed and hearing a tapping underneath of black shoes, laces undone, and I thought of her looking down, hanging over the edge of her mattress and seeing the shoes and knowing that the dead did not stay dead and that she wanted her father to return but not in the threatening visible but invisible, graveyard tap, tap calling way of his shoes. And my mother was going to help, really help, and I was pleased. Bella lived way uptown and my mother had to take a long subway trip to get there and another to bring the child to her therapist and then another to bring her home. On the subway my mother would talk to Bella and tell her the plots of Broadway shows, *Annie Get Your Gun, Oklahoma,* and *Guys and Dolls.* She would bring Bella presents. Clothes that she had bought for her or books with pictures of animals or of far-away places. Bella wanted to go to the Arctic circle and see for herself the polar bears, or so my mother told me.

After the therapy session my mother would take Bella out to a Schrafft's near the Jewish Board of Guardians offices for ice cream. Bella Moscovitz became my doppel, my shadow, my sister who was not my sister. I never met her although I asked. At first my mother kept every appointment. Each

Thursday afternoon she gave to Bella and when I came home from school she was not in bed with the scotch on the night table but instead returned later, exhausted from the traveling. But then one Thursday my mother had a dentist appointment and so she couldn't take Bella who missed her therapist that week and then a few Thursdays later my mother was going to a big party and she needed to go to the hairdresser that afternoon and Bella missed another appointment and then my mother had a card game that was changed from Wednesday to Thursday and on that week she canceled Bella as well.

I became worried about Bella and her need to get to the therapist. What did Bella do when she missed her appointment? Had she grown to expect my mother, to wait for her? Did Bella lie on her bed when my mother didn't come and try not to look under the mattress for her father's shoes? Was Bella getting better or didn't it matter if my mother stayed at home? Was Bella going mad because my mother was inconsistent?

On Saturday morning while my mother was waiting for a phone call from her brother we played our game: *inconsistent (nice, notion, stone, scion, content, sin)*.

And then one week my mother got a phone call from the Jewish Board of Guardians, Bella had taken a knife and threatened her own mother and had been removed from the home and sent to a school for disturbed children in Westchester. My mother was given the address and told she could write and visit there. A few weeks later my mother did visit. But Bella would not speak to her. My mother never went back. Bella and her dead father and the shoes that pursued became a part of our story, my brother's and mine. She was a shadow sibling that we didn't know, an absence, a hole, a stark confrontation with the fact that good intentions are not enough, not nearly enough. Although surely my mother meant well.

i become more american than thou   When I turned thirteen my Aunt Sylvia sent me a present. It came in a big box. I unwrapped it and found inside three used (one slightly stained) Chanel suits. My mother told me they were treasures, even second hand they were wonderful gifts. The only thing was I didn't need a Chanel suit. I needed cashmere sweater sets. I needed poodle skirts and black and white saddle shoes. I also needed iodine and Mercurochrome because I was forever scraping my knees at gym. After we lifted out the Chanel suits we found another gift from my aunt. The bottom of the box was lined with several layers of sanitary napkins. My aunt no longer needed them and didn't want them to go to waste.

I started going to a new high school in which I was one of a handful of Jewish girls.

The teachers at my old school were complaining that I was no longer listening. Was I deaf? I had been tested. The doctor considered that I might have some hearing loss due to scar tissue from the tonsillectomy. At the end of the forties before medicine had a proper respect for the destructive power of radiation they radiated into the throat to remove the offending tissue. Large machines pointed at my head. Loud whirring noises occurred as I lay on the table. I still paid no attention at school and so Hardy's mother suggested to my mother that I go to a well-known all-girls school with Hardy.

Ah how my world changed. There were debutantes there. There were cotillion goers there. There were blonde tall basketball players and lovers of Latin and Greek. Their apartments unlike mine had old faded oriental rugs on the floor. The furniture was likely to have worn places. Lampshades had burn spots. My friends' mothers wore sensible shoes and tweed jackets. They worked for charities like Planned Parenthood or Prison Reform. They wore little makeup. They did not have mink coats that came down to their feet. Their gold bracelets did not rattle when they walked. These mothers and their daughters were real Americans and I admired them enormously even if I could not attend their parties, join their clubs, or attend their dances which were not open to Jewish girls.

I drank in this Protestant world and tasted a quiet dignity, a respect for the privacy and surprising parameter of the self, a reserve or a coolness, the very opposite of my mother, the very opposite of the liquid Hebrew that my brother was chanting in the home. They did not lament. They had stiff upper lips. Around them echoed the voices of Emerson and Thoreau, Milton and his Paradise Lost. When you listened to them ordering a sandwich or making weekend plans, you heard Caesar coming over the mountains with Vercingetorix captured in a cage as well as Ulysses S. Grant drinking in his tent, not speaking of the horrors he'd seen. Their voices contained Sherwood Anderson whose characters—schoolteachers, rejected women, failing salesmen—made up an imperfect America that was mine in a way that it could never have been my immigrant father's or my second-generation mother's.

Had I not perfected my reading skills on books about pioneer girls captured by Indians? Did I not know Walt Whitman's "When Lilacs Last in the Dooryard Bloomed," the first five stanzas by heart? Did I not believe that restraint was beauty and democracy perfectible if we followed the path of Jefferson, Madison, and Adams who were all men with straight backs who lived in houses with tall white columns, who spoke to God in a firm unaccented English?

I was determined to camouflage myself. Draped in the American flag I would go forth and homestead a piece of America and bravely, against locusts and drought, against savages and beasts, I would conquer. This was my plan. I also intended to go to college and play field hockey till my ankles collapsed.

Although I was now enrolled in this gentile school I still attended Viola Wolf dancing classes for Jewish offspring. Viola Wolf was a large woman with a heaving breast, long purple satin gowns, and gold and silver rings on her fingers and lavender powder on her upswept hair. Her classes were held in a limestone building right off Park Avenue somewhere in the sixties. The walls were covered in velvet wallpaper. The pianist wore a tuxedo. There was nothing aimless about dancing school. The stakes were high. The smell of sex was almost eliminated but not quite. Kisses were stolen on stairwells, in the cloakroom. Boys talked about whether you would or wouldn't kiss them on the mouth, let them touch a breast. If you did you were a whore and your reputation went bear. If you didn't you were a prude and your reputation went bear and the boys migrated to someone else. Some of them were just afraid that a girl would scorn them. Most of them were afraid they wouldn't know what to do or how to do it.

If I had failed at Viola Wolf my mother would have grieved. I didn't. In my class there were sons and daughters of neighborhood Jews who learned in that building how to tango, how to foxtrot, how to do the Mexican hat dance. Everyone had to wear white gloves. The girls waited to be asked to dance and we sat on gold chairs with red velvet cushions and stared into mirrors with the reflections of ourselves on the opposite wall. We had our own Christmas dance at Viola Wolf's with holly hanging from the ceiling and arrangements of evergreen with Christmas balls placed on the piano.

For each holiday dance the girls had to have a date. The boy would come to the door and bring a corsage which was to be pinned on the waist of the dress. I had my eye on a boy named Bobby Newman who had a promising smile and was part of the desired group, hierarchies having established themselves within moments of our first classes. Bobby Newman took me to a Christmas dance. I was wearing a yellow satin ball gown which was strapless and pinched at the waist. Under my dress I wore a tight corset that pushed up my breasts and squeezed my ribs against my lungs or so I thought. Bobby Newman brought me a white orchid. I pinned it to my waist. At the first dance he pulled me in close to him and the white pearl head on the pin pressed deep through my dress. It smashed through the corset below, it penetrated right through the slip, and pierced my skin. I felt it, a pain, sharp and clean. He swung me out and I twirled around and then he brought me in close and again I felt the pain. After the first dance I went to the pink-walled ladies' room where a maid in a black uniform with a white apron was waiting to hand me a towel to dry my hands after washing. I looked into the mirror and saw a blood spot spreading across my waist. It wasn't a microscopic spot, it was a splash of red on the yellow satin. Blood was shame. It wasn't ever supposed to show. Blood on the satin was a sign, a mark. I tried to wash it out but instead I stained pink a larger area. What to do? What did I do? I don't remember. I know that I came home and threw off the dress and hid it in my closet. Blood was the deepest darkest shame of all.

In all the fashion magazines women had short noses, most had blue eyes, straight hair, and rosebud lips. There were no African women in turbans, no coffee-colored women in saris. There were no articles on gay and lesbian marriages pro or con and while the United Nations was already in its headquarters in New York City, and decent liberal people wanted Jim Crow to end, there were only the two known illicit abortionists, one in Pennsylvania and one in Puerto Rico, if you got into trouble and if you got into trouble it was very bad. Girls did not have sex before marriage without damaging their reputations, without ruining their lives, without risking their future children, because abortionists all too often left scars, caused hemorrhaging, and changed frightened girls into barren women which is why I went with my mother to have my hair straightened at a hairdresser on 125th Street up two flights of stairs with peeling wallpaper on either side, within sight of the railroad train carrying commuters to Westchester.

I wanted to look like everyone else. I wanted silky straight hair even if it was Jewish black not corn-fed blonde. I did not feel that my curls grew from my head in ethnic joy but rather that they revealed a certain separateness, a shamefulness, a less-than-perfect quality. My dark head with its wiry hair was a mark of difference, my friends at school called me Brillo-head, a tell-tale sign that referred backward to our family past, not forward into America. My mother thought so. She had told me so. She was ashamed of my hair. At the beauty parlor where we were the only white-skinned females around I sat on a high chair as a sulfurous-smelling cream was applied in sharp jabs across my pink scalp. The cream stung. The smell made my eyes water. I sat with a plastic cap on my head and waited for the chemistry to do its magic. I was a foreigner here in this beauty parlor where the women spoke with the South in their mouths and everyone looked at me and my mother as if we had offended them in some way that could not be erased. The burning on my scalp continued under the plastic cap. Some of the cream had leaked onto my forehead and a red burn mark was spreading outward. "It hurts," I told my mother. She laughed. "Everything we do for beauty hurts," she said. "You have to expect that."

Finally the beautician came and took off the plastic cap and I was given a shampoo which pricked my sensitive head as if small needles were being inserted in random patterns. I was put in curlers, tight pink curlers. I was given Vaseline for the burn on my forehead which threatened to form a blister. I was combed out and there it was, perfect straight hair. Not exactly soft and silky but yes a solid wall of hair, smooth as it had never been before. On the cab ride home my mother crooned, it was worth it, it was worth it. It was. My friends at school admired it. My Aunt Libby said I looked far better than she would have believed and she gave me a lipstick called scarlet blush.

About a week later the first hairs began to fall out. They were in my brush and they were on my pillow. Within a few weeks I had fully exposed bald spots all across my scalp and soon it was clear to everyone that my new straight hair was a temporary acquisition. Small new bristles grew up on my scalp prodding the remaining strands of still straight hair to rise as if on a bed of nails. I was ashamed. My mother looked at me and sighed. At least your nose isn't Jewish she said, be grateful for that. Such was the age of conformity which came just before the Age of Aquarius.

my brother converts in a manner of speaking

My brother on the other hand was disturbing my mother by taking his pre–bar mitzvah training very seriously. My mother was planning a big party with music and food and invitations for all her relatives and friends. His voice, however, as he prepared his bar mitzvah portion seemed to pierce the space between our rooms, a rope flung up to the heavens.

I come up the elevator after school one afternoon with two gentlemen both headed for our house. One is the Hebrew tutor who pushes himself back against the elevator wall and avoids looking at me. The other is Mr. Otto who takes my hand and kisses it.

Mr. Otto is a small nervous man who had come to this country from Vienna via Palestine where he had arrived only to be placed in a camp in Cyprus by the British. His father's pre-Anschluss linen business had been appropriated by his chief employee and of the Ottos only the small fluttering Mr. Otto survived the war. Now he sells linens he orders from Antwerp, lace-trimmed nightgowns from Alsace, monogrammed sheets from the north corner of Holland. He shows samples of his wares which he pulls theatrically from a large suitcase that he carries up and down Park Avenue. Mr. Otto has spread out across the beds different clothes, yellow and pale blues, embroidered with flowers, white rosebuds on white vines. Mr. Otto tells my mother that he lives alone in an apartment in Queens. My mother offers him a drink. "Oh no, it wouldn't be right," he says. "I'm just your servant." "It's not like that in America," my mother says.

My mother wants to buy her analyst a pillowcase for his couch with his initials embroidered on it. She decides against it. "You are not," she says, "supposed to give your doctor a present." "Why not?" I ask. She sighs. It's a deep sigh. "Do you still think about suicide?" I ask. She doesn't answer me.

The young Hebrew tutor for my brother took him to the Bronx on Friday afternoons for Sabbath services and he spent the night at the tutor's house since he didn't want to travel again until sunset on Saturday. My brother felt at home there in a way that he had never felt at home at home. His weekends away were fine with me. I did not miss his company.

His analyst when consulted did not object to his going to the Bronx once or twice a week for more intense preparation for his bar mitzvah.

15

we try the tropics   My mother tells me that her analyst has
suggested a vacation. She should get out into the world he has implied, not
in so many words of course. He himself is going away for a few weeks in
March. We go to Nassau. My brother hates the sun and water and he will
not go. He stays at home with the cook and the maid and a poor single
woman cousin who while much pitied was hardly respected. My father and
I and my mother fly off to a resort. This is the first time I have been in an
airplane. I am dazzled by the palms and the hibiscus and rum drinks with
parasol twizzle sticks.

My father tells my mother she should have lost a few more pounds before trying to squeeze herself into a bathing suit. I am in the room next door.
I am not surprised to learn that my mother is going to take dinner in her
room and I am to join my father at the hotel bar. He is wearing a white suit
with a blue silk tie. He sits on the bar stool with his legs extended and his
hands around a dry martini. I sit on his other side. He isn't talking to me so
I am not surprised when a man approaches from his other side and sits at
the stool nearby. The man asks my father something. My father turns his
head away. The man leans forward and whispers something in my father's

ear. I don't hear it. I am watching the green foam on a Grasshopper the bartender is pouring from a silver tumbler. Suddenly my father stands up and lets out a cry like a trapped animal. He raises his arm high, pulls it back, and punches the fellow in the face. He punches again and again and the other man falls to the floor, women in strapless dinner gowns are screaming, men are rushing over. I bend over the man who has fallen to the floor. I want to help him. My father shoves me to the side. He lifts his fists high. He is screaming, "Faggot, fairy. I'm no pansy." The man on the floor is crying like a child. I see the tears rolling down his face, collecting at the corners of his mouth. "Daddy," I call out, and throw myself against him, hanging on to his waist with all my might.

We are out of the bar standing on the deck overlooking a sandy tongue of the Carribean, the beach chairs, the striped umbrellas are folded up for the evening. "Goddamn fairy," shouts my father. Pushing me away he straightens his jacket and walks off along the path lit with blue and pink bulbs hanging in the branches of palm trees. I notice there are drops of blood on my white sandals.

The next day my father leaves for New York. My mother and I stay on. She explains to me what her analyst had explained to her. The best defense is an offense. Perhaps he protests too much.

On the way back to New York my mother who is afraid of flying takes two tranquilizers and several scotches before we board. I have to steady her and lead her to our seat. She can't sit by the window because she finds it too frightening. I am at the window. She is asleep, deeply unwakeably asleep. We are taking a night flight. I see a flame coming from the engine outside my window. The plane is on fire, I am cold with fear. But I watch and the fire seems steady, no more after a few minutes than before. What should I do? If I tell the stewardess that the engine is on fire and this is normal behavior for an engine I will be ashamed. If in my fear of being ashamed I allow the plane to continue flying and it crashes and everybody dies it will be my fault for not alerting the pilot for fear of being ashamed or being wrong. I turn the moral dilemma over and over in my head. The sky is dark, the only light is the small flame from the engine right outside my window. I get up and tell the stewardess. She doesn't laugh at me. But on the other hand the flame was normal, contained, noncombustive. We arrive in New York and the stewardess has to call to get a wheelchair for my mother, she cannot walk. She barely wakes. Her speech is slurred. I am ashamed and ashamed of being ashamed.

my very first funeral   My Aunt Bea whom I had seen no more than once or twice in my life lost her husband Dan. Dan Kreisberg was his name. The funeral is held at Riverside Chapel on the West Side of Manhattan. My father is paying for it and he won't go to Queens. My mother told me that it was very generous of my father to bury his sister's husband but the money would come from her bank account. She said the top-of-the-line casket wasn't necessary. My father clenched his jaw so tightly the skin beneath his nose turned white.

The chapel is not very full, the grieving widow takes up a substantial part of the first pew along with my father and her lawyer son, my older cousin with whom I have never exchanged the most commonest of pleasantries. In the second pew sit my mother and brother. The rabbi who had been hired for the occasion appears from behind a curtain and intones about the good man whom the world has lost, hard working, devoted to his family, and honest to the bone. I can hear my huge Aunt Bea sniffling in the pew ahead of us. Her large purse is on her lap. She opens and closes it to fetch tissues. I am worried that I don't look sad enough. Will everyone know that I am not a genuine mourner? It's not my fault. I never knew him, I want to say. I am wearing a hat my mother has put on my head. It has a veil. Perhaps I am invisible behind the veil. The rabbi talks in that I-speak-for-all-eternity voice, the one that makes your feet numb but also alerts you to the seriousness of the event, in case you misunderstood and thought death was just a rehearsal for the *Ed Sullivan Show*. The rabbi speaks of the courage of the departed's wonderful wife, the support of family, the comfort they should find among the mourners of Zion. The audience is restless. My mother opens her gold compact with the ruby bouquet of flowers at the center and powders her nose. Powder falls on my black skirt. "Now," says the rabbi, "the time has come to say goodbye to Harry Feingold." My Aunt Bea jumps to her feet and her pocketbook spills its contents which include several candy bars right out on the floor. "That's not Harry Feingold," she points at the black and gold leafed coffin at the rabbi's feet. "That's Dan Kreisberg."

There is a silence in the room. A shuffling sound from the assembled. My mother puts her white gloved hand over her mouth so no one can see her expression. When she puts her hand down there is red lipstick all over her glove. The rabbi spreads his white index cards in front of him. He shuffles through the pack. "Ah," he says. "You're right, I'm doing Harry Feingold at one thirty, indeed this is in fact Dan Kreisberg." He coughs, pauses dramatically. "The time has come he said to say goodbye to————." This time he got it right.

My father said later that he refused to give him the whole fee. He didn't deserve it.

The entire funeral was no more than twelve minutes. I decided to plant a tree in Israel in Dan Kreisberg's name. Of course they didn't really name the trees. And then I didn't know him. My father said he was a jerk, had always been a jerk, a small-time jerk. But what exactly did he mean? Perhaps that he left my Aunt Bea dependent on the goodwill of her brother which could not much have eased her grief. My father hated fat women. He said so all the time—bruisers, he would call them, women who shouldn't come out in the daytime he would say. Fat women give off the odor of rotten eggs, he said. I knew that wasn't true. I had sat right behind her. My Aunt Bea smelled of bath oil and peppermint Life Savers.

My mother says that my Aunt Bea wears a size 24. She's as big as a Cadillac, she says. My mother says my Aunt Bea has no self-respect or she wouldn't have four chins. My father says he can't eat when he visits her because he feels sick to his stomach looking at her. But he gives his sister money for a trip to Florida. He pays the college tuition for his nephew whom I have never met. My mother says Aunt Bea should go to a psychoanalyst. My father says he won't pay for it. My mother asks, "How many rhumba trophies does one woman need?" I erase my Aunt Bea from my family portrait. She's out.

my brother said it and he meant it which was neither expected nor welcomed   Johnny announced his intention to become a rabbi. My mother laughed. It was sweet she thought like a five year old wanting to be a fireman. "He'll outgrow it," said my Aunt Libby. He's such a serious child, said my Uncle Sy. But my brother keep repeating it, to anyone who would listen, so my mother called my brother's analyst and asked if she didn't think it was peculiar, his wanting to become a rabbi. "It's just early adolescent excess," said the analyst, "a normal enough occurrence through this passage." " Don't overreact," she told my mother who reported the conversation to me. My mother's psyche was jammed at overreact and knew no other way.

The rabbi gave my brother a Hebrew name. "Big deal," said my father. "Abracadabra," said my father. "Right off to the gas chamber with the likes of you."

The bar mitzvah was held in early December after my brother's thirteenth birthday. I was nearly seventeen. I thought that this bar mitzvah was a primitive pow-wow, a rite of passage like sending a Sioux into the forest till he found his totem animal in a dream.

On the appointed day the family gathers at the Park Avenue Synagogue. My brother looks strange in a long tallis reading his portion. I don't want to look at him so I stare at the stained glass windows, gift of Mr. and Mrs. Harvey Steingold, and Mrs. Louis Schwartz (*war, harsh, cart, wart, chart, art*). I am wearing a blue taffeta skirt with a crinoline underneath, one that pricked the skin on my thighs. I have spent two hours at the hairdresser. The heat of the dryer has left a red mark on my neck. I didn't invite any of my school friends. What would they think? I am not impressed until I hear my brother sing the melodies as he reads from the Torah. Something in the sound of his voice, in the way he moves his head back and forth and his shoulders covered by the white satin tallis stoop and rise, something about the shine of his eyes behind his glasses, made me grieve for the dead and feel like a stranger.

The white yarmulke that circles the crown of his head shines like the midnight moon. It has a design of gold threads at the edge. My brother's voice sounds as if a stone is falling, turning over and over down a narrow dark well, flashes of receding sunlight followed along the plummeting way. It brings a lump to my throat. It is very clear my brother believes whatever he is saying. I pity him his simpleness while a fungus of envy, all unwanted, wraps itself around my heart.

This was for me, despite my advanced age, my disinterest in religion, a difficult day. It was his after all, not mine. I was the attendant, the maid in waiting, he was the king. It was not pleasant. At the reception I keep a fixed smile on my face. "You must be proud of your little brother," said the assistant rabbi. "His Hebrew is the best of any bar mitzvah boy's I've ever worked with." "Yes," I nod and open my mouth in my new silver-band-free smile. My father circulates among the guests, and my mother dances with her brother, smooth and easy. The tall vases are filled with irises and gladiolas on the tables. My Aunt Sylvia said, "He'll get over this nonsense now just you watch." There are the envelopes full of checks and cash piled up on a small table in the hallway and wrapped packages wait for him in the cloakroom. I want to be generous. I want to be pleased for him. I am not. He is receiving more attention, more praise, than I can bear. I bear it because I must.

I did admire his new blue suit. I did like the striped tie he was wearing like my father's.

I dance with my father. He is a sleek jaguar hunting in the moonlight. I float in his arms, press my face against his chest, smell his tart after-shave, and observe his immaculate white shirt, his slicked-back black hair with a part so straight it could have divided the heavens from the earth. His hooded eyes give away nothing. We dance the foxtrot, we dance close. He twirls me out, I dip arching my back, a good dip. "Do you think the Jews are safe in America?" I ask. He stops dancing. He stands in the middle of the dance floor, rigid. "If anyone tries anything," he says, "I'll get a gun. I'll blow their heads off. I won't wait around. I'll mow them down. I'll go into the hills. I'll cut off their balls. I wouldn't sit still like those sheep." He waved his arm off to the side where the guests were sipping champagne and eating strawberries and blueberries served from crystal bowls that sat on beds of ice on the buffet table.

I'm just making conversation, hoping he will find me interesting. But I am flushed with pleasure at his words. He will protect me, my heart sang. He wants me to live. I ache all over with gratitude or is it love? We begin again to dance. I am the right partner for him. I respond to the lightest most imperceptible touch on the small of my back. Then I see his eyes searching about the corners of the room. "Look at those dumb broads," he said to me as a flock of my mother's canasta partners rose from their table to refill their plates.

At the end of the party after most of the guests are gone, I see my brother opening his presents at a table littered with napkins and empty wine glasses. He makes neat piles of the books he has received. I am cold as ice. His God, his religion, his people, his presents . . . it is not fair. He is not as worthy as I am. Everyone must know. I am the important child. I am ashamed of myself but the taste in my mouth remains sour, bitter, harsh. I watch the way he touches his presents and opens them slowly, carefully, reading the card, and smoothing out the wrapping paper. I know I am hateful and hate filled. I can't stop myself. How can there be peace in the world if I am how I am about my very own brother? The atomic bomb will surely fall on our heads one day.

I go home to lunch with a school friend from my girls' school. We eat with her mother. The maid serves soup in individual tureens. I am careful to put my spoon on the side of the under plate. My friend's mother says to me, "You have such nice manners for a Jewish girl." Thank God I think to myself, I know what to do with my spoon.

I didn't notice the exact moment when my brother began to look like a stranger. But finally I saw that his face except for the usual acne clusters was ashen as if he were raised underground like a tubular vegetable. There were dark circles under his eyes. You could see them behind his thick glasses. This happened shortly after his bar mitzvah. My brother wore a black hat on his head or his yarmulke, uncommon, perhaps unheard of on Park Avenue.

My brother fooled them all. He didn't stop going to Hebrew classes in the Bronx after his bar mitzvah was over. He insisted on being tutored in Yiddish. He found someone who could teach him Arabic. Soon he claimed that the food in the house was inedible because the kitchen was not kosher. He would eat only fruit on a glass plate and drink only water. My mother would give him money for his dinner which he ate alone at the Madison Avenue Deli ten blocks away. He packed a kosher lunch for school also purchased at the Madison Avenue Deli. From Friday afternoon till Saturday after dark he stayed in the Bronx, sleeping on the opened couch of his Hebrew tutor, where Shabbat was observed and the dietary laws were followed to the most precise and obscure of letters, two sets of dishes, two bars of soap, two different sponges, one for meat and one for dairy. You should not boil the kid in the milk of the mother. My brother told me that. He told me that while I was eating a ham sandwich. "That's disgusting," he told me. My mother was fond of ham. Emma the cook made a large glazed ham at least once a month. My mother liked pork chops and applesauce. Emma made roast pork with steamed onions. Greta had said bacon was good for the liver. I imagined the little lamb cooking in a pot with his mother's milk steaming up and I knew that there was something cruel, indifferent, cannibalistic about the sight but considering that the lamb was already slaughtered and wouldn't know if his body were basted in milk or wine perhaps it didn't matter, certainly not to the lamb, then who?

Perhaps the law was there in the Jewish text to remind human beings that they could not just destroy with their sharp teeth, with their empty stomachs at will, that the creatures of the world deserved respect. "And what about the asparagus?" said my mother. "Perhaps we should dress each stalk in a pinafore so it doesn't appear naked before us at the table?"

On his special diet my brother gained some weight. He got a permanent excuse from gym because of the asthma.

"Godammit," yells my father, "he looks like he just got off the boat." And he did. A certain greenish color in the cheeks that came from avoiding soaps, avoiding the shaving kit that he was beginning to need, accompanied by the shapeless black pants that he wore with a cheap dark jacket, an always spotted white shirt, and a thin blue tie with the flag of Israel printed on it over and over again, all hand-me-downs from his Hebrew tutor in the Bronx finished off the effect.

"To just get off the boat" is not a neutral phase. It is not a description of disembarking at a port, it is a pejorative referring to a newcomer who hasn't learned the ways of the new world, who is still stuck in the mud of the past, still a creature at the bottom of the social order, language wrong, clothes wrong, expectations of what is right and wrong, wrong. To just get off the boat is to have the dust of the old streets still in your hair, still in your nostrils, it is not to know about Jack Benny and Ingrid Bergman, not to know about the Rainbow Room or the names of the suburbs like Great Neck and Woodmere, Harrison and Rye. It is to be a pedlar, an outsider, a creature not of the Enlightenment but of the despised past where one was despised. It hurt my father to see his son look as if he just got off the boat because he himself had arrived as a child and learned as quickly as possible to hide that fact. To the swift learners went the rewards. The melody of the synagogues on Friday nights, the sight of the men walking home to a Sabbath dinner after prayer, so many blackbirds sailing on rooftops through narrow alleys, cows and moons floating in the air, fiddlers dancing, nothing about this seemed charming to my father. In his mind's eye the scene was painted in weakness and blood, with the contempt of the others stinking like dung in the barnyard and everywhere the abhorrent vulnerability of his kind.

My brother's appearance revealed my father's hidden history. He did not like to look at my brother. He avoided going down the elevator with him at any time of day.

"Your brother is going to be short," he told me. "Like your mother, he's a shrimp." I was taller than my mother, a good height for a girl. I knew he despised what my short brother had become. It seemed as if my home already riven apart was now dividing itself into ever smaller and smaller fractions.

Other boys at the Park Avenue Synagogue took their bar mitzvah as the open gate, a release from the peculiarities of Jewish life. They enjoyed Saturdays in the park with a baseball. They took up musical instruments or girls or became members of the debating team or the track team. My brother walked closer and closer to God. I began to think he would really become a rabbi. My mother laughed nervously at the idea. In her whole life she had never known anyone who had become a rabbi. She did not consider this one of the esteemed professions. It reeked of low salaries and indentured service to the more enterprising. Her father had founded a hospital. He had given money to an old age home, he was a donor not a beggar. It was as if my brother had aspired to become a butler or a hairdresser or a fireman, as if he were planning to create a stock market portfolio out of his daily doorman tips. And besides there was something backward about it, something that seemed un-American, as if the ship of our family fortune had suddenly reversed directions, leading us back to the small town in Poland where the rabbi and his students had been the cream of the crop, the top of the heap, the envied, the valued, the cherished, the ones sought out for the hand of rich men's daughters. As if a reverse wind was blowing us to that place where the fate of the powerless was bleaker than even the worst of pessimists had imagined.

I imagine him in the Bronx at a small shul with its worn pews, with one small stained-glass window that has been repaired because a passerby threw a rock some years back. I imagine him opening the Torah and with a silver pointer given him by one of the older men who were always shuffling

through the drafty hall or huddled over a text in the room behind the ark behind the eternal light which burned in its golden holder thanks to the electric bulb that one of them kept replacing on the first of each month. I think
of my young brother, breathing shallow from the dust on the seats, focusing
his eyes on the letters of the page. Was God in his soul? Did God enter with
the melody of the prayers? Was my brother happy there? I imagine so.

And I imagine not. His expression whenever I saw his face was sour. He
seemed angrier than ever. In all the rules of his religion he did not seem to
find order or peace. But then perhaps I have a sentimental view of religion.
His certainly was stern and judgmental and inflexible. His was a religious
sensibility of the morally discerning mind more than the merging embrac-
ing heart. He was not wallowing in the I and Thou and he was not whirling
like the Hasids with the force of the spirit taking him up to the stars. But
maybe there was comfort in the rightness of saying the words again and
again—maybe in the things done as they had always been done he found a
lifeline, a rope that bound him backward and propelled him forward.
Maybe he now believed that someone in the Bronx, someone in the heavens was watching out for him.

He continued playing the piano. He continued his four times a week visits to the analyst.

My mother told me that she was afraid something was terribly wrong
with my brother's mind. She had reasons but she wouldn't tell me what they
were. They were too terrible to repeat. They didn't come from his analyst.
But what? I pleaded with her. She cried and put her hands over her ears.
Was my brother crazy?

My mother tells me that she has bottles and bottles of sleeping pills hidden in the house. Where, I beg her to tell me where. She will not tell me.
She promises me she will not use them without discussing it with me first.
I tell my Aunt Libby. She says to pay no attention. "Nobody in their right
mind would give up a day of their lives on this earth," she says. But is my
mother in her right mind or her wrong mind? I ask my mother if her analyst
knows about the pills. He does. "Is he worried about you?" I ask. "I don't
know," she says. "He hasn't said." " I think you should get a divorce," I say.
"Then you'll be happier." My mother sighs. My mother kisses me. My
mother holds my hand. She won't kill herself I am sure. She loves me too
much.

There is a fight going on at the dinner table. I put my hands over my ears. I ask to be excused. I pretend I have to make a phone call. I too raise my voice. My brother won't eat anything from our kitchen. He sits at the table like a block of wood. I can't tell what he is thinking. His eyes are dull behind his thick glasses, that soft faded blue of afternoon winter sky. My father calls my brother a parasite, a bloodsucker. He thinks the Hebrew lessons which have now become Talmud lessons should be stopped. My brother's analyst disagrees. My mother weeps over her lamb chops. The maid who is serving the meal pretends not to notice. My brother gets up from the table and goes into his room and slams the door. I intend to eat my dessert. I bring a book to the table. I read.

My brother is in his room listening to his collection of classical music. I prefer Frank Sinatra records. I'm expecting a boy to invite me to Yale for the weekend or if not that at least Exeter or Andover. I too talk in the halls on Monday mornings about the long train trip up, the cigarettes smoked in the boys' bathroom, the scotch sipped from Coke bottles. I have gone a few places and have brought back, crimson and white, blue and white, orange and black wool scarves. I wear my collection with pride. I have purchased stickers of men's colleges and put them up on the mirror of the bathroom I share with my brother, Harvard, Yale, Princeton. My brother scratches off my stickers with a razor blade and pastes on the mirror pictures of famous rabbis. They all have beards. They all wear black hats. They all have bleak watery eyes. I don't take down his pictures. I understand they are important to him. But I am embarrassed to bring my friends home. How will I explain this, in the bathroom, these pictures of old men?

16

i have a date with history and escape   It is
1952. I am the star of the school basketball team. This is not because I am
so tall but because I throw myself after every ball. I am unafraid of banging
myself into walls. I frequently do. I am unafraid of bumping or falling, my
elbows swing, I scream for the ball to be thrown to me, I play each moment
as if there will be no others, as if the earth is holding its breath waiting for
me to shoot from the foul line, to dash, sweat pouring off my face, across
the gym, a space in which I feel curiously safe considering the ever-present
bruises on my hips, knees, shoulders. We duck under our desks in training
for the fall of the hydrogen bomb. We are issued ivory dog tags with silver
chains with our names and blood types on them. Then North Korea invades
South Korea. We have an assembly at which the Indian ambassador to the
United Nations tells us that our newspapers have lied to us. It was South
Korea that invaded North Korea. That is what it says in the newspapers in
India. My father says that's commie bullshit. Is it? I read everything in *Life*
magazine, in *Time* and I listen to the radio late at night. Who is telling the
truth? Is there such a thing as truth? If the bomb falls will I have missed a
good life or a bad one?

My father says that anyone who remained a communist after the Hitler-Stalin Pact should be given a frontal lobotomy. Then my father is given some piece work by Roy Cohn, who has been plucked from the district attorney's office to work on the McCarthy investigating team, now Roy Cohn, darling of the New York political machine, apple of his mother's eye, bridge player at the A level, had become an anticommunist warrior, a boy wonder, a defender of the flag. The pinkos, the commie symps, the commies themselves will get theirs. My father says they should be strung up, chopped up, and their severed limbs delivered to their children in old newspapers.

Then I am invited to meet the younger brother of Roy Cohn's colleague and friend David Schine. The younger Schine is a sophomore at Harvard but he seems to be having trouble getting a girl to go out with him. I have been suggested. I am told to go to the Stork Club after school one afternoon to have drinks with the Schine boy. The team has a basketball game with a rival all-girls' school. I do not have time to go home and change although something tells me I should. My mother has given me taxi money so I will not be late.

I arrive at the mirrored, white-tabled, black-walled Stork Club in the late afternoon with my book bag holding a copy of Ovid, a collection of Hazlitt's essays, and my algebra homework, still wearing my sneakers, in my school uniform which is a short blue cotton jumper with a white little girl blouse. I have brushed my hair, wiped my face in the bathroom, and put a Band-Aid on a cut on my chin. I have applied thick red lipstick. Even under the school uniform a person could see I had a female body.

The headwaiter takes my camel's hair coat and along with my book bag he checks it in the cloakroom. He shows me to a table at which the younger Schine is waiting. He is short and plump. His face has broken out in a spray of red blisters. It seems as he rises to greet me that his eyes are out of focus. His fingers clasp the red swizzle stick as if it were the gearshift in a downwardly spiraling airplane. He mumbles. He looks away. We sit down. I sigh. He has nothing to say. He eats all the peanuts in the dish before us and orders an ice cream sundae with a cherry on the top. The waiter brings it in a silver dish and a plate of cookies as well. "Do you think the waiters here are communists?" I ask in order to break the ice. "I don't think so," he answers and looks around furtively. I try again. "What's your favorite subject?" I ask. "I don't like any of them," he answers. "Will you go into the hotel business when you graduate?" I ask. "Maybe," he says but looks mournful. "I would like to build a hotel," I say, "in Siberia." He says, "I don't think you can. It would be too hard to heat."

Suddenly the waiter comes over with a silver wine cooler brim full of ice. There is a bottle of champagne in it. The waiter opens the green bottle and pours its contents into the tall thin-stemmed glasses that have appeared at our table. I am aware of the fact that my socks have lost their elastic and are slipping down around my ankles. The younger Schine must have a soul. I try to find it. It is well hidden. No wonder he needs his brother to find a girl for him to date. The lights in the Stork Club are dim but gradually I can make out one other occupied table across the room. At it are sitting Roy Cohn and his friend David Schine. The older Schine is like a Greek god, blond and tall, firm and thin. His face is bland but perfect like a model's. My wayward superficial heart jumps to a new rhythm. The older Schine has no brains so my mother has said but I would like him to take me into the cloakroom and give me a kiss, just one quick kiss on the lips. "Do you think," I ask the younger brother, "that it's possible that South Korea invaded North Korea?" He looks misty eyed. "I don't like politics," he says.

Roy Cohn comes over to the table. He greets me like a long-lost friend. I play my part. The older Schine waves from his table. He had sent the champagne. At last it is time to go home, to retrieve my book bag from the cloakroom. The younger Schine asks me to come to Harvard for a weekend. I agree to go but I then don't. My father says Roy is angry at me. Roy will be president of the United States one day and I will regret my disloyalty. I understand the politics of the situation. I am sorry but not that sorry. I remind my father that in America there are no arranged marriages. I live in the land of the free, I remind him.

my mother finds me a sister i don't want and my brother finds that he doesn't want his sister   My mother has been picked for a special canasta game. Vladimir Horowitz and his wife Wanda, the daughter of Toscanini, had come to East Hampton while my mother was vacationing at a seaside cottage, and they had asked around for the best player anyone knew. Again and again my mother's name had come up and so she became involved in a game with four or five other players that met twice a week for the next ten years. In the game were the Horowitzes, their interior decorator and his life-time partner, and a friend of my mother's named Sally. The Horowitzes lived right near us in the nineties just off Fifth Avenue in a limestone house with a large piano in the living room and everything in the house was hushed and still as if the building itself were waiting for the maestro to play.

Vladimir Horowitz had stopped playing in public. My mother explained to me that he had suffered a breakdown, a great performing anxiety that was now depriving the world of one of its greatest master musicians. His analyst had suggested cards as a means of soothing his inner turmoil. My mother told me that Vladimir Horowitz was afraid he would soil his pants while playing and the shame of it, the potential shame of it, kept him off the stage. Will the analyst cure him? I had asked. It's not so easy, said my mother. Maybe he could wear a diaper, I suggested. He won't, my mother explained. He doesn't want to play in public. My mother did not know any-thing about music. Her favorite song, the one she hummed to herself in the bathtub, was "I'm Carmen Miranda and I'm here to say I love bananas in every way." But she was delighted to be playing cards with a celebrity and they played an exciting high-stakes game, the kind she liked. She won too, most all of the time. She would come home from the game and turn her purse upside down on the bed and hundred dollar bills would fall out along with nicotine scraps, lipstick-stained tissues, Chicklets that were chewed when she was trying to cut down on smoking, her good luck earrings that pinched her ears so she carried them in her purse, a silver cigarette case with her monogram embossed on the lid.

The Horowitzes had a daughter named Sonia which was unfortunate for me because she was just my age and I was her intended friend. I was se-lected to take her to the movies on Saturday afternoons and to bring her to parties with me and to help her find her place among her peers. This was not easy. Sonia had an awkward walk, a body that seemed oddly without age or gender. She was gruff and not eager to be my friend. She had other things on her mind. She was not a musician. She did not have the hands for it, my mother said. She was not a reader. She didn't have the concentration or the patience for it. She seemed wrapped in a thick cloud far away. She embar-rassed me. Was I kind enough? I doubt it. Did I really try? I doubt it. But when my mother said, "Take Sonia with you," I did. I understood that Sonia was a part of a package that was crucial to my mother, something that brought her happiness. "Think of her like a sister," said my mother. I tried or at least I intended to try.

Then one night when her parents were asleep Sonia went downstairs and went to the kitchen and took a sharp knife and climbing on the back of the sofa reached up and slashed the Picasso painting that hung on the wall. She slashed it more than once and in the morning when her mother and father came down to breakfast they found the ribbons of canvas hanging limply in the frame. There was no repair possible. This was a very expensive temper-tantrum. This was a sacrilege.

"Why did Sonia do that?" I ask my mother. "Sonia is ill," says my mother.

So Sonia went off to a hospital and I never had to take her anywhere with me again which was a relief except that I often thought of Sonia. "Was she ill because there were too many geniuses in her family?" I ask my mother. "Was she ill because Wanda had no time for her?" I ask. "Was she ill because her father won't play anymore?" I ask. I ask my brother because he has an analyst of his own and might understand things that I don't. My brother says his analyst doesn't want to talk about Sonia.

That a Picasso had been destroyed moved me very little, but that Sonia raged in the middle of the night and broke the bonds of civil behavior was frightening enough. Why had Sonia destroyed the Picasso? Who was to blame? Was the family wiring that had produced musical geniuses so delicate, so close to madness that the little girl child was destined for disaster? Sonia, who should have been, was almost my sister, disappeared and I wrote her a letter telling her to get better soon but she never wrote me back.

Meanwhile my brother was obeying the rules for turning on lights and rules for eating and the rules for prayers after meals and rules ran like the red and black squares of the chess board regularly, repeatedly, predictably, endlessly across his days. The knight never takes three squares forward and two to the side. The bishop never makes a horizontal dash. So did his soul comfort itself by staying within the laws, a pattern determined long before our coming into existence, a way of hiding within the folds of the past, every breath already examined by an earlier sage, every rule with fourteen explanations, all valid, all available to a person literate and obedient. As in the music he so loved the spaces between were measured, calculated, calibrated, repeated, sundown, sunup, seven days, the weeks between Passover and Tisha B'av, always the same.

Every morning before the maid served us breakfast and we went off to our schools my brother said the morning prayer to God in which among other things he thanked God for not making him a woman. Since he did this in Hebrew I was not offended and even if I had understood I would not have been likely to notice something unkind in this prayer. It might well have seemed sensible to me, certainly reasonable enough.

Also my brother who shared a bathroom with me yelled when once I left some panties stained red on the rim of the sink. "Never, ever, do that again," he said between clenched teeth. "I cannot live here if you do that," he said. He was serious. I could tell. I was ashamed. After that I was careful. I locked the bathroom doors. I threw underwear into a paper bag at the bottom of my closet rather than risk leaving any signs that might confront him with my biology.

He would wash the doorknob on the inside of the bathroom before he would use it. Perhaps I had touched it. He washed the surface of the sink and the toilet with a detergent that he kept in his closet.

Then when he would pass me in the narrow hall between his room and our mother's he would press his body against the wallpaper as flat as possible. He would not touch my hand or sit next to me on a sofa. I worried that I smelled badly. I worried that I must be oozing or reeking. I would stay on the other side of the room from him because if I did not he left the room. He would no longer speak to me if it wasn't absolutely necessary.

Once we are in the elevator together. I have come into the lobby of our C-D section and see him waiting for the elevator. The door opens. We both enter. As usual he keeps his eyes averted and his head down. "Why won't you look at me?" I ask. The elevator man whose name is Kevin and has big ears on an impish frame says to my brother, "Look at your sister, she's getting to be a fine girl." My brother glares. "You don't understand anything," he says. I don't.

My brother had learned the laws of purity. Every culture has a sense of the pure and the impure. Every culture makes certain foods, certain places, certain things taboo, off-limits, impure. Here we have the vainglorious heaven-defying attempt of the small but brain-humming human to seduce his gods, to protect against the random forces of flood and wind, of disease and war. It doesn't work of course but every culture marks something off as sacred, valued, precious, cows and scrolls, feathers and bones, and something other, opposite as impure, defiled, deadly, pigs and menstrual blood for example. Out of this impulse come all kinds of interesting art, patterning of spoons and coloring of vessels, wall hangings and madly grinning headdresses of bark, feathers, hides, furs, beads. Out of it too comes the Jewish laws of purity which made my brother lean away from me and made me feel unclean, as if my whole body were like the sanitary napkins that I so carefully wrapped and disposed of in secret. In our family my brother was the only one who understood these taboos as an expression of God's will. If only I had gone to a ritual bath and been blessed by prayer instead of feeling merely stained by my own messy biology.

One afternoon I was sitting in the chair by my mother's bed as I always did as soon as I returned home from school. My legs stuck out from under my blue jumper uniform, my dark heavy as yet unplucked eyebrows growing across the bridge of my oily nose, and my chin mottled with a cluster of small red bumps, my mind on Milton's *Paradise Lost,* my ear attuned to my mother as always. She sitting in bed, wearing her satin robe with the lace collar, with a half-done crossword puzzle, with a mystery story lying on the silk coverlet, with her pack of Camels on the night table, an ashtray on the bed, a lit cigarette between her fingers. It was not yet five o'clock. At five o'clock I would bring her a scotch and water. She was checking her watch. Not yet.

Then she told me that my brother's analyst had an explanation for my brother's extreme avoidance of me. She had been to see Dr. Bussel that day. Dr. Bussel thought the religious injunction against touching women was just a cover, a plausible excuse that provided an apparently rational or at least culturally normal (not on Park Avenue in the early fifties) way of controlling his fear of his own desire for me, his own response to my sexual existence as it rang bells waking his forbidden, frightening, risings of the sap, running of the hormones, pulsing of newly released testosterone. My brother's analyst told my mother that her son had built a high fence to protect himself against his most terrifying, not allowable, unforgivable urges toward, not away, but toward, his sister.

Was this true? Had he told his doctor something that led her to this conclusion? Was I complicit in his unclean thoughts? What to make of this? I had kissed a boy. I had gone to dances with boys. At parties I had pressed close to a boy's body while we danced cheek to cheek and felt his penis flutter and swell and I had made out on someone's couch when the lights were out, hands moving across breasts contained by corsets, a lot of moisture and lipstick running. But I still did not quite understand how it worked.

Now I became afraid of my brother. I pressed myself against a wall if I saw him coming. Now I closed my door if he was in the house. I left rooms that he walked in. Was his sexual interest in me an expression of love or was it something else like the dogs in the park in heat jumping each other in a frenzy of biology? Was he saying all those prayers so that he wouldn't attack me in my bed? I begged my mother for locks on my doors. She had the super come and put them in. Did he despise me because once a month I bled or because he yearned for me in a way I could hardly imagine? Could both be true at once?

My brother practiced the piano when he was at home. He was not so skinny anymore. He had grown round in the hips and his hands were plump. There was always a gray shadow over his upper lip. Once in a while he would come to the threshold of my room and tell me a joke. He would laugh at his punch line, a sweet, gurgling, laugh.

17

when fate comes knocking don't answer the
door   My mother took me to Billy Rose's Little Club for lunch one
Saturday. The room was decorated in red and white striped wallpaper. The
maitre d' welcomed my mother like an old friend. The tables were small and
lined up on either side of the wall. There was a black carpet and a bar with
crystal glasses and a shimmering of white lights that made the place look
something like a carnival, something like the inside of a jewel box. We had
salads my mother and I and as the coffee was served she called over the
tarot card dealer, the fortune-teller, the much rouged lady who was sitting
at the bar wearing a long gypsy dress and spangles across her chest. The
woman spread out her cards. My mother leans over to talk to her. "Should I
be faithful to my husband?" she asks. I hold my breath. "Should I leave
him?" she asks. The cards are shuffled, some birthdate and birth hour information exchanged. The cards are once more shuffled and once more
spread out on the tablecloth around the water glasses, around my half-eaten
roll. "Take action," says the tarot card dealer. I close my eyes. I feel a pressure on my chest. I remind myself I am too young to have a heart attack.
"Yes," I say. "Take action."

My mother's eyes grow watery. She puts on her dark glasses. "Maybe now," she says, "I'll leave him. Maybe now I'm finally ready." My mother orders a chocolate cream puff for dessert.

Every winter my grade at school held a class dance. This compensated those of us who were not invited to the society dances that the majority attended. This was a democratic event which was always held at the Plaza Hotel in the grand ballroom. We had a band, Lester Lanin would come in person. The palm trees were decorated with red and green balloons. The little tables had peppermint-striped candy canes at their center. Each of my classmates arrived with a date, perhaps a brother or a brother's friend or a cousin or a real date from one of the prep schools. We did not have our own music in the early fifties. We had "Tea for Two and Two for Tea," we had the conga line, the box-stepping slow foxtrot, and we had "The Last Time I Saw Paris," we had "You Say Tomato and I Say Tomato" and we had the lindy hop and the charleston which were not ours but were adopted as a way to fling the body about, a way to show off and let go and perhaps it was a way to announce to history that depression and world war aside the flapping would not ever stop.

Across the room I see a tall and handsome boy with soft black hair that hangs loosely down his neck. He has long arms that he flings about like a heron lifting his wings. I see his white face, strained, and his thin lips nervously moving across his teeth. I think of Albert Camus, of French intellectuals drinking absinthe, smoking Gaulois in dark cafés. When he sits down at a table across the dance floor I take off my corsage and walk over to him. Placing my flower in front of him I stare into his face. He cuts in on me in the next dance. So I rush out to greet my fate, not content to wait for it to claim me. We dance together wildly. Other couples get off the floor to watch us charleston. His legs move so fast you can hardly see them. He dances in rhythm but to his own rhythm at the same time. His dance becomes a lyric poem. Although I occasionally trip on my own feet I too have a kind of abandon. My old athletic conviction that my body can safely break the laws of gravity allows the music to well up inside of me as if I were an unruly wood nymph greeting the dawn, or maybe I was Zelda dancing with Scotty. Then the musicians take a break. Paul and I are given Lester Lanin beanie hats with the name Lester Lanin in script on the brim. I am out of breath. Paul says he needs a cigarette.

Leaving my date to wander around looking for me behind the palm fronds I go with this boy named Paul outside on the Plaza steps. The lights of the city glow hard white, the cabs pull up under the marquee and depart carrying women in furs and men in black tie, and there is a cold white glow over the steps. The doorman has gold buttons on his red uniform. Everything shines, every time we exhale a white cloud follows.

I am bare shouldered. Paul takes off his rented jacket and puts it over my shoulders. He speaks in whole paragraphs without pause, he quotes Shakespearean sonnets. He talks about Sartre and philosophy. His spindly arms gesture as the words tumble out in long and gracious sentences and he stares into my eyes as if he was begging for my attention. He needn't have begged. He talked about Byron who did just what he wanted with his days. He tells me that *Swan Lake* is the only ballet in the world that is worth dying to preserve. While we are talking he drinks straight scotch from a silver flask that he pulls out of his pocket. The ash of his cigarette glows from the end of a long black cigarette holder. My virginal skin has goosebumps and not just from the cold. My nipples stand erect.

Better and better: he turns out to be a poor boy living in a one-bedroom apartment in Brooklyn. His southern mother came from a pedigreed family that had fallen on bad times due to his river boat gambler grandfather. A traveling band had come to town and his mother had run away with the piano player. The young couple had settled in Brooklyn. Shortly after Paul's birth there had been a divorce and his grandmother had arrived to rescue her daughter and grandson. There was no going home and so now the grandmother supports her daughter and grandson by working as a receptionist at a big law firm. The grandmother, the daughter, the grandson all share the bedroom and from the fire escape Paul can see Manhattan shimmering across the river. His story is so beautiful, makes me think of *Death of a Salesman* and *Streetcar Named Desire* that it brings tears to my eyes. I can see the frail southern belle, the pot-bellied piano player who lures her with tales of the big city and good fortune that await her there, the devoted grandmother who mounts the high stairs to the elevated train every day and returns exhausted, carrying bags of groceries in the evening. I can see the piano player in the two-bit dive where he now works three nights a week ducking his bald head down while the customers go right on talking and the glasses clatter behind the bar. I am where Paul wants to go and he has come from where I want to have come from. There is a link between us. We are both in motion.

Paul has won a scholarship to one of New York's private boys' schools. His schoolmates are the sons of bankers and lawyers and real estate lords. They have summer houses in Oyster Bay or the Hamptons. Paul has just returned from a weekend in someone's mansion on Lily Pond Lane. He had played billiards and fallen down drunk in the dining room of the Maidstone Club. "I am destined," he whispers into my ear, "to marry a rich woman." I am offended. I believe in true love and I believe in Paul Robeson but I want to be sophisticated, worldly, appreciative of such open evil, such obvious corruption.

If the music had swelled behind us on the Plaza steps it would have been familiar music, new orchestration but the same old melody. As it happened I miss the connections.

How different he is from my father I think.

He tells me that he had been drunk during the SAT test and had not completed it, staggering out of the test room to fall asleep on the subway back to Brooklyn and so was going into the army instead of on to college. I gasp. Fate stands over him with her little scissors ready to snip the line of his life. I can almost the smell the rising smoke above the battlefields in Korea. He is the only boy I know who is going off to basic training. That too blesses him with the glow of large consequential matters. He has long elegant fingers and as he kisses me that December night on the steps of the Plaza I taste scotch and smell the strong odor of nicotine that has stained his teeth. I see a weariness in his red-rimmed eyes, as if he had already died but like a zombie was not allowed to sleep. I am now a heroine in a Hemingway novel. I am trembling, not from cold, not just from cold. My soul has been hit by a tidal wave stirring up things from the bottom, wrecking and smashing as it goes.

Standing there on the steps of the Plaza, I watch as a horse and carriage pull up to the entrance. The driver wears a high black hat. The passengers in fur carrying Christmas packages alight, the doorman puts up his red-gloved hand to hold the mistletoed reins, and the horse, old, frayed, bow-legged, lifts his tail high and drops large smoking turds on the street.

We go out on several dates. I discover that he sometimes goes into a closet and takes a wooden hanger and waves it up and down and back and forth in order to calm himself. I cherish him. I know his heart is ill. I believe that I could, if given a chance, shield his fragile spirit from the winds that blow by. He reads me poems he has written. One of his poems begins, "April is the cruellest month, breeding/lilacs out of the dead land, mixing/ memory and desire . . ." This is the most amazing poem. I am awed. But then he doesn't call me again. What have I done wrong?

He left for the army and I forgot him or almost forgot him or should have forgotten him.

off with their heads, said the red queen

My father with Roy Cohn's help had found a job as an assistant DA for the Southern District of New York. The family business was taken care of by other lawyers but his retainer remained the same. Through Roy Cohn my father became part of a circle that included Judge Irving Saypol and short, thick-chested, polished like an apple happy-faced Judge Irving Kaufman who was trying the Rosenberg case. Judge Kaufman and his family lived at 1185 Park Avenue. The FBI assigned bodyguards for the two younger Kaufman boys. Every morning when I would come downstairs I would see the FBI guys waiting for the school bus with the boys. When I came home in the afternoon the boys were often out in the middle of Park Avenue in the grassy area over the railroad tracks playing some kind of ball game with their young bodyguards. On the warm days the jackets would be off and the muscled arms would lift up and down and the calls of the game would float toward me and I would stare for a longer time than was decent at the guns the men wore strapped to their waists stuffed into their holsters.

In other parts of the city people were ready to weep for the Rosenbergs. In Union Square speeches were made. Could they be sentenced to death? Would a Jewish judge do it to his own? How could he not? My father says they deserve a slow death. He calls me a commie dupe. The cruelty of the execution lights small fires in my brain. In the wake of the trial there would be another son without a father as if there weren't enough already.

Everything human will perish in a nuclear war, everyone over the age of two had the facts. "If the bomb gets us it's because of the Rosenbergs," my father says. Judge Saypol croons the word *America* into my ear when he comes to dinner. "Loyalty, loyalty," he bangs his fist on the table, toppling the drink in front of him. Nevertheless I sign a petition that was offered me by a man at the bus stop with a thin black beard and a feverish look in his eyes. The petition calls for mercy for Julius and Ethel. The young Kaufman boys continue to play ball with the FBI guys all through the spring.

The judge was a short man with fine dark blue suits. He was so clean and well shaved, his striped tie so fine, his dark chauffeur-driven car reflected the morning sun as if Walden Pond had been transmitted to Park Avenue. I thought of the Rosenbergs waiting to die and thought of the blood flowing through their arteries and the flatness of the prison light that cut out all the shadows, and the loneliness of their last nights and the fear they must have felt for their children and the sadness of the thing weighed in my mind along with the pleasures of life that belonged to me, most in the anticipation of adventure, buying Bermuda shorts to pack for college in the fall, whispering with a friend about what another had done behind the curtains with a certain person she had met at a party.

That Ethel Rosenberg was counting the last full moons her eyes would see made me feel unsafe, like a fish in a drying pond. That everything lay ahead of me prompted me frequently to dance naked in front of the long mirror on my closet door. My father said that Roy Cohn would be president of the United States in another ten years and would finish off the last of the commie bastards. My father was hoping his service in the DA's office would lead to a judgeship. Now he went to Tammany meetings and introduced himself as Roy Cohn's close friend and relative. One was as true as the other.

There were flowers growing in the center of Park Avenue and the heavy brass mailbox on the building wall with its ornate, golden vines and clusters of metal grapes stood as always, securely anchored to its place, more bank vault than wishing well. It kept its mailbox watch night and day. The valley of death stretched along the avenue, a grayness, a shiver, a cold reality emanating from prison slid along on its snake belly down the public street.

Shortly after my graduation from high school, white dress and white shoes, the Rosenbergs were in fact executed. All that day and night policemen stood outside our building, protecting the Kaufman family. My father said good riddance and my brother said he didn't care one way or the other and my Aunt Libby said that she was going to a party at the Harmonie Club that night but I did not feel safer in my bed and kept checking the sky for unusual flashes of light, mushroom clouds, radiation glowing.

i feint toward a jewish path—my brother continues down his All that spring I spend hours in the Metropolitan Museum of Art. I am not looking at the paintings which are fine enough but not what I am seeking. I had decided that if I were an Israeli soldier on leave I might come to New York and go to the museum and walking the halls and feeling lonely I might be happy to meet an American girl. It occurred to me that such a soldier, a veteran of '48, a fighter pilot perhaps, might ask me to be his wife and take me to Israel with him and I would grow tomatoes in the desert and drive a tractor. I already know how to steer a speedboat. I walk the halls of the museum and sit on the benches in all the galleries but I never meet an Israeli soldier. In fact no one talks to me.

No use scolding me now for the peculiar form of passivity this prefeminist vigil exposes. I was forming an escape rope out of whatever remnants of material I had. If another train was coming down the tracks it was still too far away for me to hear its whistle and even if I lay down and put my ear to the ground I would have heard nothing more than the sound of my own breathing.

My brother, with the help of his analyst, has convinced my mother to allow him to go for the summer to Camp Ramaz where he can continue his Hebrew studies and have kosher food. At this camp they observed the fast day of Tisha B'av, which falls during the summer. It marks with the collective singing of Lamentations, the destruction of the second temple, and the beginning of the exile of the people from their domain. At Camp Ramaz they said the long blessings before and after meals. They sang the *Hatikvah,* the Israeli national song, and they did not have a horse show or baked ham for dinner.

While I do not remember my brother sending me a postcard from camp and I do not remember any comments about the experience he may have made I do know that it is unlikely he joined the boys playing baseball, unlikely that he went on hikes in the woods. More likely that he stayed in his cabin or joined in groups studying the Talmud under the trees. He came back as pale as ever. His eyes blazed at me as if the history of our people were somehow my fault.

18

escape: a beginning effort   I had lived my whole life on Park Avenue and still I felt rootless as a dead dandelion, white puffs drifting with the changing directions of the wind.

I sat at the end of my mother's bed, ashes fell on her bed jacket, ashes overflowed the Spode ashtray and floated toward the rose-colored carpet. I watched her, a plump little sparrow, with dozens of tiny bones all probably broken, now unable to fly, held in permanent captivity. If I leave her what will she do? She is thinking about investing in the theater. She loves the theater. She could become a producer. She'll start by being an angel. She says her analyst is encouraging, not directly of course, but she can tell he approves. So do I. Can she find happiness on Broadway? Why not, I think. I hope.

The fall of 1953 I went to Smith College in Northampton and the first week there the president of the college railed against the anticommunist alumnae group led by William Buckley's sisters that was urging him to fire three professors whose guilt (Communist party affiliation or sympathy) had not been proven. We sat in the chapel, a host of young women in plaid Bermuda shorts with cardigan sweaters and gold pins, some belonging to boys' fraternities miles away. The president slammed the Bible shut and the sound of the heavy book under pressure of an angry arm reverberated through the carefully proportioned, polished and painted, simple but awesome chapel in which the entire student body had gathered. Then there was a movement to fire the president himself for slamming the Bible.

I read Aldous Huxley and wanted to try peyote. I went to the infirmary to see if the college could obtain some for our educational use. They turned me down.

Saturday nights girls would sit in the lounge of their dormitories and boys would come through picking out the girl they would ask for a date, curfew at ten. From this experience I know what the puppy in the pet store window must feel like. Everywhere in the living rooms of the dorms you could hear the nervous giggle and see the ingratiating smile, followed by the "I don't care if you pick me look." It was a strange mating rite more frightening I suspect than being carried off by one's hair into the cave of a club-wielding humanoid. The humanoids at least most likely did not slug down shots of bourbon in their beer when they got you where they wanted you. Mostly I remember the smell of beer, the sense of shame that hung over us all weekend and didn't begin to dissipate until the following Wednesday.

In the lecture halls girls were knitting argyle socks for their fiancés and after every few professorial sentences a sharp rolling metallic sound would rise, a dropped needle sliding down the incline. It was on those needles that girls of the fifties rushed to impale their futures.

For reasons hard to understand I did not feel liberated by my escape from my parents' dinner table. Instead I found myself spending long hours in a coffee shop at the edge of campus eating jelly doughnuts by the dozens. By mid-October I could hardly fit into my clothes. I had bangs that I let grow down over my eyes so that I had to push them up in order to see. I rode my bike with one hand on the handle and the other ready to push aside my curtain of protective hair so I might avoid oncoming objects. I had a gold circle pin like everybody else. But I didn't feel like everybody else. What I didn't know was that nobody else felt like everybody else either.

Someone in our dorm is stealing things. It isn't me. But the housemother thinks it is me. She tells me that kleptomania is an illness. I know that. She asks for a confession and offers psychological help. I laugh. Everyone thinks it's me. I am still talking about the Rosenbergs. I play field hockey. I am on the water ballet team, but I have no school spirit. Instead I have a dark desire to go to Paris and drink absinthe. I'm not afraid of going blind. I don't blame them for thinking I'm the thief. But I'm not. Then they do a room check and in the room of a quiet unassuming girl who has a boyfriend at Dartmouth and straight blonde hair and a sweet smile they find the missing pearls, the cash, the leather gloves, the stockings. The housemother apologizes to me. In the middle of the night I take all the silverware from the dining room and hide it in the reading room under the cushions of an unused couch. No one dares ask me if I am the culprit. Eventually the housemaid finds the silverware. But I am avenged.

A boy from Dartmouth takes me out. His father is the editor of a newspaper down south. He is strange and sad and he writes poems and he's on the swim team. He says that when he is in the water his mind is empty and free and that he wants to spend the rest of his life underwater like a fish. When he was at prep school he tried to hold his breath underwater long enough to drown but each time he would bob back up to the surface. It's harder to die than you would think he tells me. He sends me long letters and encloses his poems. I don't always understand them. Sometimes I can't make out his handwriting. But we are attached. This is comforting.

Then he calls me from the hospital. Voices have told him to harm himself. Voices are telling him to go home and take a gun to his father's office. He speaks in great loops of words that flow from his mouth into my ear and I am afraid of him. I am afraid for him. Then he doesn't call me anymore. What happened to him?

I transfer to Sarah Lawrence.

My father said he didn't trust me and asked for my key to our house in Rye. What didn't he trust me to do? Be a good girl. What was a good girl? This was up in the air as far as I was concerned. But I did know that a girl could die from an illegal abortion. Pregnancy without marriage was a disgrace that knew no bounds. I would sooner have immersed myself in gasoline and lit a match than expose myself to such a potential disgrace.

Every encounter with the opposite sex held the threat of annihilation, no matter how pleasing it was. Sarah Lawrence had a curfew after which the gates were locked and you couldn't gain entrance to the dormitories. But my first night on the Sarah Lawrence campus my mother called. She was calling from a cocktail party. I could hear the sound of laughter and ice in glasses and the whirr of movement at the far end of the mouthpiece. "My God," she said, "I've just met Dr. Rose Franzblau." (She was an advice columnist in the *New York Post*.) My mother said, "Dr. Franzblau told me that there are no virgins at Sarah Lawrence."

In 1954 she was wrong. I knew that for a fact.

My mother believed with other mothers that my worth on the marriage market was contingent on my virginity. She explained this to me over and over again. But Dr. Rose Franzblau was aloft on the wings of change. Virgins were soon to become an endangered group whose numbers were diminishing by the hour.

I was happy at Sarah Lawrence where no one was chasing communists around the campus paths and free thought was admired. I wore a black leotard and heavy brown sandals. I now had a uniform of my own although I thought I was a nonconformist, a dedicated member of the opposition. To what? To the boys who were going to wear gray flannel suits, to the rows of identical houses that were beginning to ravish our countryside, to the status quo, to the identityless America that Gertrude Stein and her brother Leo had fled years before. I believed in Albert Camus and the existential choice. I believed in Jean-Paul Sartre. I may not have been entirely clear as to what they were saying, but the negative, the anti–status quo theme I got. I wanted to die rather than live an ordinary life. I thought I had found the land of the free.

Escape, while the true subject of every memoir including this one, is almost never through the obvious portal.

my brother and i go to europe but not together   My brother went on a summer trip with a Jewish group to Europe. They traveled to Rome and Paris and Poland finally to Israel, newly minted kibbutz-blazing Israel. In Paris they stayed in the Jewish quarter. They passed through the Louvre on the run and they had all their meals in a kosher café behind some still-destroyed synagogue. In Rome they visited the Jewish cemeteries and the Judaica shops inside the old ghetto walls. In Poland they went to Auschwitz. My brother's Europe was the place of exile, of galut, of expulsion and exclusion.

My (after my junior year in college) Europe reeked of Latin and Christ, it spoke of eons of artists, of Gothic and Romanesque, of Renaissance and Enlightenment, of Voltaire and Garibaldi. My Europe was the glory and the gory of mankind fresh out of the caves yet reaching for the stars. My Europe was made up of Thomas Mann and André Gide, it was haunted by Baudelaire and Rimbaud. I met a man who had translated into French Rilke's letters. I had drinks with a young boy who had met Auden while traveling in Spain. I went to the Uffizi and stared at the many madonnas, the crucifixes, the piétas, the saints punctured by arrows and bleeding from foreheads and palms. I saw the flesh-toned colors, the perspectives, the shadows of Giotto, the bulging muscles of Michelangelo and I saw the ceiling where the hand of God reached out to Adam. I was impressed by the Gothic arches, by the vaults and the naves and the hushed footsteps and the huge brilliant stained glass.

Nevertheless it seemed peculiar to me that such a ridiculous idea, a resurrection, a virgin birth, a God that sacrificed his half-human son, that this should be the inspiration for so much decoration, so much heaving of stone and chiseling of bas-reliefs.

The lushness, the weight of time, the sense of power that gushed from even the smallest crevice of the least imposing of apses altered my eyes, made me weary and sad. All this brushwork, all this gold engraving, all those curling snakes covering silver boxes holding the dried bones of a saint's pinkie, what was it really? Not more, I thought, than the trail of history, covering up its cruel tracks with the collusion of the local artists who needed to eat after all. I knew what had happened to the Jews of Europe. I did not let my guard down. Here I was at the center of civilization and everywhere I heard the rattling of the cattle cars on their tracks and the sound of black boots pounding shnell-shnell on the stairs. My trip to Europe was not as different from my brother's as I thought.

Except that I met a boy named Larry in a café who said he was a writer, so far unpublished. He had spent the winter on a Fulbright to Finland. He had a strong face with the beginnings of a beard rough around his high cheekbones. He had sad blue eyes and carried a tattered, stained copy of Hemingway's *For Whom the Bell Tolls* in his back pocket. He wore a blue and white shirt like a French sailor. He took me to his small attic hotel room on the Left Bank. Out the window I could see a tangle of pipes and smokestacks, the slanting corners of buildings, the geranium plant of a neighbor. Down in the courtyard a woman was screaming at a child, a man was singing out to housewives to come and sharpen their scissors.

I lay there on the coverlet eager and afraid. I must have been more afraid than eager because as hard as he tried, as strong as he was, he could not enter my body. I had gone into a spasm and shut the entryway. I hadn't meant to. I thought perhaps I was malformed. I thought perhaps I had no entryway. We rushed downstairs to a taxi. He was pale as a ghost, worried that he had hurt me in some way. We went to the emergency entrance of the American Hospital and waited for a gynecologist. I was examined. The gynecologist explained it to me with great patience and very slowly as if I must be somewhat retarded. I was normal, perfectly normal, just needed to relax, to open myself up, to allow this to happen. I also received birth control information. It was the latter that probably made it possible for me to become a woman of experience.

Larry and I traveled together to Spain. He carried his typewriter with him and cradled it like an infant on the train. As the train stopped at stations along the way I would run out and buy us sandwich *jambons* from the stands on the platforms. There was smoke in the air and dust on the train windows. There was romance in my heart, but perhaps not the romance of man and woman, just the overexpectations of anyone entering a new country. It was hot in August. In my silk Bergdorf Goodman slip, the pink one my mother had given me as a goodbye present, I stood on the balcony of our cheap hotel in Barcelona, with whores coming and going from the neighboring rooms as he read me his stories. They were stale as old bread, flat as matzos. This was too bad. I was prepared to love him forever. I had my plane ticket home.

I showed his picture to my college friends but I never wrote him although I had promised and I had truly meant it when I said it.

I loved Europe and I hated Europe. Something opposed to Europe had already been imprinted in my blood. It was the white steeple of the New England church standing like a sentry on the village green. It was the spare lines of the Congregationalists, the Methodists, the Lutherans who put a single candle in the church window in December. It was the white clapboard, the black doors, the clean cold air of New England whose God was not friendly, intimate but whose presence perhaps in judgment, perhaps in warning hovered over the rising hills, the dark mountains with their small towns nestled by the winding rivers, the mills with their broken windows and rusted pipes, the inns with wood burning in the fireplaces.

My all-girls' school (As I walk through the Valley of the Shadow of Death—Oh to be in England now that Spring has come, in this green and lovely land) made me into a pretender, a borrower of other people's memories. But my brother as he boarded the bus for Camp Ramaz, as he traveled around Europe, eating only in kosher restaurants, what was he but an imposter too, pushing his way in where he had not been expected to a world from which his ancestors had fled.

in which my key to the house in rye is returned

My father had still not received his judgeship. He was now back in practice as the lawyer for the family business. He had a few other clients who were mostly supplied by Roy Cohn. These consisted primarily of very nasty divorce cases. I wrote a letter to Roy Cohn and told him I thought his behavior on the McCarthy committee was vile and that he was the antidemocratic force I most feared. I mailed my letter to him in Washington. A few weeks later my father received a call from Roy telling him that he had received my letter and promising that my father would have no further crumbs from his table if I ever wrote to him again. My father called me. "How dare you. How dare you." He screamed into the phone. I did not dare again. When I signed a petition passed around the campus I wrote my name as illegibly as I could.

One sun-drenched Indian summer day I decide with a few of my friends from college to picnic at our house in Rye. We make peanut butter and jelly sandwiches and packed a thermos of iced tea. We have chocolate cookies in a tin from someone's aunt. I hope my father will be at the house but if he is not I plan to simply spread our lunch on the lawn and wade in the pools of saltwater that appear at high tide. I have a Chevy convertible with a top that once down is reluctant to go up. We arrive at the driveway of the house just before noon and see two cars. One was my father's—the other car? We walk to the door. I call out, "Daddy are you there?" Silence. Perhaps he is out front by the water. We walk around the house. No sign of him. I try the door. It's open. I walk in followed by my friends. "Here is our dining room," I say, "and here is the living room." On the electric green and white swirling patterns that cover the couch my father's tennis racquet lies abandoned, outside its press, all akimbo. "Daddy," I call again, and again there is no answer.

I go up the stairs my friends all following me. "Here," I said is my room still decorated with white polka dots and a sweetheart rose-patterned wallpaper. There is my own dressing table with its white tulle skirt and a mirrored top with little flowers etched around the edges. "Here is my brother's room," I say and open the door. "Great view," admires one of my friends, (why did he get the room with the better view? He never looked out.), and then I open the door to my parents' bedroom. I open it wide, I step inside, so do my friends right behind me, and there in the bed I see first a man's legs naked and writhing, then a woman's arms and her silky black hair on the pillow. Then I see them turn toward the intruders, my father's face on one of the naked bodies and Elisabeth's surprised face on the other. My friends are frozen and seem unable to move as I push them out the door. Gently I close the door behind us. We run and jump down the stairs. No one knows what to say.

We take our sandwiches to an amusement park a mile or so down the road. We sit underneath the turning Ferris wheel and nobody says anything. "So that's why," I say, "he wanted my key to the house."

And I must have been right because a few days later my key arrived in the college mail in a white envelope, no comment added. I never told my mother. What after all was the point? I never used the key. The blue waters of the sound had been polluted anyway by the sewage from the industrial town of Port Chester a few miles away. The small islands of rust-colored rocks that rose each low tide and sank little by little as the hours passed would do so without my watching them.

Now in my bag I carried a diaphragm, daring, rebellious, ready for love, action, life. I looked in the cafés on Macdougal Street at the soulful eyes of young men writing deep thoughts in notebooks. If I had been able to carry a tune I would have been a singer of Negro spirituals. If I had been a pianist like my brother I would have played the coolest jazz in the hottest spots.

The doors to America were open for me. My brother was left behind still believing that God cared whether he kept the Sabbath, whether he sepa-

rated meat from dairy. He kept his shoulders hunched now in a sort of per-
petual student's crouch. If you looked at him you saw rows of black hats,
black-coated young men rocking back and forth on the wooden benches of
ill-lit, paint-chipping, tiny windows covered with brown wrapping paper,
houses of study in towns with unpronounceable foreign names now emptied of Jews with cemeteries vandalized and left to the random growth of
weed and briar. He avoided sunlight, valued mind over body, lived to study
not the other way round. The only modern thing about him was his analyst
and I suppose his record player. Although I thought I might I never told him
where I had caught my father or with whom. We were never in a room just
the two of us, together.

19

over the top, into the deep end, whoops a
daisy, the piper is paid   Back at Sarah Lawrence Col-
lege in the fall of 1956, looking for adventure, I found my way to the West
End Bar on 115th Street in Manhattan where the poets and misfits of Columbia University were gathering at night to drink and fight and plan the
heist of literary America. Allen Ginsberg and Jack Kerouac had recently
huddled in the dark booths and written odd words on the men's room wall.
The smell of pastrami and sauerkraut rose from the glass cases at one end
of the horseshoe circle bar. There was spilled beer on the floor and the toilet in the ladies' room was stopped up. The high stools, the dim stark light,
the big-breasted girl in red bathing suit calendar tacked into the wall,
warned of bad neighborhoods, long whiskey nights and promised nothing
but the seamy side of America's tracks.

There sitting on a side of the bar, his black hair falling across his eyes,
waving those familiar long arms, near the silver kegs of draft beer was Paul.

"Ah," he says, "a maiden from my lost youth." "Listen," I say, "How could
you steal from 'The Wasteland' and tell me you wrote that poem? You're a
fraud, a con." He puts his large head down on the table. "You caught me," he

smiles. "I did," I say. "Buy me a drink," he says. "You're a rich girl." I buy him a drink and then another. Paul's eyes are already pink from whiskey. His legs can hardly support him, smoke swirls through his nostrils and out his mouth. He coughs constantly. Something tragic, something that speaks of genius and sorrow fills the air around him. His thin body carries with it the romance of the tubercular, of a Picasso blue period jagged mournful clown, and his face with its wide forehead, its slightly protruding chin reminds me of a Roman gladiator—ah, so beautiful.

I meet his friend Carl André, who takes a five dollar bill from his pocket and puts it in his mouth and chews awhile and then swallows. "There," he says. "I ate my last dollar." I buy Carl André a drink too. He has dropped out of some fancy prep school and come to New York to drift, to wallow, to sponge, to be. A tiny boy, his name is Peter Kleinschmidt, a published poet, a favorite of Lionel Trilling, tells me he has sexual secrets, terrible sexual secrets. He does not love women, he tells me, otherwise he might love me. There are others, a crowd at the bar. Every night, starting before the sun makes its final dive over the Hudson River they gather. They draw on napkins, like Ed Koren. They are assistant professors with great burdens, like paralyzed legs or Korean War traumas, or fathers who disinherited them. They are screamers and yellers and slip me plots for novels written on toilet paper. They all want to go to Paris where the lightness of air prevents madness, so they believe. They have bad memories from childhood. They tell stories that go on and on and soon no one is listening but me.

Paul has been to Paris, Sartre's Paris, Fitzgerald's Paris, Gertrude Stein's Paris. Spared the Korean battlefields he worked during the war at the *Stars and Stripes,* the army magazine. He now has a British accent, a real lord's accent. He had lost his mother who had died of a heart attack. He lives still with his grandmother in Brooklyn. She is still answering phones. He is studying philosophy, logical positivism. "The bomb will fall," he says. "The games of the mind are all that remain to us in the short time we have." I believe him. I feel a sharp pain in my side. His mother has died. He is alone. I am wanting, wanting, wanting something I can't find the words for. I drive him home to Brooklyn.

It is 3:30 in the morning. The dark water lies beneath us. I am the only car on the bridge. The moonlight shimmers in the water. There are great steel beams above me, crisscrossed at my side. We stop at the all-night

White Castle on one of those streets with warehouses looming behind and gas stations on every corner. I buy Paul two burgers and we talk of suicide. Noble, Paul thinks. Cowardly, I think. I am worried. Is he thinking about suicide? I buy him a double milkshake. He has deep shadows under his eyes. Later I drive myself back to the Sarah Lawrence campus in Bronxville. I am awake, alert, listening to every sound, roll of tire, call of bird, and as the dawn turns the sky the color of anemic gums I park my car and spring out ready for the day, overflowing with courage.

At the West End Bar evening after evening I find Paul at the bar, already running up a tab.

I am home on vacation between terms. My brother tells me a joke. Every night for thirty years a man goes out into his backyard and prays to God. "God," he says, "answer my question, just one question," he prays. At long last a voice comes from the heavens. "So ask your question, already." "God," says the man, "is that really you?" "Ask your question," booms the voice. The man says, "Why did you make women so curvaceous?" The answer came from the heavens, "So you would like them." "But God," said the man, "why did you make them smell so good?" "So you would like them," came the answer. "But God," said the man, "why did you make their skin so soft and their breasts so beautiful?" "So you would like them," came the answer. "But," said the man, "why did you make them so stupid?" "So they would like you," said God. My brother laughed his small smothered laugh, his pixie smile lighting up across his face, his shoulders raised up and down as he shrugged and shut the door.

I followed Paul from bar to bar, down to the White Horse Tavern in Greenwich Village, up again to someone's house in Morningside Heights. I followed my star. He was the exact opposite of the soft-in-the-center, well-protected boys I had always known. He had no business waiting for him. He was too fine for the ordinary professions of law or medicine. When you looked at him you knew that he intended to pay no mortgages, tuition, insurance, or taxes, plant rosebushes, drive a station wagon, watch football games. He liked fine things, like camel hair coats and fancy silk shirts but he considered them his due, as if he were a faded member of the British nobility whose country estate no longer produced revenue but still kept up the annual pheasant shoot.

My face was always turned to Paul's. He invoked the spirit of Wittgenstein, the words of Rimbaud, quoted André Gide's letters from Africa, spoke of ennui and the absurdity of political passions of any kind. Behind us the glow of the tested bombs on the Bikini atoll glowed or was that simply the lights behind the bar flickering to signal the 4:00 A.M. closing.

Once a gaggle of engineering students came into the West End Bar. I was wearing my black sweater with holes in it.

One of them talks to me. Paul comes over and blows smoke into his face. "What are you doing with that fag?" says the engineer, some fancy ruler sticking out of his book bag. Someone trips the engineer. Soon there is a fight and a swarm of bodies pretend to violence. At the end as the police pull up to the door, Paul comes out from the men's room where he had retreated and the engineers leave quickly. Paul says to me, "Philistines and bourgeois, the salt of the earth, we should treat them kindly."

Paul tolerated my company. Sometimes he found me interesting. He needed hour-long baths and at least one shot of whiskey before he could leave his apartment and head off to the subway for the night. It would be almost dawn when he would leave the bar, taking one last drink before the return trip to Brooklyn.

We are at the West End Bar. Paul is in an argument about the implications of the last three pages of Thomas Mann's *Buddenbrooks* in German. He is standing on the bar shouting out his opinion. I have already bought him two packs of cigarettes, two roast beef sandwiches from the grill. He is weaving. He falls. He stands up quickly but there is blood streaming down his face. I hold his hand. I pull him along till we reach the nearby hospital. The young intern asks me to wait outside while he puts stitches in Paul's scalp. When we return to the bar Peter Kleinschmidt reads aloud a poem he has written about a fallen God killed in the Trojan War and mourned by a nymph. I am that nymph. I know it.

We go to a party at a would-be filmmaker's apartment which he shares with four other students. We bring our own liquor. The poet anthologist Oscar Williams is in the bedroom where we throw our coats and he's handing out copies of his anthology to anyone who will take one. I take two. At the party Paul sees a girl with long straight yellow hair down to her waist. He moves through the crowd toward her. I pretend not to notice. I see him lean toward her, into her. I see that she is impressed. I see him put his arm around her shoulders. I feel a crack in my chest, a split in my head. I try to drink. I don't sip. I throw back my head and gulp. The liquor burns my throat. One scotch, two scotches, a third as I see Paul and the girl disappear into a bathroom together, and suddenly the room spins, my stomach floats up behind my eyes and all is bile and rue, and I fall on the floor.

I remember nothing: to black out is to die temporarily. I wake up in my car, where someone has carried me. It is morning and students are coming and going from class and the stores are open and the lights are changing from red to green and people are crossing the streets and the bank is open and the subway entrance is crowded as the people emerge like paramecia on the march. They are wearing clean clothes. I am sick still. I smell. Such is the condition of unrequited love. I never drink again. I go right on loving.

Peter is not at the West End Bar. He is always at the West End Bar. From the phone in the bar I call his apartment. He answers. His voice sounds thick, heavy, monotonous. "It's over," he says. "I cannot bear it any longer." "What?" I say. "Everything," he says. "You're a poet," I say. "No," he says. "I'm a failure." It's deep winter. We walk through the cold the few blocks to Peter's apartment. We ring the bell. He doesn't answer. We wake the superintendent. We open the door. There is a stale odor in the room as if the garbage had not been taken out for weeks. Peter is lying passed out, barely breathing on his bed and by his desk we see wisps of smoke still rising from his wastepaper basket. He has set fire to all his poems. There are none left, nothing but crumbling blackened bits and pieces. Peter is all right but his poems will never recover. Paul says, "I'd rather fall on my sword than accept failure."

Paul was like a black bird crossing my moon, a harbinger, a warning, as beautiful and compelling as the darkness itself. He said he would die before he was Keats's age if he had not accomplished work that equaled the master's. He said that the best kind of women for sex were whores and he said that he had known many in Paris. He said that if Ingrid Bergman were a woman then I was a member of a pygmy tribe grinding my food with a rock. He admired long leggedness, society girls with gold pins in their pale silky hair. But when he needed a ride back to Brooklyn as he always did and his hands were shaking and behind the dark glasses he was rarely without night or day his eyes were streaked with red and the excited wave of his hands slowed to the wilt of yesterday's flower stems, I was there at his elbow. Like moth to flame, as if destiny had called my name and was accepting no deferrals, evasions, or absenteeism, I rose to the occasion. I counted myself among the blessed.

The madness was more mine than his, the blame entirely mine. He never lied about who he was or what would become of me if I hitched my hopeful wagon to such a lurching star. I pursued, he tolerated. His poverty was a mantle he wore like a magician's cape. In his long-fingered hands it became operatic, a high note reminding the God in whom he doubted of all his stupidities.

He told me he had not won the Adenauer fellowship to Germany that he was counting on and in his grief he spoke of death and how welcome it would be. He spoke of his fear of being a failure for the rest of his life that this rejection surely confirmed. He disappeared on a bender that lasted four days for which he borrowed money from me which I raised by selling at a pawnshop on Eighth Avenue my mother's gold with lapis stone ring slipped from her jewelry box.

Paul told me he visited a whorehouse and spent my money there. It saved his sanity he said and I believed him and was relieved that madness had been driven away by something as small and unnecessary as my mother's gold ring. Then the following week we learn that he had in fact won the fellowship. His grief had only been practice, just in case he had not won.

So we both went to Europe. Sailing on a boat that took six days for the crossing I stared at the gray waves of the ocean not so much afraid as numb. My mother had wept when I left her at the dockside but as the boat pulled out and she got smaller and smaller I turned away as soon as I thought she couldn't see me. My mother thought that I was studying French at the Sorbonne. Instead I set up an apartment on Paris's boulevard Montparnasse with Paul. Such daring, such boldness, such an avant-garde statement that made in 1957.

In order to pay for the apartment and put up the security I had to borrow five hundred dollars from my cousin, my Aunt Sylvia's son Howard. He had his own apartment at 65th Street off Park Avenue. He was now an executive in his father's business that would be his soon enough. I implied, I suggested, I hinted that I needed the money for an abortion. The truth was even worse and more impossible to explain. He gave it to me but then no sooner had the boat sailed off than he told my mother who wrote anguished letters to an imaginary address all through the long summer.

I had thought that Howard who had a closet full of dresses which my mother knew because she had supplied his twice-weekly maid and who wore flamboyant flowered vests to the opera that scandalized my mother and her sister Libby and her brother Sy, would have kept my secret, since he had secrets of his own. He might have kept faith with me but he wanted his money back and my mother paid him in full which I would not have been able to do, not as promptly as I had promised.

In Paris Paul drank and wrote stories. I sat in parks and waited for him to return from his outings or to stop working. I was patient. By midsummer I knew I wanted to go to Munich with Paul. He wanted me to pay for myself. His fellowship would not be enough for two. I had to tell my mother what I was doing. She would not send my winter coat unless I agreed to get married. She would not send me money unless I was married. Paul thought it was a joke. I pretended to think it was a joke.

Why did Paul agree to marry me? Perhaps because I told him every day that he was a writer his generation would have to match. I married him because he was my Pegasus. On his back I would escape, arrive, begin. Love may be blind but I saw clearly enough. I just couldn't stop myself. Like a racing car driver I circled around the track faster and faster, steering but not steering, thinking but not thinking. It was that kind of love I had.

I married so that the artist male could absorb me, grant me by association a pass into the holy light of creation, cathedrals, and unstained national flags. I made of art too much. It became my golden calf. I was willing to sacrifice my not quite virgin self on its altar. That was my love for Paul or most of it. He is not like my father I said to myself. He has language, poetry.

I have a lame excuse. A female in 1957 had been quite conditioned to express her ambitions through a male. Girls who wanted to be doctors married one. Girls who wanted to be politicians married one. My excuse is that

I thought that art, art as I worshipped it, as it gave meaning to my life, was male not female and I would need a male if I were to get close to the sacred fire. The leaking hole in this excuse is that Amelia Earhart did not marry a Saint-Exupéry and wave him off from distant runways. Mme. Curie did not marry Louis Pasteur and cook him chicken soup. I drowned where others swam quite competently. I thought myself special. I was ordinary, dangerously ordinary.

When I married Paul and when I planned to have his child I was engaged in an act of theft. I wanted his talent for myself and falling in love this way provided cover for my larceny. Far from the victim I was the architect of my own erratic desires.

That summer I was twenty-one. My father flew to Paris for the wedding. My mother was too afraid of planes to join him. We had a wedding lunch at the restaurant Maxim's. The mayor of the little arrondissement in which we said our civic vows announced that he had never had a divorce in his arrondissement in all his many years as mayor. Immediately I felt guilty. I began to sweat, staining my dress with visible circles of distress. My brother who was traveling with yet another group on his way to Israel came to the wedding lunch with us. He wouldn't eat the food. His French was excellent or so it seemed to me. He had learned it in high school and hadn't yet had much practice but his good ear served him well. He was openly impatient with me if I mispronounced or misconjugated a verb or my noun endings didn't agree. He corrected me again and again. For the wedding he wore a blue jacket and his face was not quite cleanly shaven. His hips were heavy and he spoke English with a hint of a Yiddish accent, one that he affected, certainly not one that he had learned in our mutual home. My husband's British accent was also adopted.

I was embarrassed by my brother. Nevertheless I looked at him across the table over the glass of champagne and I felt grateful he had come, happy to see him, hopeful, perhaps he cared about me, perhaps we had a bond, unbreakable between us even though I felt the Jewish aura washing off him, wafting toward me, as if I had betrayed him, marrying as I was. I did not touch my brother. I did not kiss him on the cheek.

My new husband was not impressed by him.

Paul had written a story that summer that we lived on boulevard Montparnasse about a young man whose philosophy professor convinces him that the world is random, that only logic survives investigation, reason is the only protection man has against the chaos of time and space. The young student in the story loses his faith in a God who cares, loses belief in a preordained moral order, and reels around the campus in mourning for the former object of his prayer and his respect. This student in a Dostoyevskian fever of regret purchases a gun and rushing into the lecture room kills the professor. There is no moral order, there is no reason for him to hold back his hand as he takes revenge on the bearer of bad news, the philosophy professor with a distaste for the irrational.

The story itself was not quite right. It was ambitious but it failed. The reader could too easily see the heavy-handed large-vocabularied author pulling at the strings. The emotion of the story rang false. Does anyone kill because they lose their faith? Don't we struggle on with the same moral restrictions whether we consider ourselves God's chosen or believe that we are ignored by an expanding or contracting universe? The sentences in the story were eloquent perhaps brilliant. The narrative however was stilted. I believed that time would bring Paul the perfect story, an expectation as sensible as expecting the Holy Grail to show up at the bottom of your cereal box.

After the celebratory lunch my father gave us some money to go away for a few days. My new spouse took the money and went on a week-long drunk. He visited the bare-light-bulb hotels with urine-smelling hallways where the prostitutes of Montmartre led their patrons. He slid off bar stools at the Hotel Ritz, and drank from a bottle lying on the cobblestone walk at the side of the Seine watching the *bâteaux mouches* with their tiny lights floating by. The darkness of the thing that haunted him was far more real than I had believed and the biochemistry of his soul more irregular than I had understood. Something nasty had its hands around his throat and would not let go simply because a girl was in love with his way with words and fancied herself a muse with a willingly-paid-for high-cost biographical footnote in literary history. The hole of his illness was far grittier, worm filled, than I had known.

I sit in the café down the street reading Henry Miller's *Tropic of Capricorn,* wondering why I find it mildly boring and waiting patiently for his return.

johnny becomes gene and reverse-converts in a manner of speaking   In the fall I went on to Munich and my brother went to college. He stayed in New York to continue seeing his analyst. He went to Columbia and moved out of the house into the dorms. My mother sent me a long letter saying that she was going to leave her husband, my father, at last. But then she didn't do it. She sent another letter. "What better, after all," could she hope for at her age? But she has become a theater angel. She is investing in Broadway plays. It is exciting. She has new friends who want her to produce a play, to be the producer. Her analyst thinks that she is at last growing up. So she writes me. My father she tells me wants to be paid back for the wedding luncheon at Maxim's. He won't buy me any pots or pans or furniture on my return. Do I care? I do not.

In Munich, now twenty-one years old and a married woman, I sit at the window of our apartment on Baraviaring where Hitler's masses had met and cheered. I do not think of my brother.

Nor did he think of me. But he did take the required core courses for freshmen. At Columbia University on upper Broadway he walked past the city-soot-stained bronze statue of Rodin's *Thinker* and up the long steps of Butler Library and into the carrels where the dust in the air rising and falling as books were moved from their shelves and replaced, dust that years before would have constricted his lungs, made him pull for breath, now bothered him hardly at all. What was in the books gave him the Enlightenment itself, reason and science, rational thought and the wealth of discovery. Darwin and Newton, Chaucer and Homer, man and his attempts to make peace with the threatening skies, Zeus and Voltaire, Thomas Jefferson, Herman Melville rushed into his mind and brought with them the doubts and the questions and the burning heat common to all those who feel betrayed by an earlier idol.

Since he never told me, since this is one of the many things he never told me, I can only guess how it happened. How Odysseus vanquishing the Cyclops, tied to the belly of a beast, escaping the darkness of the cave through the legs of the blinded giant, stirred in him a desire to join in the journey, a desire to ride through the peril-ridden Mediterranean Sea, to rescue Helen from Paris, to move at least for a temporary visit from Mt. Sinai to Mt. Olympus. Perhaps it came to him that Prometheus bound to the rock with the vicious raven forever eating his liver was an explanation of original sin not so unlike the expulsion from Eden. Perhaps as he and his classmates discussed Socrates and his cup of hemlock, civic order and the subversion of ideas, he saw that the Talmud was one of the human paths, not the only one, and with that admission the absolute power of the rabbis was undermined. If the Torah was one of the truths, one of the great books, not the only one, then the power of religion lost its exclusive hold on his spirit. If it was not absolutely God's word that you must not boil the kid in his mother's milk then the whole pack of cards wobbled and fell. If Thomas Mann was a great writer and if Pasteur was a savior because he found the TB bacillus in milk, then the world of the small synagogue, of the Sabbath service, of the tallis hanging from beneath the shirt, of the covered head and the reading of the same scrolls year after year, was just one human possibility, not the only possibility. How quickly it happened I do not know. How many term papers, how many more trips to the analyst before it happened I do not know. He had a new analyst now, a man. (My mother told me.)

Before the completion of his second year my brother grew cold to his former love and began to speak of superstition, of parochialism, and all this just before he fell into Proust the way an eager bride on her wedding night falls into the arms of her destined mate. He wrote paper after paper about Swann and the Baron de Charlus.

A century ago a million Englishmen had combed the rocks by the seashore to examine the exact forms of snails, butterflies, bugs, as voyages around the world brought back word of strange customs and other gods, some with many arms and elephant heads, others made of stone dragged to the edge of blue gold beaches. The word finally reached my brother, who once again would turn on the light switch on a Friday night.

Maybe his rebellion had simply, like a storm, exhausted itself, leaving a hole that was filled with his love of language. He now turned to French and Italian, German and Spanish. He abandoned the rigor of his religion that kept him focused on the heavens instead of the sorry state of his family dinner table. Perhaps having moved into the dorms at Columbia he no longer needed to find a home in God. Perhaps it was just time for him to give in and ride with his times, to return to his place in history.

Falling away from God so abruptly had to be like ripping a bandage, accompanied by pain. It must have seemed like a bitter divorce, a backward and forward, good days and bad days as he gave up placating this God who demanded constant praise in return for a dubious promise of mercy. As he gave up loving the God he had hoped would love him, and as he no longer believed in the sanctity of the words of the rabbi's, he must have been bereft. He must have turned away in a burst of anger, leaving behind a trail of bitterness to mark the path where his God hopes had been. Unlike the character in Paul's story he didn't shoot anyone.

"Arise, O God, judge the earth; For thou shalt have dominion over all the nations.—O Lord, Thou God who requitest evil, and bringest the wicked to judgment, shine forth." So the psalm says. But now my brother was no longer waiting for a sudden coming of the Messiah. I who did not believe, who came into my adulthood without the expectation of heavenly reward or earthly guidance, who scoffed and ignored, I was not as bereft of comfort from one year to the next as my brother must have been. And as much as he needed God, his loss of God must have ached him. Although he never told me so and perhaps I am only imagining a mourning following on this de-conversion, perhaps he shed his religion easily, like a snake leaving behind a no-longer-needed skin.

What he kept was his slight Yiddish intonation, his pale face, his almost hunch, his unathletic roundness, his jokes.

He tells me this one: A patient in a mental hospital had argued that he must be served only kosher food. He went on a hunger strike until he got his way. The director of the institution gave in, despite the extra expense. A few days later the director was strolling on the grounds when he comes upon the same patient sitting in a chair and eating a ham sandwich. "What are you doing?" yells the doctor. "I thought you were so religious we had to bring in special food for you and here you are with a ham sandwich." The patient answered, "Doctor, did you forget I'm meshuga?"

He still seemed uncomfortable, nervous even with his peers and his pale blue eyes flashed out from behind his thick glasses with a look at once bellicose and yearning, a boy about to yell at someone, a boy who needed a cup of cocoa and a gentle hand.

In the dorms he made a few new friends, some who liked his jokes. Some who admired his language skills. Some who played chess with him. He insisted on living in a single room. He got a letter from his analyst to secure his privacy. He was offended by the authorities at the college. They required that he, like all the other students, take a musicology course. He knew more about music than could ever be taught in a universal college requirement. He went to the dean to get himself excused. The dean refused and my brother railed and howled, wrote letters accusing the dean of stupidity and cupidity. My brother refused to go to the course. The stubborn dean refused to release him from the requirement. Years later he would talk about the arrogance of that dean and the stupid bureaucracy of the university and the babyish simplicity of the course. Years later it would rankle in his heart, this demeaning of his mind by petty tyrants insisting that he take that music course.

At college he changed his name from Johnny to Gene. He was out of the house. He became again as he was at birth: Eugene F. Roth, Jr. Johnny was the name of a boy child. Johnny was the name of his past. Johnny was rejected and Gene was what he was called. I tried to remember that whenever I saw him. I understood that it was important to him to be Gene and not Johnny. I trained myself to call him Gene but in my mind he became nameless, referred to when my thoughts slid his way as "my brother." This avoided for me an uncomfortable dislocation. My mother still called him Johnny. My father still called him Johnny, my uncle and aunt still called him Johnny. But I agreed with him. He wasn't a Johnny who calls to mind an all-American boy holding a baseball bat in hand, or a World War II hero as in "Johnny got a Zero." He wasn't a Johnny-come-lately or a boy who would fish in the river, his dog by his side. He wasn't a man who would play poker with his friends, who would sell you a car or join the Rotarians and dance with the homecoming queen.

He wasn't quite a Gene either or at least I never felt it, not deep in the bones where the name of a mother, father, sibling rests, barnacles covering it, gathering strange patinas of tide and wind, instantly evocative of nursery smell, setting off bells that call to sanctuary or warn of impending danger. Gene never exactly became for me his name, a name of a family member, evoking the dank of the cellar in which one rushes at the first report of tornadoes over the plains.

I did not see much of him through his college years. For me he was a Johnny-Gene person who had no particular interest in seeing me. As I must have reminded him of a childhood more woe than joy so too he reminded me of a place I wished I had not come from.

He did not go to fraternity parties. He had secret meetings with boys he would not name to my mother. He told me I would never be an educated person because I had no grasp of calculus or chemistry. Because my French was flimsy and I had a bad ear for languages. He did go to concerts with a friend or two. He did not ever go to the football stadium or the tennis courts. He looked down on the jocks and the would-be lawyers or bankers and all the fraternity boys. He despised stupidity. They were stupid. He dismissed most of his professors whose intelligence always seemed questionable, far less than his. He also made fun of their accents in French or Italian or German.

If anyone, student or professor, made a grammatical mistake in a foreign language he immediately corrected it, a look of scorn, a hum of contempt followed. It was as if he heard linguistic errors the way most of us hear the scraping of a fork on a plate or chalk on the blackboard or a violin in the hands of an amateur.

He had a permanent excuse from gym, doctor's letter: asthma. He may have abandoned religious orthodoxy but he was no Hellenist, at least not the body-is-important kind. He didn't shave properly. He shrugged his shoulders oddly.

He tells me another joke. Rothschild is traveling through Minsk and stops for breakfast in a small Jewish café. When he is finished the waiter brings him the bill. "Twenty rubles for two eggs!" shouts Rothschild. "That's impossible! Are eggs so rare in these parts?" "No" says the waiter. "But Rothschilds are."

20

my brother, the doctor   My elegant husband, my tall handsome husband, my artist, my writer, my passport to immortality, is drinking up all the money I make as a receptionist at a public relations firm. We sell the silverware my Aunt Libby had given us as a wedding present. The money finances a four-day binge. I wait for him by the window each night. Each night I fall asleep in a chair. By the fourth night I am certain that he lies dead, knifed by a man in a poker game, beaten to a pulp by a pimp whose woman he has refused to pay. I imagine that he has been run over by a truck, bus, train. Each of these possibilities appears in my mind complete with image, blood and crushed limbs. I go to his desk. I am careful not to let a tear fall on the typewritten pages. His brilliance is here at his desk, whatever roams the outside world is not his soul, but his shadow, or so I want to believe.

During the day at work I am exhausted. I force my hands to type, my voice to answer the phone. I call my mother. I want to tell her that Paul has disappeared. I don't tell her. What can she do to help me? He returns and I sleep. He returns and he sleeps but then for days on end he doesn't get out of bed. The shades are pulled down. He eats only what I bring him on a tray.

His skin is pale white. He shakes his hands in front of his face. He takes a wooden hanger and shakes it back and forth hour after hour. Finally he goes back to his desk.

We sell the silver chafing dish. We sell the antique lamp my mother's friend Helen gave us. "I have to go out," he says. "If I don't I'll go crazy. I have to get out to a bar." I am worried. I have bought an entire *Encyclopedia Britannica* from a door-to-door salesman. If I can't make the monthly down payment, the company has threatened to take it back. "I can't pay the light bill. I can't pay the cleaner for the clothes I need to wear to work," I try to explain. "There just isn't enough money. You can't go out." I say this calmly. I don't want to frighten him further. "Borrow it from your mother," he says. "Sell something else." I don't want to ask my mother for money again. She would give it to me. But she looks so sad, so anxious when she writes me a check. She doesn't say I told you so. But she is thinking that I too have betrayed her, ruined her life, ruined my life. I can't ask her again. Paul takes money from my purse.

"What do you do with the prostitutes?" I ask when he returns early one dawn. "I can't explain," he says. He puts his head in my lap. I hold him. The mind is a cesspool. I know that. Swann loved Odette the way I loved Paul. I know that too.

My mother plans on buying us an apartment at 1045 Park Avenue ten blocks away from 1185 Park. I don't want an apartment on Park Avenue. I can't pay the gas bill. Paul wants an apartment on Park Avenue. He goes with my mother and her decorator to pick out a cabinet and a sofa and they buy tables. "Paul has such European taste," says my mother admiringly. "He could be a decorator," says the decorator. I try to get a better job. I fail a typing test. I want to live in the woods with Paul. I want to live on the prairie. I want to live barefoot by the sea. My mother grows fonder and fonder of Paul as they spend the afternoons shopping together. My mother buys Paul an expensive oriental rug for his birthday.

We move into the apartment at 1045 Park. We are on the fifth floor. Paul has a new blue blazer my mother has bought him. He is elegant. He belongs on Park Avenue. I think it makes him happier living here. He is working better.

Paul says he cannot live without fame. He needs it the way more ordinary people need oxygen. Fame is shy and holds herself back. I borrow from my friends. Finally it happens. The lights are turned off and then the gas. We live on Park Avenue, but we live in the dark and eat peanut butter and jelly sandwiches.

Paul has written a play. I raise the money for an off-Broadway production by asking all of my mother's friends to contribute a little bit. My mother puts up a small part. We find a producer. We find a cast. We open the play in a little theater on the Lower East Side above the Lithuanian meeting hall. The actors are bad. The director is clumsy. The sets are dreadful. But the play, the words of the play are brilliant. It's not just his wife who thinks that. The early reviews rave. The later reviews rave. In the dawn after the opening we walk down the street with the swagger of the barbarians coming to conquer Rome. Nothing will stop us now. I am the wife. He is the toast of the town. In a few weeks his picture will be everywhere. We are invited to dinner with famous directors, with famous actors, Irene Selznick invites us to her country home. Lee Strassberg invites us to a party and we meet Vivien Leigh and Jason Robards and all the legends in the theater who want Paul to write parts for them. We are photographed at Sardi's. Paul gives interviews to *Vogue* and the *Daily News* comes to our home and photographs him standing on the oriental rug next to the sofa. He has a white flower in his lapel. "How come," says a reporter, "you have an English accent if you were born in Brooklyn?" Paul says, "I had a British father who lost his entire estate in a gambling debt and is now wrestling alligators for tourists in the Everglades." "Oh," says the reporter and writes down every word. He wins an award for the play. It's making money. Enough so that I pay off the entire amount I owe the *Encyclopedia Britannica*. I am twenty-four. My husband is twenty-five. Keats died at the same age.

My father takes Leonard and Kopatkin to see the play. They appreciate it or so they say. He is proud to be related to Paul. He invites him to the club for dinner and Paul gets drunk in the bar, but that's all right with my father. My mother is happy. Her eyes shine. She has invited Vladimir and Wanda Horowitz to see the play. She herself has invested in a Tennessee Williams play, in a William Inge play, just small amounts. She doesn't have the courage for more. She is still talking about producing a play of her own. Many hopeful playwrights and producers send her scripts. She reads them but she can't decide. I encourage her. She says, "Money is not to be thrown around."

I ask Paul for my reward. I want a child. I want a baby whom I will mother perfectly. This is a story that will after all end happily ever after. Paul does not want a child, what he wants is to put Chekhov to shame, to outdo George Bernard Shaw, to shrivel the memory of Oscar Wilde, to stride across the literary landscape a giant with big boots, but he sees the justice in my request.

In the midst of his triumph I become pregnant. I continue at my job, throwing up in the bathroom before work each morning from morning sickness. Will Paul stay with me? The baby will have his genes. The baby will be a writer too. My ambitions for my unborn child are not modest.

Even my brother was proud of his brother-in-law. We met him one night after the house was dark and we went to eat at a Jewish deli in the neighborhood. My brother told us that he had decided to go to medical school and become a doctor. Perhaps he wanted to be a healer like the analysts who had been the carpeting on the floor under his life for so many years. Or perhaps he wanted to be a doctor like the doctor who tended him when he had asthma, an authority, on the right side of the disease, not the patient but the powerful adversary of the illness. Perhaps his decision was influenced by the worshipful way my mother regarded the many doctors she consulted for one symptom or another, perhaps he decided to become a doctor because doctors were separated from their patients by pedestals and screens, by professional jargons and special powers to administer potions, to admit to hospitals, to declare and define, to make pronouncements over life and death.

My mother in this respect was not a typical Jewish mother.

She said to him, "You won't have any capital if you become a doctor. Doctors are always living on what they earn. Why won't you go into the shirt business? There's always a place for you there." My brother turned sullen. He shook his head. His left the room. He said to me, "Never. I'd rather die than work in the shirt business."

She said to him, "Go to business school. Then you can become an investment banker or an executive of another company. You can always play the piano," she called out to his retreating back. "You can go to concerts and you can read your Proust or whatever as much as you like, but you'll be safe, protected." "Safe from what?" my brother said in a voice that seemed to threaten and sneer at the same time. "Everything," said my mother. "I'm not going to pay for your medical school," said my mother.

In the end after a consultation with his analyst she agreed to pay. In the end she told me her analyst explained to her that her fears of bankruptcy were irrational, phobic, neurotic and that her son wouldn't lack for anything if he became a doctor.

my mother needs a doctor, not an analyst, the other kind   I have a baby. My mother buys nursery furniture for our apartment at 1045 Park Avenue. I quit my job. She will help us meet the bills till Paul's next play opens. The baby needs to be fed at all hours. I need sleep. I no longer go with Paul to parties or if I go I come home before midnight. I put the baby on a bed with the coats. I run in every few minutes to make sure the coats have not fallen over the child's face. I see Paul with an actress in the corner. I don't care. I am in a hurry to get home. I need to sleep.

As I walk along Park Avenue pushing my baby carriage my mother walks at my side. A friend of hers stops us. "What a fine—," My mother interrupts. "Don't say it," she begs. Then she adds, "The baby's funny looking don't you think, the eyes are too close together?" The friend looks puzzled as my mother urges me to move on. "Don't let anybody," she cautions me as we walk on, "say good things about the baby. Praise brings on the evil eye." My mother shudders. She is really afraid of the evil eye. I am not. "Does your analyst respect the evil eye?" I ask. My mother is ashamed and doesn't answer me. For all I know he does. For all the good he's done he might as well.

I am off floating in the milk and the touch of my naked body to the baby's skin, the baby's fingers curled around mine. I am drifting in powder and bubble, croon and weariness, although I know that I will have to reach dry land sometime.

And then early into my brother's first year at medical school my mother, after many-months-long delay in which she spent her usual hours in waiting rooms to obtain reassurance about her sometimes fast heartbeat, her possible blood sugar level, her possible intestinal infection, her chronic cough, had a mole removed from her leg. It was a small dark irregular mole on her inner calf. The mole seemed to be growing. Sometimes it oozed small dots of blood. The dermatologist did his work. He then went off on a three-week vacation. Although I don't know it I no longer have to wonder if she will kill herself.

When he returned he called her into his office. She was fifty years old. Her skin despite cream after cream was no longer fresh. She was trying to lose fifteen pounds and so she had been for the past thirty years. She had read every medical article printed in the *Reader's Digest* on every surgical triumph, the victory of the will-to-live types, the positive thinking gurus, the vegetarians with their prophesy of one hundred years of life. She knew better than all of it. She trusted only her own forebodings. They had been with her all her life.

She agreed to an operation that would spare her leg but leave it hollowed at the calf. The night before the operation we all had dinner at a Chinese restaurant. My mother's lip trembled. My father talked about a divorce case he was handling for Roy Cohn. This was a divorce in which the wife had hidden all her rubies and diamonds and stocks in a safe and then had the safe removed to a secret place. Roy Cohn was defending the man whose intended new wife (who until recently had been his masseuse) wanted the jewels. The case made the gossip columns in the *Daily News.* Over the moo shu pork and the sweet and sour shrimp my mother looked at me with a bitter smile. My brother was whispering in my ear the statistics of melanoma survival. They were not good. Paul was drinking one martini after another. Soon he was reciting from memory Plato's essay on shadows in a cave in a loud voice although no one was listening to him.

It was not my mother's pending operation that had driven him to drink. He then began to ask my father about the divorce case. Was the rich divorcée in need of company? What exactly did she look like and where did she live? The thirty-two-room mansion in Short Hills and the place in Mallorca interested him. My father was pretending he knew all about Plato and was already applying his philosophy in his Roy Cohn divorce case. My brain hardly worked. It would be all right, I said to myself. I couldn't imagine anything else. I wouldn't listen to my brother. He was sweating from the lights of the restaurant, from the weight of the food. My father ate only white rice.

Everything else smelled bad to him. "You'll get sick, you'll see," he kept saying to me as I ate with a certain greediness, appreciating the green color of the snap peas, the white creamy texture of the sauce over the fish, the dark brown sesame-soaked beef with delicious strips of orange rind circling the plate. I had learned to concentrate on my food.

She was in Beth Israel Hospital. In the lobby was a portrait of my grandfather, her father who had been one of the founders of the hospital back in the very earliest days. I waited on the hospital floor for my mother to be returned from surgery. A man was screaming at a nurse who was trying to get him to fill in a form stating his religion. The nurse kept explaining to the man that all they wanted to know was what kind of minister to call if he should need one. He kept wailing in an heavily accented half-Yiddish, half-English that this was a free country and he didn't have to tell anyone his religion if he didn't want to. "It's not a secret," the nurse said to him. "I won't put it," he was weeping. "Leave him alone," I said. "You have to leave this area," the nurse said to me. They told my mother they had gotten rid of all the cancer. "The odds," my mother said, "are not good." "I've never," she adds, "had any luck."

I rock the child as I wait at the window in the early hours of the morning for the sound of a taxi coming up Park Avenue. A single car makes a hushed sound along the empty lamplit street. I press my face to the window and stare downward. Is this Paul? Will he come soon? I listen for the sound of a car door opening. If I don't hear it I lean back in my chair and wait for the next rush of tire along the pavement. I watch the changing traffic lights. How many more switches from red to green and back again before he returns? More than 100, less than 25? All that can be made out of the word *sex* is the modifier *ex*. Will the next cab bring him or the one after that? Will he make it home before 4:30, before 5 o'clock? I am patient like a lizard waiting for a fly to come within striking distance of its tongue. Waiting is not difficult. I know how to be patient. While I am waiting I hum a tuneless tune to keep the child asleep, to soothe myself. I am still like a china cat on the mantlepiece, listening and listening for the sound of an approaching taxi in the street.

For a while my mother seemed fine. My brother entered his second year of medical school. Then in March about six months later my mother vacationing in Florida with Libby found a lump in her groin and the two sisters flew immediately back to New York. There was another major operation. Nodes were removed. Again there was a long wait in the corridors of Beth Israel Hospital. There was swelling of limbs. Without lymph nodes ankles become puffed, formerly shapely legs become like tree trunks. My mother wrapped her damaged limb in a rubber tube which when plugged into the wall inflated and squeezed the fluid in the leg somewhere else. My mother used the tube for several hours each morning and evening.

Everyone told my mother she was fine. The cancer had been all re-moved. My brother consulted with the doctors. He was a participant in medical conferences between internist and surgeon. My brother told me that the Talmud says that it is a great sin to tell a person they have a fatal ill-ness. I'm not so sure. I don't like lying to her. I lie. "Everything is fine," I say. She nods but I know she doesn't believe me.

I sit on the beach that summer at the end of Long Island with my child and watch the waves remove the wet sand from the shore and return it with the next surge of the sea. Paul is in L.A. exploring screenplay offers. He calls to tell me of a starlet who licked him on the ear at a party. He asks me to wire him more money. I cash in some company stock my mother had given me on the birth of the baby. I wait in line for a long time at the West-ern Union office in order to wire the money to the Beverly Hills hotel. I con-sider my marriage to Paul. It is not boring. I have a ticket to a lifetime front seat, no-net high wire act. Bourbon gave him the courage to walk the wire and bourbon made his head spin so he might fall.

Am I a mighty enough angel to spread my wings beneath him and carry him off to a mountaintop? Will he ever turn his attention back to me and this child he had never wanted and had, most reluctantly, against his own best interests, created? He sends me a postcard of Marilyn Monroe. On the back was written, "If she is a woman, what are you?" It was true I didn't hold a candle to Marilyn Monroe. I wasn't particularly offended. I look into the child's eyes. I listen to the child's words. I am wrapped in the child. No one had told me the excitement, the wonder of it.

I am ordinary and ordinary is a miracle. This I do understand. My mother says, "Why didn't you go to L.A. with Paul? What's going on?" "Nothing," I say. "He's working," I add. She doesn't believe me. She suggests I go see her analyst. She is willing to pay for it. I refuse although I want to accept. Could masochism be catching like TB I wonder? Could it be in the genes? How do you get it?

All through that summer despite the rubber tube that pumped around my mother's leg she played canasta almost every day. The cards flipped and turned, money was bet and won and lost. She played high-stakes backgammon on the patios of friends. She knew the odds of each throw. She was a gambler with a perfect eye for when the opponent would weaken and close. She doubled and redoubled as soon as she smelled an advantage. My mother played that summer as if the shuffle of the deck could delay death indefinitely.

The family next door had a son my age named Joe who from a childhood accident had a wide streak of white hair among his black ones. It startled the eye in such a young man. Joe Abraham was working in his father's investment firm and that summer every weekend he stayed with his parents and in the early morning sunlight did situps in the backyard. My mother found him sweet.

As an act of friendship, in hopes of pleasing her neighbors, or provoked perhaps by some evil impulse, my mother gave Joe Abraham the name and phone number of a girl named Sally who was the daughter of her stockbroker. Sally was a full-bodied, full-lipped young woman. The one time I met her she was wearing tight pedal pushers and a halter top and had stopped at my mother's cottage to convey an invitation to dinner from her parents. She was spending the summer at the beach tanning carefully, reading *Vogue*. She had long much-brushed forest brown hair which was pushed off her face with a black velvet band. She showed my mother her notebook of dream dresses she had designed herself. My mother knew and I knew that Sally had been to the movies several times with my brother. Would it have become serious? Did my brother have hopes of wooing her? Did he like her at all? My brother had never up to that time had a girlfriend that I knew about. But perhaps this was the moment when his long years of therapy would result in a happily ever after.

What exactly was in my mother's head? Why had she assumed that Sally would not be interested in her own son and might therefore like to meet the neighbor's son? Of course it is true that Joe Abraham was perhaps a better catch than my plump-faced, thick-glassed, hunched-over, uncomfortable in his spectacularly unmuscular, antisunlight, and unexercised body, already balding, shy, and somewhat pedantic unless telling a joke, brother. But even so—.

I and the child are at my mother's small seaside cottage. The day is damp and gray. The fog has come in from the sea and everything feels wet. My brother has come up to visit. My father does not like the seashore. He is staying in Rye. Over the tuna salad we have for lunch at a small table in the living room of the house my mother casually mentions to Gene-Johnny that she has introduced Sally to Joe Abraham and that the two of them seemed to be getting along well and are going out again that Saturday night. My brother stands still stiff as a corpse. He holds on to the arms of his chair so tightly that his hands begin to tremble. Drops of sweat come out on his high receding forehead. He lunges across the room and grabs my mother by the arm. "How dare you, how dare you." "You whore," he shouts at her. His eyes are wild. His glasses tilt to one side. Is this Hamlet? What is this? The child who has been climbing in and out of a chair cries and runs to my side. Gene-Johnny throws my mother against the wall. She screams and begins to sob. He pushes her again hard and then he punches her in the face. She falls into the corner of a high bureau and there is blood coming from her nose mingled with the running mascara and the lipstick that smeared. She is still attached to the machine which makes a constant huffing wind noise as it inflates and deflates. My brother is about to push her again with his entire weight when I pull at his arm and beg him to stop. The child is crying on and on, a sound between a wail and a whine. He stops. He stands in the middle of the room and from his throat comes such an animal roar that I cover my ears.

Later I say to my brother, "Why did you hit her?" "It was just a small push," he says. "It wasn't," I say. I ask my mother why she had introduced her son's date to another boy. She says, "I had my reasons but I can't explain them to you." A mystery. She goes to bed and stays there for several days. My brother goes back to the city that very afternoon. He doesn't like the beach in any weather. He tells me that I will get melanoma if I continue to go out into the sun. He tells me that it runs in families and I will surely die of it because I go to the beach and run into the waves whenever I have someone to watch the child who always wants to run after me.

An August night. The Milky Way hangs right over the roof of my mother's seaside cottage. I bring my child and sit on the edge of her bed. Over the ridge in the darkness lesser terns run back and forth in the froth of the surf and tiny iridescent sand bugs wander in the tide's wake. What mother takes a girlfriend away from her son? What son hits his mother? What did everyone's analyst think? How can a mother even a sick mother insult her son's manhood by offering an introduction to another male, I do not know. Was it a misunderstanding on my mother's part? Was it perhaps that she did not believe the girl could ever like my brother? Did she know something about my brother that I didn't? Was my brother's rage an old one, about something else? Who would hit a woman with a cancer in her leg that was creeping up her body? Why did he call her a whore?

That was the last summer of my mother's life. Some family stories are like this. The facts are remembered accurately enough but the meaning will never be discovered.

The sister believes she understands nothing and the conversations live on in her mind raw, undigested, also malignant.

At my child's second birthday in December my mother comes over with a cake. She is smoking her cigarette when just as my daughter blows out the three candles, one for good luck, I see that my mother's cigarette is burning right through her fingers and she has not stopped speaking. She hasn't felt the heat, the ash, the burn that raises a terrible red blister before I call out. A few hours later she has an epileptic seizure. There is vomit and head twitching and spasms in the face and after that an ambulance comes.

There is a brain tumor. My brother consulted with the doctors again. He had quarrels with them. He was angry that they had not removed her entire leg in the first operation. He sulked and insulted the doctors. He accused them of carelessness. He told me they were responsible if she died because total amputation might have saved her. He said that her doctors had failed her. That medicine was nothing more than pretense and comedy.

21

the evil eye   That was the winter Paul's play was opening on Broadway. A slightly over-the-hill musical comedy star was to play the major dramatic lead. The play was in rehearsal. It was Paul's chance at becoming a real big King of the Hill. He was afraid and stood hours by the windows behind the curtain, shaking his arm with his wire hanger in hand, trying to calm his anxious heart, already medicated, although it was barely noon, by a few drinks.

I went to a rehearsal with the child in my arms. I heard Paul's lyric words and saw the actors moving back and forth to their assigned spots on the Broadway stage with its red velvet curtain and its golden proscenium with cupids blowing trumpets at the corners and I counted myself fortunate to be so close to the flame of history. I didn't mind being singed. In the back of the theater the child slept on and I watched as Paul, blowing smoke into the spotlight's path, whispered into the ear of an understudy. He was all glamour and sparkle, all intellect and wit, all come-on and bravura, a fountain of Becket wisdom and sharp-edged judgment. The bitter grief of logical positivism made him beautiful like Lord Byron. I didn't blame the objects of his thirst. I alone knew that the thirst was fear made concrete, or an attempt to flee fear. I knew about the predawn vomit and the shaking of the knees and the wire hanger that waited in the dark closet to be shaken in front of his face and the nightmares that woke him and the way he blinked at daylight as if he was surprised that the sun came up. I knew he needed to be taken care of, invalided as he was by the racing of his mind, and all the rest was pose.

Sometimes when the child was asleep and he was sinking into bed in the early hours of the morning I would see that love itself (which was the name I gave my plight then) could not push him up onto a higher ledge, one further away from the stink within. Other times I denied that admission and believed that my love, if constant enough, pure enough could erase all the ailments of his mind.

Then my mother was home in her bed and she wasn't able to speak. Her right arm hung limply over the covers. Her lips seemed to have slipped sideways as if an invisible hand was wiping away her features. She gestured with her left hand. She stared at me with imploring eyes. She pointed at the sleeping tablets by her bedside. She wanted more. I knew what she wanted. I was afraid to do anything. What if I were sent to jail, who would take care of the child? I sat on the end of the bed and let time pass over me. My father on doctor's advice hired a teacher of speech who might help her regain connections between sound and word. This was intended to fool her. You will get well. It was an ordinary stroke. You're getting better every day. That's what the doctor told her and my father and my brother told her. I tried to signal my mother with my eyes whenever I lied. I let her see that my fingers were crossed. The speech therapist, with conviction, played her part in the charade. She produced a sheet of letters and made the sounds again and again. During these sessions my mother stared off into space. Sometimes she would cooperate and then sounds would come from her throat unrelated to the letters before her, something close to whale songs. Then I wanted to put my hands over my ears but I didn't.

Through all the days of her dying the chiffon inside curtains were always pulled closed even when the sun was slapping down on the avenue below.

My mother was not fooled. I knew it. I brought my child to stay in the room with her and with me. The child sat with my mother's jewelry box and pulled out all the beads and pins and gold bracelets and pearl necklaces and tried them on and rolled them across the floor and I sat there as I had for years, my mind wandering, my attention riveted. My father went to his club. He played squash with his friend Leonard. He had dinner with his friend Kopatkin. Now Kopatkin came to the house and sat on the living room couch letting his cigar ash fall on the rug. "Annie dear," he would say to me with a conspiratorial wink, "a little more martini if you please." He told me a joke: At the funeral of the richest man in town, a stranger was observed crying louder than any of the other mourners. One of the townspeople approached him, "Are you a relative of the deceased?" "No," said the man. "Then why are you crying?" "That's why," said the stranger. Kopatkin giggled and opened his mouth into a wide smile. I saw the shreds of cigar on his tongue.

My father took his usual long walks. He had his usual breakfast of prunes and juice. A nurse was hired to stay with my mother all night and another arrived in the morning.

My Aunt Libby came to sit with me sometimes. My Aunt Sylvia came in and out. My Uncle Sy told me that if I said anything at all to my mother about her impending fate he would never forgive me. His internist had said you must never, ever tell a patient an unbearable truth.

Her analyst calls to find out how she is doing. I tell him. He asks if he can visit. My father says no. I ask again and again. "All right," he says, "but make sure he doesn't tell her the truth. I don't trust the son of a bitch." Do analysts lie? Will this one? Is he a son of a bitch? Her analyst came. I answer the door. At last I see him, a large man with a big jaw line and teeth that are crooked. He has kind eyes or is that my imagination? I say to him, "Don't tell her anything." He says to me, "She knows, of course, she knows." The nurse was sent away when he came. The child and I waited in the den, the den that had been my room just a short while ago. When he left I went back to my mother's side. She seemed quieter. Her left hand was not jerking. She closed her eyes and fell asleep.

Then Paul's play had its opening night. He was in a bar across the street. I was in the back of the theater. Was it going well? There were the critics, Brooks Atkinson, Richard Watts, and others in the fifth row center. There was the director and his wife and they greeted me as if I were a friend. But that's the way it is in the theater: pretend turns to pretense and failure will result in obliteration and Paul with his shock of hair falling over his high forehead, with his blue eyes hidden behind his dark glasses, was the poet master clown, the illegal pretender to the rights of citizenship in their do-main. I ached for him. After the curtain closed we went to a restaurant to wait for the reviews. There were little bulbs in the restaurant's shrubbery blinking like stars in the sky. The waiters were running like whirling der-vishes with drinks. The first review was on television, the commentator found the play pretentious. More drinks. At just before midnight someone arrived at the party with the next day's *New York Times*. The review was read and passed along from table to table, along the line at the bar, and the room became suddenly quiet, somber, and people gathered their coats and left without saying goodbye. Paul wouldn't look at me. He moved away from my hand. "I won't be back tonight," he said. "I'm gone." How could I help? How could I bear it, the way he was feeling, a panic and a dread, a shame and a fear flooding his system, overwhelming his reason, sending him into the night wounded and alone? I could do nothing but wait for his return. There might be other nights, other plays, other reviews. I knew that but I knew that he did not, not in a way that would hold back the terror that was now claiming him for its own.

My mother knew that the play was opening. "What were the reviews," her eyes asked me. "How was it?" I told her that the reviews were mixed. This was not true. They were universally disastrous. She shook her head. She knew that I was lying. She knew. I could tell from the expression on her face. She could tell from the expression on my face. Ashes, ashes, all her hopes were ashes. All the unnameable things she had always feared for me were now going to happen. She knew it. Paul went on a five-day bender. By the time he returned the play had closed.

The child walks her child walk over to the nurse sitting in the chair by the bed. "I want to try on your white shoes," the child says to the nurse. The nurse is a proper professional nurse whose job is to watch the patient, not play with a child. "No dear," she says. She has thick legs and slightly swollen ankles and very big tempting white shoes. My child goes back to the box of beads on the floor but a few minutes later she is over by the nurse's feet and in a quick motion she pulls open the lace on the left shoe. The nurse looks down. "No, no," she almost shouts and moves her feet in short jerky mo-tions away from the child. The child looks surprised and pauses a second. She pulls out the lace on the right shoe. My mother in the bed makes a hol-low rasping sound, like the wind in a canyon. The child begins to cry. "I want to wear the white shoes," she whines. I carry her out of the room. When I come back I notice the gray in my mother's hair. The roots have grown in about an inch. It's as if the hand of death is coming upward from her brain and signaling us. She would have been ashamed had she been able to see the dead white thick roots of her hair. The nurse brushes her hair and applies lipstick to her mouth. It is a kindness, part of what she is paid to do. My mother has a convulsion and vomit rolls down her chin. Death is not like the opera or the movies where music swells and light comes in at the window.

I take the child to the park. I am pushing her in a stroller. We go to the zoo and look at the seals swimming in the pond. I buy the child a pink balloon and tie it to the side bar of the stroller so the child can see it if she turns her head. A man and woman walk past their noses red from cold. They are pressing close to each other as if nobody else were in the park, as if nobody walking by wouldn't feel a chill of exclusion as they strolled past. The balloon floats steadily above the child's head. We stop at a stand where a bearded man with a gray wool scarf over his ears is selling hot dogs. The air is cold. We exhale white puffs like the Little Engine That Could. The child wants a box of Cracker Jacks. I push the stroller close to the stand. One of the green and white umbrella points flicks at the balloon and in an instant there is a loud popping noise and the balloon is no longer sailing above the child's head but sits, ragged shreds on the wheels of the stroller. The child has had this happen before. There is no shriek. The child looks up at me and says as if observing the weather, "Grandma has gone pop like my balloon."

Not quite yet, but soon enough. Even small children understand death but they hide the fact from us out of an instinctive politeness, knowing how little we can bear. Each peekaboo game is a rehearsal for the real thing.

I had wanted to be there at the moment my mother died. She is no longer conscious of those around her. So I do not need to keep her company. We have already lost each other. But I do want to be there in that room because I want to see, observe, know, watch, grasp the moment that the quick become the dead. I believe that some truth, something I need to know, will occur, some explanation of soul and body and their terminal symbiosis will be revealed if I am right at my mother's side when the passage occurs.

Was this cold and unfeeling of me? Was this curiosity born of the pleasure that it was not my own life ending just then?

My mother had another convulsion and then a few hours later another
and then in the early hours of the morning the nurse called at my apartment
to say the end might be near. My brother had been notified and was already
on his way. (Why was he called first?) I woke the child and went over to the
apartment. In the predawn hours the gates at 1185 Park were still shut. I had
to ring a bell and a disheveled night doorman let me in and another ran the
elevator up to our floor. Although still in pajamas the child was completely
awake, wanting the jewelry box with the gold beads. The aunts were called.
The uncle arrived. My father was wearing his purple robe from Sulka with
his initials on the pocket.

Hours later, when the rest of the city awoke and dressed and went about
their day I went into the kitchen with the child to fix her a second breakfast.
While I was out of the room the exact moment of death came. When I
came out of the kitchen the nurse was on the phone calling the doctor, my
father who was out for his morning walk in the park was due to return in
moments. Leaving the child with the maid and the cook I stood by my
mother's body and tried to put her hand in mine. I was afraid of the way her
body felt, an inertness that startled, a flatness as if dimensions were disappearing as I sat there. I took back my hand.

My aunts were there. Everyone was waiting for the people from the funeral home to come and take away the body, but my mother was in bed,
dressed in her silk bed jacket, a clean nightgown underneath. My aunts
were going through the closet and had packed up my mother's two most
fashionable wigs (that was a season for wigs) and they had taken her dress
pocketbook, the one with the gold handle and they had a shopping bag
packed with hats and scarves and white gloves. My mother lay on the bed
without comment. I picked out of her closet a dress for her to wear at her
burial. It was blue silk. It had a rhinestone border at the low-cut neck. It
was a party dress. She had not had a chance to wear it. If she wore a dress
and had a bad night, an unlucky night, a sorrowful evening, she would never
wear that dress again as if luck attached itself to your clothes. The dress she
was buried in had not yet been tested. This seemed to me the safest choice.

As we waited for the men from the funeral home to come and take away
my mother's body my father went through my mother's dresser drawers and

swept up her jewelry, took the diamond ring off her finger, and said he was putting it all in a vault for safe keeping. He said he didn't trust her sisters who now were in the kitchen packing up silver trays and serving utensils they said they had lent my mother. My Aunt Libby took the green jade picture frame that held my grandmother's photograph from my mother's desk where it had been for my entire life. "It was mine, originally," she said.

My uncle said to me, "Take your mother's mink coat home." "I couldn't," I said. "You can," he said. "It's too small for me," I said. "I don't need it," I added. I didn't think this was the moment to explain to him that I was not going to live on Park Avenue for the rest of my life. I didn't belong. "Take it," he urged. My father said, "If she doesn't want it, she can leave it." My uncle was pale and his voice was hushed. We were becalmed in a passage, caught in the transition tide. I took the coat. That night I used it as a blanket on the child's bed. The next day I hung it in the back of the closet. Paul said he might pawn it. I said, "No, please, not yet."

In the small room outside the chapel where we receive mourners before the funeral starts, I see my mother's hairdresser and her manicurist, Mrs. Hummel who did the waxing, Mr. Otto who brought the linens. I see the canasta partners and her current stockbroker. In the main room I look in the open coffin and see my mother lying on a blue satin cushion. Her color has returned to her face. But something is wrong. She looks like a doll in a box. My brother stands by my side. I put my hand on his shoulder. He moves away.

We went to the cemetery far up the Saw Mill River Parkway and from the top of a hill a person could see the Hudson River and the high rusted cliffs of the palisades. Paul and my brother Gene and I were in one long black limousine. Paul was drinking from a silver flask he kept in the pocket of his long cashmere coat, the one my mother had bought him.

Blanche Phillips Roth was buried in a plot she had bought. It had four spaces, one for her husband, for herself, and one for each of her children. Everyone buried as far as the eye could see had a Jewish name.

Melting pots there may be in America but not in death, there the paths separate and no one speaks of brotherhood. The ferryman who rows the body across the River Styx is named O'Malley, Schwartz, Rodriguez, or Worthington the Third depending on the identity of the corpse.

The plot overlooked the Hudson River and though it was March and a blowing bitter cold wind bit at our necks the view of the rust-colored palisades and the moving slate-gray water clotted with blocks of ice was pleasing enough. "Make it short, rabbi. Nobody wants to stand here all day," my father snaps. Nevertheless the rabbi takes his time. I watch the coffin go down into the earth. I wonder if the maid has remembered to cut off the crusts on the sandwich she will give the child for lunch. I feel numb. "Grieve," I tell myself. But I am relieved it's over. Everything, the sickness, the not speaking, the convulsions, the things that didn't work out, the marriage, the analyst, the less than good children, everything is over. I want to grieve but I am frozen. I watch myself trying and trying to grieve. It is not a pretty sight. I am in pain, This must be true, but the pain if it is there is so deeply buried in the hellish circles of the soul that it can't find its way to the surface. Am I also dead?

At the grave site Kopatkin stands next to my father, my brother stands between Kopatkin and Leonard. My Aunt Libby and my Aunt Sylvia and my Uncle Sy stand together on the other side. I go stand with them. On the way back from the cemetery where we were going to greet family and friends at 1185 Park Avenue Paul sits on the jumpseat of the limousine and blowing smoke across the black velvet seats asks me in a loud voice, "How much money, exactly how much money are we going to get? How soon are we going to get it?"

I hear him. I don't say anything. My brother hears him. My brother goes on looking at the window. Did he really hear him? Does he think that Paul is joking? I know this is not a joke.

I see Paul sitting there in front of me and I find him vulgar, unappealing, disgusting. I know it is conventional of me to think his mention at this moment of the inheritance is vile. I know that he is simply playing against the sentiment of death in the most avant-garde, dada, Apollinaire, Mallarmé, manner. I know that he intends to be shocking, not cruel. But I know he also means it. He wants the dollar amount. He wants my mother's money. The thought runs through me like an electric current. It brings me back to life. He cannot have it. He will not have it. I will never let him have it. I look at his dark glasses and I hate them. What are they but pretentious props, defenses against looking anyone in the eye, avoidance of responsibility for what you do and who you are. I look at his skinny long body and I hate it. I look at his formerly beautiful mouth and I hate the way it appears, hard, artful, unreal. He is a fake, a construction, a hollow man. He never looks at his child. He is without manhood. What man doesn't look at his child? I am not sad for his sadness. I don't excuse the liquor as balm for his jumbled head. I think he's spoiled and selfish and drunk too often. He will shrivel in the daylight like a vampire so let the sun shine on down. I am no longer proud of his words on paper. I don't care anymore. Whether or not he is a great writer I don't care. I don't care anymore about writing. What are writers but vain and vainglorious egos gone wild with presumption, with ambition. How bitter is ambition. How stupid of us to grant fame to mortals who lack sufficient morality to shoe the foot of an amoeba. He is a worm of a person, a small figure, a failure on all levels. I want the gods to grind him down under their heels. Let his liver curl up like a leaf in a fire. Let him have one last cigarette, blindfold him, and push him into the mud. I sit there quietly but instead of grieving (or is that my way of grieving?) I hate and hate my husband at last. I do remind myself that it is my fault that he is my husband. I have pursued him, backed him into this marriage. For this I also hate myself.

And back at the apartment at 1185, already the halls and the rooms feel stripped, emptied of their habits, their accustomed sounds, false rooms, no more than a stage set for the after-the-funeral meats and drinks that are laid out on the table by the maid and prepared by the cook. My mother's friends come up to me and express regret. "She died so young, she had so many years ahead." Did she? I'm not so sure. She was fifty-two years old and so much had passed her by. More passing by lay ahead. This was the tragedy, not the cancer. I nodded and kissed and hugged. I noticed that people turned away from me and back to talk of other things. The rabbi calls me into a corner. He pulls out a pamphlet from his inside jacket pocket. This is for you he says. Call me and we'll talk about it. The pamphlet is about the disastrous and increasing evil of intermarriage which is now at a 9 percent rate. It speaks of the need of the Jewish people to stay together after the holocaust. It speaks of out-marriage as treason. I find the rabbi in the living room in conversation with Sandra Leonard who is asking him whether the Ten Commandments apply in all cases. I hand him back his pamphlet. "My

mother has just died," I say. "I have nothing to say to you and I never will."
It crosses my mind for a moment to stay married to Paul forever, just to spite
the rabbi. I know that's ridiculous. Some people are just clumsy. I should
forgive the rabbi his unfortunate timing. I don't. I don't stop hating Paul. I
just also hate the rabbi. I wish on him boils and trenchmouth and a double
hernia.

No one knows how to grieve, I think. Then I am in my mother's bedroom
and I look at the empty bed and the chair beside it and I am filled with her
absence. It comes up behind my eyes and makes me blink and blink. It
comes into my stomach and causes a spasm that will not let go. It enters my
brain and makes me feel weak and short of oxygen. I am cut off. I am alone
except for the child. I am aggrieved. But am I grieving? Is pity for myself
grief? In the room with me I feel the evil eye. It bores into me whichever
way I turn. Is this warning of doom the thing we call grief? Will it ever go
away?

My mother was not brave but she was a person, a real person, a smeared
and weepy person. Of course I remind myself, that's who dies: people. Cold
comfort.

22

the advantage of a having a lawyer in the
family   My father the lawyer had prepared her will in the last
months of her illness and he had left himself everything as her spouse. The
small portion she has allowed to be divided between my brother and me is
held in a trust with my father as trustee. So Paul will have nothing when he
leaves me. It is three weeks after my mother's funeral. He wants to go. He
has already found a woman who is a curator of an art gallery who will take
him in. I want him to go. I know he must go. The child will not notice he is
gone. I am sad at the failure of my marriage but not as sad as I would have
been if the marriage had continued.

He moves out. I walk around the apartment at 1045 Park Avenue staring
at the bookshelves now emptied of his philosophy books, our French books,
my theater books. I walk on bare floors. The rugs are gone. I take the child
to the park. I watch cowboy shows on television. The child and I are beginning again, each without a parent.

Why was his remark about my inheritance the one that opened the door?
The final straw is only the last one, not necessarily the most significant. In
1962 I was too old to be a flower child but not so old I couldn't hear them

chanting as they were drifting toward me over the hill. Paul's remark shamed me. I was ashamed of what I had become. I should have been. You can say that love is always a good thing but sometimes love is a whip you use to beat yourself. Love can make you ashamed. Love can be a way to shame yourself.

I gave Paul all the antique furniture my mother had given me. He had nothing and I had no interest in furniture. I considered moving to Appalachia and becoming a public health nurse.

Then my Aunt Libby came to visit. She sat on the wicker chair I had purchased to fill the empty living room and I sat on a cushion on the floor. The child was throwing crayons everywhere.

My Aunt Libby asks, "How could you give away the furniture, the French eighteenth-century desk, the English lamp, the sofas? What's wrong with you?"

"I want," I say, "to live in a cabin in the mountains and pick blueberries from the bushes behind my outhouse." "In that case," said my Aunt Libby, "I'll take back your mother's mink coat. You'll only get blueberry stains on it." She went to my closet and took the coat which was too small for her. I didn't care. It wasn't any concern about animal rights that provoked my indifference, it was the fear I had that mink was an extremely dangerous animal when dead.

Did I know my mother? Did I make a picture in my mind that is constructed out of reality but is rearranged so that it does not correspond to the real woman, the Blanche Phillips Roth that chain smoked and read mystery novels and went to the theater or to a party wearing her double strand of pearls and her hair done in strawberry blonde waves? Was she a coward for not leaving my father? When she died in 1962 on the very eve of the feminist second coming was she the last soldier on the battlefield to come home in a body bag? Did I understand her or misunderstand her? It's hard to know.

On Park Avenue, in my bare apartment each morning I would wake with the sensation that I had spent the last hours in a grave in a box lined with blue satin, husbanding my breath while banging on the coffin lid.

I go to Tijuana to get a divorce. I take the child with me. We stay at a hotel in the middle of town. I bring a supply of bottled water for the child. In the hotel there is a smell of cesspool leaking. There are whores and their customers, doors slamming, shouting and cursing, goings and comings all through the night. I can't sleep. I watch the moon sliding over the red hibiscus. I watch the great cactus with its needled arms sitting in a sand pit in the inner patio of the hotel. In the morning on the way to the courthouse I stop at the front desk to pay the bill. When my back is turned the child goes over to the parrot cage hanging by the cigar case and reaches in and grabs a piece of corn tied to the cage. The corn disappears into the child's mouth. The parrot shrieks and flaps its wings and slams itself against the cage. I turn around. I am afraid the child will get sick, will die from some foreign parrot fever. I hold the child in my arms tightly. I scold. I spank, I find to my surprise I am crying. To hide my red eyes at my court appearance I buy a pair of dark sunglasses.

The law court in Tijuana grants my petition for divorce and it is over, this marriage. The child and I fly back to New York.

hansel and gretel in the big city   My father allowed me to continue to live at 1045 Park Avenue, although the apartment now belongs to him. He let me use the money my mother had left me to support myself. It would last a few years. After our mother died my brother decided to leave medicine and instead become a professor of comparative literature. The following fall he went to New Haven and planned to do his graduate school thesis on Proust. Medicine he said was bogus, offering false hope, incapable of honesty, corrupt to the core. Medicine he said was full of fools and he didn't want to be in their company.

Once in a while he would call from New Haven. "How many graduate students does it take to change a light bulb?" "How many?" I ask. "One, but it takes nine years." Before the second term began he was complaining to me about the stupidity of this professor or that. They all seemed to have serious lacunae in their educations. Before the second term ended he was disenchanted with graduate school. Medicine could not save my mother and for that he would never forgive it. On the other hand graduate school was full of hair splitters, angels on the head of a pin counters, people who did not understand the simplest point, who made mistakes in pronunciation of the languages in which they were allegedly proficient. As always around my brother there was an aura of isolation. He was quick to ridicule, quick to judge, saying the thing that was best unsaid, sometimes true, sometimes not. He was impatient with those he considered slow. There were many of us he considered slow.

He left graduate school after a year and returned to medicine. His year away from science would leave its mark. He never stopped reading in French and German. He never stopped reading Thomas Mann and was always discovering brilliant authors who wrote at the turn of the century, interesting writers, novelists of social manners and novelists who wrote of World War I, untranslated but worthy of translation. His library held French books with their white covers and red borders and the strange glue that smelled of furniture polish. He owned large German books and Spanish books and biographies of writers and musicians. He had books of Hebrew poetry and some of the Italians of the nineteenth century. The one country whose written word did not command his respect was his own. All his jokes were told half in English and half in Yiddish or at least with a Yiddish accent and a Yiddish shrug and an impish look that even behind the glasses made you think of Alice's Cheshire Cat, of something friendly and not so friendly at the same time, something whose tail has been caught in the door but who won't give anyone the satisfaction of a howl.

He lived in a large modern glass high rise near his medical school in New York overlooking the East River that led under the Manhattan Bridge out to the ocean, past the Statue of Liberty and he felt that his place on the globe, his spot on the time line, was second rate, ersatz, corrupted by commerce and eternally dull. He did not do the twist when it came into fashion, he did not root for the home teams, not baseball, not football. There was still a trace of Yiddish inflection in his speech. There was still that odd pallor of the yeshiva student on his cheeks. His body was soft from lack of exercise. When he was not at medical school he went to concerts. He told me that analysts were not real doctors. They were not scientists. That real doctors had contempt for analysts, that real medicine was based on hard provable facts. He too now believed that psychiatry was a false path. "I wasted my time," he said. "I wasted hours on that garbage." I would have argued with him. I didn't see it that way, but he was not easy to argue with. He became easily sullen and would hang up when it was my turn to make a point.

He would call me nearly every week often to tell me of a new disease he had learned about that particularly struck women in their twenties. Also he would tell me about the more bizarre, more outlandish, more dangerous diseases that he was seeing under his microscope. After I talked with him it would take me a while to feel the heat of the sun on my arm, to again recognize that the water in which I bathed my child was a warm soapy bath, not a pool of microscopic life forms each willing to devour our hearts.

One Saturday he came to my apartment and went with me to Central Park. The child sat on a blanket and he took her picture. He was good with cameras. I hadn't thought I could do something so technically complicated so I had never touched a camera and did not have any pictures of the child. He sat with me and we had ice cream popsicles from the vendor and it was just the start of spring and there were dogwood blossoms on the trees at the top of the hill and he said he couldn't stay long in the park because his allergies would start but he sat for a long time anyway and whatever we talked about it didn't make the earth tremble but I saw him, his gray blue eyes clear behind the glasses and he told me a joke in Yiddish and then translated it for me in English and then told me another that the first had reminded him of and I was glad of his company. I wanted to tell him something so interesting that he couldn't leave the park, would spend the entire afternoon with me and my child, watching as the child chased after some bugs and dug with a stick in a mud hole near the roots of a bush. "You should learn Yiddish," he said to me. "The best jokes are in Yiddish." "Will you teach me?" I asked. He blushed and looked away. "You have a tin ear," he said. Which was true. I have always kept the picture he took that day in the park of the child because he took the picture for me. The sweetness of the thing rivets me even now.

a stepmother several nicks after the nick
in time   In the weeks after my mother's death I asked my father if he wanted to take me up with the child to the house in Rye. I wanted to sit on the rocks. That's where he spent his weekends. He explained he couldn't take me. He had a friend, a special friend who was coming. Who?

One thinks of poets as being in a risky venture but in fact their work may be more secure than most. At least they very rarely make enough to lose everything. People who make sweaters however can be in for very hard times. This is what happened to the Siegal business, so I was told. The father who had his factory in Vienna died and the son who was Elisabeth's husband did not have the gift of survival in a fickle America where sweater sets could go out of style and markets moved like the wind down a heaving storm-driven river. The Siegal business which supported Elisabeth and her four now mostly grown children was bankrupt. The speedboat was sold. The three cars were sold. The estate was about to be sold. Gert Siegal needed a job.

The Phillips family, the employers of Gene Roth, his in-laws, might find a place for Gert somewhere in the clothing business. Who should ask? Elisabeth should ask. A place was found for Gert Siegal in someone's sweater business, now he was an employee and not an owner. All this I was told.

The following summer my father takes a cottage in East Hampton. I am visiting friends with the child. We are walking on the beach and we see my father and a woman coming toward us. It is Elisabeth. She is covered against the sun in a white shawl and dark glasses. She carries her sandals in her hand. She is careful not to let the waves wet her legs.

Elisabeth is now divorced, my father explains to me. She and Gert have remained friends. This makes sense to me, after all she had saved him as he had once saved her—even steven, as they say in the playground. This explains why my father never wants to come to my apartment for dinner no matter how often I ask. He is busy.

The first September without my mother, the first September I was without a husband, the fall that the child began to climb into every available man's lap and croon to him, "Be my daddy," that season my father invited me to his club on a Thursday night for dinner and announced that he was going to marry Elisabeth and he did. My brother and I were not invited to the ceremony. They wanted it to be private, him and her and her children. When Thanksgiving arrived my father explained to me that there was no room for me and the child at his table, my mother's former table, Elisabeth had such a big family.

Elisabeth needed to sleep at least until noon. This was a war plan to avoid the marks of age. If I came to visit my father with the child she was asleep or out. She would not leave food for us. We did not stay long.

After a while we stopped coming. When I was remarried some few years later she did not come to the wedding. She was in Boca Raton away from New York's cold. New York was cold that winter.

Elisabeth did not want to live at 1185 Park Avenue. They sold the apartment and bought a new one, smaller, more modern, downtown on Park Avenue. This was understandable. I went back to the apartment for the last time before the new owners were to take over and walked through the now empty rooms. I kept opening windows to let the air in although it was winter. I looked at my mother's decorator-bought furniture, the Chinese silk screen, the eighteenth-century chairs, the long blond art deco dining table. It was all being moved to the new apartment. I didn't want it. My brother didn't want it. That was good because we weren't offered it. I did stuff my mother's ashtray, the one that sat by the side of her bed, into my pocket, but then I felt uneasy and put it back. I left.

A few weeks later I received a small package in the mail. Inside was a tiny china dachshund, black with brown spots like Guppy, my dog. The china dog was mine, hard to remember when it came into my possession, but I do know it was on a shelf above my desk all through my childhood and was packed away when the room was redecorated into a den when I went off to college. Folded inside the box was a note on lavender paper. "I thought you would want this," the note said. "Your mother was holding this tightly in her hand when she died." It was written in purple ink and signed "Elisabeth," with a flourish.

Only I knew my mother was not holding a china dog in her hand as she lay dying. What she had in her hand at the time of her final convulsion was her diamond ring which I had seen my father take off her finger in the moments after death. It slipped off easily because my mother had at last lost weight. My father had reset the ring in a wide gold band. He had given it to Elisabeth who was now wearing it on her fourth finger of her left hand along with my mother's diamond circle wedding ring.

I decided this gift from Elisabeth was an attempt to comfort me, an offer of friendship. I invited her to go ice skating with me and the child but she declined.

I write a novel about my mother's death and other family matters. My Aunt Libby buys up all the copies in her local bookstore so her friends cannot read it. The store orders more. My Aunt Libby is not speaking to me. My Uncle Sy is not speaking to me. My brother is angry for a while but then forgives me. My father is grim. He decides to avoid the subject when he sees me.

Elisabeth was a wife who unlike my mother understood the deal. She did not demand that my father pay attention to her. She did not have money so he did not feel like a consort. She did not have opinions on politics or business nor had any ideas ever caused her to question or interrupt someone. She was not clever at cards or good at the stock market. She didn't understand the odds or the way you paid taxes or how you got a driver's license. She was simply languidly pleasing, plump white flesh on the arms and a black bow holding back her smooth bear-colored hair. She did not challenge or accuse. She did not require anything more than that the bills be paid and that she be allowed to sleep ten or twelve hours a day, a black sleep mask pulled over her face. I thought this might make my father into a new man.

But soon he called her names. He yelled at her whenever he pleased and her hands began to tremble and her smile became less steady. Still no doubt she was a better wife for him than my mother; at least with my mother's money to support them both, that was true. They began to spend winters at their newly purchased apartment in Boca Raton where my father would take long walks along the ocean's edge and Elisabeth would sleep on the chaise until it was time for her massage. The building was a high rise that blocked the view of the water for all the houses behind. There was Muzak in the elevator and wine-colored carpeting on the lobby floor. Their apartment had a large gold-framed mirrored bar and all the sofas were covered in white leather. Elisabeth spent long hours in the building's sauna and wore large straw hats so that her pale skin would never be exposed to the sunlight.

We, my second husband and our three younger children, go down to visit. We stay at a motel in nearby Delray. We go to dinner at the Boca Raton club where my father has a membership. He has invited us. There are little green lights around the pool. There are splashing pink lights on the stucco patio. There are blue and yellow lights on the trunks of the palm trees. The Florida air blows over us, warm and gentle. There is an ice sculpture at the buffet table. As we wait for the waiter Elisabeth's fingers pull and twist the fringe of her shawl. She is wearing her diamond ring, hers and my mother's. The children are given menus. The waiter arrives and turns first to the oldest child. The child says, "I'll have the steak, with french fries and a Coke." My father leans over and shouts down the table, "How dare you, who do you think you are ordering the most expensive item on the menu? What makes you think I want to buy you a steak?" Elisabeth puts a hand on my father's arm. "It's all right," she says very calmly. My father turns on her. "It was your idea to take them to dinner. You see what they want, you see how they are."

My husband rises from the table and I rise with him. The oldest child is white like the fluorescent lighting in a hospital operating room. I carry the youngest who burrows into my neck. I look back at the table. Elisabeth's lips are trembling. My father calls out after me, "You've spoiled your children. They have no sense of value, the cost of things." My husband gets our car from the parking valet. We eat fried clams at a seaside place.

The next day I walked alone on the beach with my father. As the water pushed up between my toes I could smell the coconut suntan oil I put on my shoulders and my face. I could smell the seaweed on the shore line. I could smell my own sweat. It was good to be walking with my father.

"Daddy," I said. "What do you do that you like to do here in Boca?" "I walk," he said. "I swim in the ocean every day it's possible. I don't mind the rain or the cold." "You're a strong man, Daddy," I said and I meant it. He smiled at me, a tight quick smile, but a true smile: a sign I believed that he liked me.

His sister Bea dies. She needs to be buried. She has died without funds. So my father buries her next to my mother in the plot that my mother had bought that had come to my father in the estate. Would my mother like to be lying through all eternity next to my Aunt Bea? Of course not. But since neither my brother nor I believe that the dead could be socially inconvenienced we let it go. Does my Aunt Bea take up more than her one-fourth of the plot? Probably. On Halloween night does the ghost of my Aunt Bea do the rumba on my mother's grave? Maybe.

Al Cohn dies. He leaves explicit instructions to his wife Dora that he wants to be buried with his own family in their modest plot in a Queens cemetery. Before he died he asked Dora to honor his final request. He asks her to sign a letter agreeing to his final resting spot. She does.

However when he dies he is buried with Dora's family, in the imposing mausoleum in Westchester. Oscar Wilde said, "If you marry for money you earn it." I fully believed that Al Cohn had earned his.

science: a modern miracle   My brother became a
hematologist. He worked in his own lab at Montefiore Hospital as a re-
searcher on sickle cell anemia. He was a practitioner of deductive reasoning. He worked with mice and test tubes and machines that whirled blood
samples around until they separated into their component chemical parts.
He worked with a lab assistant sometimes when the grant money was good
and without when the funds dried up. At lunchtime he went into the doctors' cafeteria and exchanged jokes with the other doctors. Sometimes he
would call me to tell me a joke. I would hear his half-swallowed crinkle of a
laugh through the receiver. Once he called me up to read me "'Twas the
Night Before Christmas and all through the house" in Yiddish. He told me
I had to do a better job sterilizing baby spoons or washing down counters after preparing chicken. He frequently listed the common microbacterial dis-
asters that awaited me because I was sloppy and inattentive and had no real
understanding of the invasive world of germ and food chain. He would call
and leave a message on my machine about a novel that had been translated
from the German written in the early 1920s that I must read. He would call
if he saw an obituary of one of our mother's old friends. He always read the
obituaries from beginning to end.

    In the pursuit of sickle cell disease he wrote a paper on *Babesia microti*
about hamster erythrocytes infected from a human source. He wrote about
reticulocytes and falciparum malaria. He went to Sicily and published a paper with his department colleagues about sickle cell disease brought by
African slaves to the European continent. Day after day he tested out a new
or old hypothesis. Day after day he waited for something to show up on a
slide, for something else to disappear. Was he lonely in his lab? He didn't
say so. When he went to conferences of hematologists in distant cities he
was frank about his negative opinions of his colleagues. He was nonpoliti-
cal or obnoxious depending on your point of view. He was not interested in
being diplomatic with government funding representatives. He corrected
their pronunciation too. He was tactless when tact would have helped. He
believed in the principle of peer review but he didn't respect his peers. He
thought people in authority were by definition fools or possibly dangerous
fools. But he was passionate. He was steadfast in his pursuit of the small
detail, the slight change, every fact that needed an explanation. The things
he saw through the lens on his table, the chemical formulas and numbers

that he methodically charted, the small animals he sacrificed in the name of information, the hour after hour of watching and thinking, the ideas that came to him while floating in the tub, the grinding work of the lab scientist, to those he was an ardent suitor. He insisted that the leads that didn't work out, the ideas that dead-ended, those too made a contribution to the discovery of cure, each added a small drop to the pool of knowledge out of which one day would come solution, revelation, explanation.

He taught me about the terrible diseases carried by a midge named phlebotomus argentipes, the sandfly that transmits the parasitic protozoan, *Leishmania donovani,* the cause of kala azar which in plague times seems to have killed 25 percent of the people in villages in India. He told me about the discovery of the cause of malaria. He was studying malaria because sickle cell anemia seemed to have evolved in Africa as a protective device against malaria. My brother admired the original, the outlaw, the nonconformist, the pioneer Leeuwenhoek who first saw the moving crawling tiny creatures we call bacteria that lived in his own mouth and so revolutionized science. My brother was a devotee at the church of meticulous observation. He was a follower of Pasteur and Spallanzani who discovered how microbes multiply. He talked to me about the devastation and death brought on by fevers, dehydration, that made life along the riverbanks of far-off continents so fragile, so temporary, so brutal and short. My brother had seen the tiny microbes and respected their awesome power while intent on learning about the chemistry of their operation, the better to disable them.

I read the *New York Times Book Review.* I read the *New Yorker* while he read *Science* and *Cell* and the *New England Journal of Medicine.* He did not want to have his son bar mitzvahed because he didn't want to give a party. He loathed large parties. He begrudged the expense. Also he was no longer in thrall, no longer enchanted, no longer believed that the truth was in the Torah. Instead he was radiant as he praised his newest microscope. I wished I had a scientific mind, an orderly mind. I wished I had become a doctor. When it comes to envy the penis is the least of it.

He told me a joke: There were two rabbis in heaven looking at a third who was sitting under a tree with a smile on his face. The first said to the second, "Look at him, he's only been here a week and already he thinks he's nothing."

He married a woman who had been a remarkable young pianist. He did not like her parents. He accused her father of invading his privacy when the couple had once stayed over at his wife's childhood home in the suburbs. The man had opened his daughter's bedroom door without knocking. My brother never wanted those people in his house, this he told me years later. Together he and his wife had a son. When he was two the boy learned the word for "cookie" in four languages. By the age of three he could tell a Yiddish joke in perfect accent. Gene-Johnny and his wife had evenings of chamber music in their home and once my brother invited a quartet of wind instrumentalists that he heard playing in the subway to give a concert in his home. He and his wife knew tenors and harpsichordists and violinists. They went to concerts. They gave a young opera soprano a place to perform and invited people who might further her career to attend. Over and over again my brother read Proust, the entire *Recherche de Temps Perdu*. He read *The Magic Mountain* in German and *Death in Venice* repeatedly. He loved the Marx brothers and W. C. Fields. He would wince if a strain of rock and roll floated off someone's boom box and into his windows. He would, if you coaxed him, go to films made in France or Poland or Sweden that played in small theaters to select audiences.

He particularly disliked the Hasidim whom he believed were basically unclean. He was convinced that they didn't shower frequently enough to prevent the spread of disease in their midst. He relished with lip-licking glee stories of religious Jews who were discovered at whorehouses or came down with trichinosis which they caught from a Hispanic maid who had stirred their kosher chicken soup. Working in the summer at the Woods Hole lab he would avoid the beach. He would not go out on a colleague's boat and watch the fractured light of the sun striking the water. He almost never walked to main street or sat down on the grass. He had allergies and stayed in an air-conditioned room.

He was heavy and full hipped and no one could convince him to exercise. He fully enjoyed other people's mistakes. He was delighted to point them out. He did not move up the academic ladder. He did not break through and solve a crucial puzzle and become renowned in his field. On the other hand he kept working, autonomously, new ideas steaming, planning papers, testing theses. He had a certain prickly strength. He played chess with himself on his computer for recreation. He listened to the latest recordings of performers of Bach and Mozart of Handel and Chopin. He knew the names of promising young violinists and sopranos and he knew all about stereo parts and audio systems. He kept his money carefully and watched it grow. He did not want more than one child. He told me he would never do to his son what had been done to him, that is me, that is, a sibling. He went to Israel for some months and worked in the Hadassah hospital in Jerusalem. He came back and told the Hadassah women that their hospital was dreadful and the leading doctors were blundering idiots.

He asks me if I know the joke about the sadist and the masochist who are walking in the woods. He says, "The masochist says to the sadist, 'Hit me,' and the sadist answers, 'No.'"

He tells my psychoanalyst spouse that psychoanalysts are worthless, not doctors at all. He informs him that he has wasted his medical training. My husband is not mad.

In 1981 a child of mine is in the hospital requiring serious surgery. My brother comes to the hospital the night before the operation. The child is frightened. The knife will slip. The surgeon will cut in the wrong place. Sleep will be permanent. Pain will be felt. My brother leans over the bed, "Think of it like an airplane ride. The surgeon is the pilot. He will take you there safely. Let the pilot take you there." The child is not afraid of planes and smiles. I am happy my brother has come. The next day after the surgery he says to me, "Don't worry, no transfusions, no extra blood, I checked the chart." I hadn't known enough to worry about blood.

My brother loves Woody Allen and Mel Brooks. He dislikes Catholic hospitals, folk music, Broadway musicals, any meal that includes fish. A stepchild of mine is getting married. My brother calls up to say he will not attend the wedding. He doesn't like this child who has just graduated medical school and who once disagreed with him about some medical issue. He doesn't like weddings. He refuses to come. When I insist he says that if he needed a kidney this child could not give it to him because the child is not of his blood. My husband asks, "You only go to weddings where the bride or groom can give you a kidney?" Finally my brother under threat of severed family ties agrees to come to the wedding. But no one is pleased he is there.

He really doesn't like weddings and he doesn't feel comfortable in a big crowd. One of our children sings for the bridal couple the Song of Songs in

Hebrew. My brother says that the accent used is not authentic, too American, the worst insult he can conjure up. He is teaching his own son Hebrew. The boy he says has a perfect accent.

just deserts   For many decades Roy Cohn gave an annual New Year's Eve party in his town house. Celebrities who had short memories or atrophied consciences attended in great number. Politicians from city hall, media people from New York, Hollywood, and Washington came. Barbara Walters came. Bankers and investors came. Beautiful young men came. Models of both sexes came. My Aunt Libby also went, year after year, long after her brother-in-law, Roy's father Al, died, after her sister-in-law Dora died. My Aunt Libby attended in her best dress, wearing all her diamond and emerald finery. Judges came to the party, eminent doctors came to the party. Journalists, the kind who liked to be seen as well as to see, came. My Aunt Libby enjoyed a good party. My father was not invited although he still did legal work for Roy. There were many beautiful young men at the party. They were found in bathrooms, in backrooms, sitting on the staircases. There was talk of nitrates and cocaine in the study served in silver dishes replenished by maids in black and white uniforms. Libby told my brother that she never saw anything like that. She herself had seen no evil. In the early eighties some of the young boys began to look sickly. Libby told my brother (who told me) that Roy seemed to have a cancer on his ear. It was removed and all was well.

My father told me that the son of a family friend had gotten into some trouble in Colorado. In the car that he and his friend were driving the police found a large drug stash intended for sale back east. Fortunately for him my father was able to call Roy Cohn, who out of family loyalty was able to make some phone calls and get the name of an approachable judge in the little Colorado town and make a deal. The deal left the other boy in jail facing a ten-year sentence but released his friend's son to make his mark in the world. This my father told me. Also he said, "Goddamn idiot cowboy judges."

Once every few months my father would accept my invitation and come to our house before dinner. He would not stay for a meal. He did not bring

Elisabeth. Repeatedly I invited her. She was unable to come. My father would have a drink, sit on our living room couch, and tell us about the latest murder case reported in the *Daily News*. He would tell us about the great stupidity of the mayor and complain about the ignoramuses who ran our foreign policy. He thought we were always giving in to the communists when we should really bomb them into extinction. "What's the army for," he said, "if not war?" He would not stay more than forty-five minutes. He never held a child or touched one. He told us who was going to win the next election and why. There were no contradictions, no discussion, no other views possible. We listened. It was like having a ghost in the house, one you can see but can't see you.

I had a seventieth birthday party for him. I invited my stepchildren and his stepchildren and the last son of Elisabeth who had grown into his late adolescence looking oddly like my father—or was that just my imagination? This boy went to my father's club with him and played golf with him and was interested in my father's opinions on the stock market. Who was his father? We tend to make too much out of literal paternity. Sometimes it's a difference that doesn't matter. My father flew up from Boca Raton for the party. But Elisabeth backed out at the last minute. She claimed stomach trouble. I had given her no cause, still I understood that she was uneasy in my presence. I didn't want her to worry about me. She was a beautiful woman with a skinny gray whippet dog, that's all. Surely her life with my father was all the vengeance I required.

The children colored cards with place names. We served poached salmon and had a bottle of champagne. Conversation around the table flagged and stalled. I kept dropping things. In the midst of serving the cake I forgot to make a birthday toast. Later my father said he was not pleased. I should have made a toast. I should have. Ah, how the unruly rude unconscious takes the upper hand.

Then cancer cells appeared, mysteriously, silently, deadly, with an agenda of their own and settled like termites in the cellar in (never say fate doesn't have a grasp of irony) my father's prostate. He was treated and perhaps all would be well. After being released from the hospital he went to his apartment in Boca Raton to recover. When he returned to New York he did not come to see my children. I invited him. He said he was busy. I called again. He was going out of town. I invited him to come to dinner with Elis-

abeth. He said she didn't like to come in to the city. They were now living
in the suburbs in a house I had never seen. My brother drove up to this new
house with his son about once a month. I offered to come and visit with the
children. "Not now," he said. "I haven't time for a visit and Elisabeth is getting over the flu." He hadn't seen the children in nearly two years. The first
year he had his secretary purchase birthday presents for them and mail
them from his office but he didn't come. The second year he forgot the
presents.

Of course he was angry with me. I had written things in still another
book that he didn't like. I had complained about him in public. I had not
been discreet. I am a writer and burning bridges behind me is part of the
cost of the work. I did not feel I had lost a father only that the barbed wire
fences that separated us had grown higher. But then they had always been
part of the landscape: that had been my complaint, the one I had made
public. I expected no profound reconciliation. I was sad that the children
were included in his dislike of me. They were innocent of my offenses and
while all previous visits with their grandfather had left little trace, engaged
no part of young mind or heart, I still hoped for a moment of genetically
pushed affection to open his eyes to the hard-breathing sweetly expectant
life that pulsed so insistently through them. "Last chance," I wanted to tell
him, "last chance."

Then a few seasons later I received a phone call from my brother. The
cancer had returned. My father had flown up from Florida and was in another hospital. I went to see him. He wasn't particularly pleased to see me.
I understood. There were nurses coming and going. Elisabeth sat on the
chair and applied cream to her hands. Her eyes seemed swollen and she
had gained weight. Now she seemed like an oversized dove blinking in the
too bright sunlight. Her Viennese accent, a slight thickening of the vowels,
dipped up and down as she spoke of the weather, admired my shoes, suggested another brand of shampoo. I thought of edelweiss and sacher torte
and wished for Elisabeth a kind man who would wash her shoulders in the
shower and laugh with her as she responded to his tickling hands.

Elisabeth shuts the window blinds and opens the window blinds as if the
right degree of dimness in the room will make everything all right. I ask my
father if he wants to see photographs of the children that I've brought. He

says "Some other time." I promise to come again. My brother talks with the doctors and then talks with Elisabeth in the hall. My brother understands everything that is happening in my father's body. He is part of the medical authority that stands above us, the travel agents responsible for the connections and the accommodations of the trip. My brother explains what he can to me. He enjoys explaining hard science matters to me and does not mind if he has to repeat something once or twice. He draws a picture of a prostate gland on a napkin in the hospital cafeteria and he gives me the medical name for the tumor, the medicines, he makes a diagram of the chemical changes in the cells. "Thank you," I say. He blushes and I catch a quick soft smile that must have been meant for me.

A few days later my brother calls. His voice is dour and grim. No jokes. What is it? Is my father worse. No, but my father has just told him that he has disinherited us—my brother, his wife and son, and me and my husband and our children. His will leaves all my mother's stock and property to Elisabeth and her children.

Whose money was it anyway? Would my mother have wanted her money to be handed over to her rival, her successor and those children? Ah, my mother dead and defiled. Also I did want the money. I knew the costs of tuition and orthodonture and summer camps would bear down on us hard and that money needs are not always irrational, laced with arsenic of folly and pride. I burned slowly. Ambivalence and guilt muted the fire. My brother erupted like a wounded bull.

It turned out that my father predictably enough had lost a good deal of the capital. There wasn't very much remaining. It was also true that Elisabeth would need to be completely taken care of at least until she found someone else willing to take up her care. My brother was able to support himself and had invested what had come to him with prudence and success. My husband and I were always living at the edge but we had grown skilled at our balancing act and we didn't expect to fall. I, about to be disinherited, was not entirely unhappy at losing this money that had proved so toxic to those who touched it. Besides I of the former black leotard and brown sandals could not, without much loss of face and indecent squirming, now mourn the money once so loudly and publicly scorned. Nevertheless I had a sharp pang of regret. Mine, mine, mine, a little voice within whispered. Then it stilled as I recalled that I had earned my own rewards and was now receiving my just deserts. A guilty writer cannot also be a wronged daughter.

My brother, who had done nothing to my father, had been dutiful (if not a son made in the father's image), remained outraged, injured. Unjustly attacked he now prepared for battle. He had always expected his share of his mother's good fortune. And he was right. My nephew and my brother should have a portion of the remnant of my mother's funds.

I try to console my brother. He will not be consoled.

Elisabeth's youngest son, the one who was tall like my father, was named a trustee for the estate. This was another slap in my brother's face. We went to a lawyer and the lawyer asked if my father was of sound mind when he had written this will: he was. He asked if we had any earlier wills in which the money was left to us. We hadn't. My father had dealt with his estate with the help of Aunt Bea's son who had become a lawyer and worked for my father, and had no reason to feel friendly toward us.

"So let it go," I say to my brother. We are not less beloved now that Elisabeth has our mother's money than we were before we knew that fact. But my brother feels like Esau, robbed.

A few weeks went by. My father had been sent home from the hospital. There was nothing more that could be done. My brother and I went to see him.

A hospital bed has been installed in his room in the house in the suburbs. He has an IV in his arm and a nurse is sitting in the kitchen reading *People* magazine. He is in continual pain although medicated. He is white as a sheet, his entire body is bloated. His stomach is hugely swollen and his legs will no longer hold him erect. Elisabeth and her sons sit downstairs in the living room furnished in gold-plated mirrored modern hotel style. I know that in the kitchen cabinets my mother's silver rests. I knew that the diamond on Elisabeth's finger was the very same that my mother had worn all her life. On the shelf behind his bed I see one of my books. My father has put yellow markers on many of the pages. My conscience aches, guilt gathers into a lump in my throat. I want to bolt from the room. I sit still in my chair. "Can I get you anything?" I ask. My father asks for water. I give it to him from the glass with a bent straw. I touch the blanket gently. I want to stroke his hand but I don't. I sit at the edge of the bed. What is it I want to say? I want to say something to make him happy. But what? I can't think of anything to say.

My brother takes me out on to the lawn and says, "Dad wants out. He wants me to help him to end his life now. He says he doesn't care anymore. He wants me to speed it up. He begged me." I am not surprised. I can understand. There is an indignity to this illness as well as pain. There is an invasion of privacy by nurse and wife and visitor that is particularly appalling to this man who has always lived with such a slamming of doors, so neatly dressed, no tears, no cries, no sneezes, no exposures of nerve or soft underbelly. This end is unbearable. "Do it," I say to my brother. "You know how. Do it."

My brother looks at me and looks away from me. "I told him I would, but only if he changes his will and leaves me a good part, a good part for my son. There's still time for him to get a lawyer and change the will and then I'll help him."

Was this blackmail? Was the getting and having, the controlling of money, to shape the death as well as the life of the man? What kind of doctor is this, one who follows his oath or one who violates it? My father asked my brother again to help him die. Again my brother said he would if the will were changed.

My father refused the deal. My brother refused to insert some higher milligrams of morphine into the IV drip. "Do it anyway," I beg my brother. He says, "It's illegal." There is a cold look on his face, and a cat that ate the canary smile, akin to a sneer on his face. There is sweat on his forehead. "I know it's illegal," I say, "but you could do it, you should do it," I add. "I won't," he says. "Don't ask me again," he says.

I didn't.

The end went on ending a while longer and then some few weeks later my father died and was buried in the plot that was now Elisabeth's property in the cemetery in upper Westchester. He was buried with Blanche our mother on one side and with Bea his sister on the other. He had told my brother that he had left instructions for Elisabeth to be buried in the fourth plot. There was no need he had explained to her to purchase a new plot when the old one, which was expensive enough, still had room. In the interest of economy he had arranged to spend eternity with his two wives, one of them the mother of his children and the other his former mistress, as well as his sister whom he had never invited to dinner at his home while she was here on this earth.

At the grave site I ask the rabbi if I may put a stone on my mother's grave. The rabbi says that such a gesture is not appropriate and is rude to the widow. My brother and his wife and I and my husband stand apart from the other mourners. Several stare at us and whisper. We do not go back after the service to Elisabeth's house where she will pour coffee from my mother's silver coffee pot and serve cookies on my mother's silver platters.

If a man robs a bank to get cash he goes to prison. If a man robs a woman of her life in order to gain money he gets away scot free.

My brother and I considered moving our mother to a plot of her own. I made some phone calls. The cost would build a hydroelectric plant in a village in Upper Volta. Since we believed in death as end not beginning, after was not the point. Sometimes I think of the three filled graves in the four-grave plot and a skin-prickling shadow falls on my day just as if I were haunted and like Hamlet had not yet done the right thing. I ignore the shadow and it goes away.

23

les jeux sont fait or it's too late now   In the summer of 1989 my brother first told me when I asked about his racking cough that he had developed an allergy to the fumes issued by the crew repainting his apartment. I suggested he move to a hotel. He didn't. He looked ill. He had lost weight. A good thing too, he said to me, and he was right. He really was too heavy. Finally he was hospitalized for what appeared to be a nasty pneumonia. I was away and he didn't tell me. When I returned he was out of the hospital. "I'm just fine now," he said.

Then he began to hint to me that he had a terrible personal secret. "Tell me," I asked. "No," he said. "I'm a private person," he said. "You have no sense of privacy," he said. This I have to admit is true. I am bad at keeping secrets, even my own. I think of them as dangerous if kept too long. My brother considered secrecy a protective shield. From what? I wondered.

We are having breakfast at my apartment on Riverside Drive. My brother tells me that he has been to visit our very elderly Aunt Libby (who is not speaking to me), and she told him that Roy Cohn has liver cancer. My brother says, "I told her the truth. Why shouldn't she know." I say, "I bet she didn't believe you. I'll bet she still doesn't believe it's AIDS." My brother says, "I heard from a lab assistant down in Washington that young boys were brought to his bedside when he was in the hospital. They tried to stop him but he went right on." "He was a murderer," I say, and then I add, "Do you think he got AIDS as a divine punishment?" I am joking. My brother stands up. "I suppose there's no point in telling a person as ignorant as you how viruses actually spread," he says. He is glaring at me with fury. His sarcasm is so bitter I want to cover my ears. I try to explain that I was just fooling around.

But then after some months he wanted to tell me. He hinted so broadly, he hinted in a context of particular conversations so often that I guessed his secret, or one of his secrets. He said, "I hope to live more years than Mother." "Of course you will," I said. "Don't be so sure you know everything, You always think you know everything," he said. I held my tongue. I might have guessed wrong. Some months after that he told me as much as he wanted to tell me. He said he had cut himself in his lab and given himself AIDS and this was a deep secret that none of his colleagues in the lab were permitted to know, no one was to know. His fourteen-year-old son was told but not allowed to tell anyone, not a friend, not a teacher. This was a secret worthy of its name. Because it was a secret he would not join a support group, not even a very secret support group for doctors, that you could contact only through a third party who would refer your name to the group leader. He suspected everyone of betrayal. This was 1989. Shortly after we had this conversation Roy Cohn died. Now I was completely clear that AIDS was no joke.

He and his wife bought a plot in a cemetery, not my mother's cemetery but another one that looked just like it a few miles away. He said it was a good place.

I visited him at the Yale University Hospital where his Montefiore doctor had been appointed head of the AIDS clinic. While I was sitting in his room perched on a stool a black minister entered and asked if he could come in and talk about Christ with us. My brother yelled at him, "Get out of here. Get out. How dare you think I want your Christ, your God, anybody's God." I was embarrassed. The young minister drew back but wasn't certain if he shouldn't try once more. On the threshold of the room, he offered to leave a copy of the New Testament for Gene to look over when he felt like. "It will be your comfort," he said. My brother was thin as a rail, an odd shade of gray, his bones showed through his arms and seemed to pierce the skin at the base of his neck. He had sores in his mouth. "You uneducated rude moron," he screamed at the minister who was retreating backward into the hall. I didn't think this was such a politic thing for a Jewish man to say. I was suffering from liberal squeamishness. It was not ecumenical. It was not in the spirit of Paul Robeson's "Ballad for Americans."

I went into the hall to apologize. The minister flashed me a big happy smile. "He'll come to Christ," he said, comforting me. "Sure," I said and thanked him for his visit.

We go for a walk in the hospital's glassed-in tree-planted lobby. He walks slowly. He won't lean on me. We talk about our Aunt Sylvia who has suffered a stroke in her late eighties which has left her comatose but alive. Her son Howard has brought her home to her apartment on Park Avenue and hired round-the-clock nurses. She has spasms and eye flutters and she moans but she has no true consciousness. Howard visits her every day. I ask my brother if he thinks this is the act of a good son or is it revenge? My brother says, "It will never happen to me. If I think my legs are going and soon I'll be helpless I'll be gone the next day."

My brother asks me, "Does Howard have AIDS?" "No," I say. Howard has supported the ballet and is a friend of Baryshnikov's and on his estate on the Florida border he has created a zoo where endangered species live in peace. "That's good," says my brother. He says, "You could probably build a hospital in Angola with what it takes to keep Aunt Sylvia alive." "It's not fair," I say. "It never is," he says. The sun slants through the glass. But my brother's face is without light. His hands are shaking and the hospital robe seems to be floating off his body.

Later when he is out of the hospital my brother and I go to see Howard's photography collection which has been lent to the Metropolitan Museum. My brother is too tired. Even sitting on the benches in each room we cannot see more than a quarter of the exhibit. My brother continued to work at his lab for some hours a day as long as he could and then he couldn't anymore. The rashes and swellings, the itchings and burnings, the difficulties of swallowing, the wear of the newly brewed medicines as well as the daily fevers that made him alternately cold or hot wore him down. His face changed. He had strangely full lips and sunken hollows at the sides of his mouth. He looked as if his eyes were huge, as if he were wearing a mask in some African dance of death. He had back pain and a nerve down his leg was compromised. He sat on his couch while the IV dripped into his veins. I visited. We watched the tennis matches on television. This was the only sports event I had ever seen him watch. Was the spirit of my father in the room? Was he watching tennis out of resignation or as I watched his face I thought he is not watching tennis. He simply has the TV set on.

I am visiting him. I have finished my cup of coffee. I reach across the table for a sip of his half-filled cup. He knocks over his cup, letting the coffee slip over the wooden table and onto the floor. "Don't ever do that," he whispers to me in his hoarse voice. "You want to die?" He wouldn't blow out his birthday candles in case the saliva in his mouth might propel HIV across the chocolate icing. He followed the reports of HIV research and drug development. He discusses his illness with his doctor like a fellow doctor not like a patient. Despite the destruction of his own crucial cells he was an ardent admirer of the virus's chemical genius. Understanding everything, each blood test, each medical twist and turn, the balances and the unbalances, allowed him to be what he was for a while longer, a scientist, a doctor.

His eyes have been invaded by a cytomegalovirus. He has an open catheter placed permanently in his chest. An IV pole sits by his couch. He attaches a line into his catheter and for three or four hours every day he lets the medicine drip directly into his chest. If he did not do this he would be blind in a matter of days. In the afternoons I keep him company. We talk about 1185 Park Avenue. Only my Uncle Sy's widow lives there still. She knits and she watches television and her memory fades in and out. "We are the last survivors," I say. "Speak for yourself," my brother says.

My brother drives to his lab every morning and works there for a few hours and then he comes home. He is exhausted. He needs to sleep in the afternoons. The medicines that may or may not be stalling the disease are weakening him. Every week he gives some blood and then calls to find out what is happening to his red cells, his white cells, his T-cells. The reports are never good. When I visit he tells me the results.

His oldest friend from college, a rabbi, called and asked to visit him. He had not looked well when they last met. "Something is wrong," said the rabbi. "Nothing," said my brother. The rabbi's wife called, "What is going on?" she said. "Tell us." My brother screamed at her on the phone or so he told me, "You're a voyeur. You just want to satisfy your own curiosity. I don't ever want to speak to you again." He would not accept their phone calls after that or so he told me.

He investigated promising medications that didn't deliver or didn't exist or couldn't be obtained. He believed it was a matter of time before a cure was found. He knew he wouldn't make it that long. He was not peaceful. He was not ready to die and he was enraged at his suffering rather like a wounded bull; he bellowed to the sky.

That summer I forget to pay him the monthly amount I owe him on the purchase of his old Honda Civic. He calls on the phone. He says, "I know you want to kill me. You've always wanted to kill me. If someone lets you into my hospital room you'll pull the oxygen plug. You'll disconnect me from my life support. You are my worst enemy and I will never allow you near me again." "But," I say, "this isn't so. I'm just sloppy about money. You know that." "No," he says, "I can tell how much you hate me. If you didn't hate me you wouldn't let me wait for the money. I know you. I know what you are. You like to see me in pain. Well you're never going to enjoy that again."

I try to persuade him to let me see him at least once more. I think I can convince him of my goodwill if we are face to face. "Goodbye," he says. "I'll never see you again." His voice is frail but firm. He means it. I immediately drop off a check with his doorman. He still refuses to see me.

Of course he was ill and what multiplying virus lay in his blood surely swam into his brain and old paranoias flourished in the morbid medicated climate of his mind. But what was I doing, not sending him the money promptly. It wasn't that I couldn't have written the check. It wasn't that I didn't know that he wasn't casual about money. It was that something vile in me; something that hid below my acceptable thoughts must have been preventing my hand from reaching for my checkbook. I knew he would be provoked by my delayed payment. I knew he felt about money that it was the tie that binds. He had so much more than I had. Did I resent that or did I simply think it acceptable to tease him the way one might a wounded tiger lying in the dirt? It wasn't acceptable. I cursed my stupidity, unconscious or not, my actions made me ashamed. I wanted to be by his side.

I knew he was not so fond of me. He had contempt for my math and foreign language ability. He thought I was stupid to ever watch any TV. He thought my pleasure in the outdoors childish. On the other hand he was attached to me, the object now of his most paranoid fantasy, tiptoer into hospital rooms and puller of plugs against the patient's wishes, murderer. I was his sister. Who else had been there from the beginning, who else understood without saying, who would laugh at any joke, who would read the day's obituaries with him looking for friends of our parents who had at last bit the dust? Who else knew that his fair shake at this world wasn't so fair. That he had kept secrets from me I had forgiven even before I uncovered some of them. That he had things to say about my children that were not so kind, mostly said out of competition, the same old competition that had not quite been settled, did not seem to me to rule out our attachment one to the other: witnesses to the same battles, children of the same parents, raised in the shadow of the Second World War before the winds of social change blew down on the country.

My younger brother, not quite my friend, not quite my enemy, whom I felt was tied to me as I was tied to him irrevocably, was refusing to talk to me, considered me his murderer. Was I his death wish walking about in the guise of a middle-aged writer with a certain squint in her eye which came from looking too hard and seeing too little? Did he hate me because I did not have this illness? Maybe. More likely he was just caught in the volcanic flow of his own fright and fury, the lava was falling hot and fast and anything in its way might get buried. I was in the way.

Then eight weeks later he called and said he would see me again if I didn't discuss the incident or any accusations he had made on the phone. I never did.

His left eyelid became swollen. This did not seem alarming to me. But he seemed very concerned about this minor ailment. He went to the eye doctor and a few days later was admitted to the hospital and they operated even though he had said he knew what it was and wasn't going to let them operate. They found exactly what he had feared, a fungus growing backward toward the brain and he came home from the hospital waiting now for something worse to happen and I visited him every few days.

He gave his wife and me very strict instructions about what he wanted for his funeral. He called me up to tell me that if I went against his wishes I would be committing an act of betrayal that would be unforgivable, criminal, revolting. I promised. I swore. I did not, as I might have in childhood, cross my fingers. He was particularly clear that the funeral home was to get no more money than absolutely necessary. "They want to make you pay, to convince you that you need more than you need. Don't let them, don't buy anything," he told me. He called me twice to make sure I understood. "Don't let them convince my wife," he said. "They're only interested in my money."

Then I came down with a cold, a bad sneezing cold. I knew his immune system was nearly nonexistent. I called on Thursday and asked if he wanted me to come over that afternoon or he preferred me to wait a few days until my cold subsided. He said wait. He said it angrily. He said it as if I had said I didn't want to come. I felt uncomfortable. I wanted to come. I didn't want him to be angry with me because I came with a cold and threatened his life. That Friday night he died. He was fifty-three years old and he had lived a longer life by some months than had my mother.

His instructions were followed. We went with his wife to the Riverside Funeral Home and picked out the simplest coffin possible. There were Hebrew letters on the lid. We asked that they be removed. He wanted no Hebrew anywhere near his body. The next morning there was a heavy rain falling. We brought our umbrellas. We went the four of us, his wife and son and me and my husband, to the funeral home. We had no service. We had no visiting time. We had no book where friends sign in and bring consoling thoughts. We went immediately in our car up to the cemetery. We had no rabbi. We had no words. We were allowed by my brother only to stand in silence as the coffin was lowered into the grave.

My brother had said that the God who would do this to him deserved only silence and he would not have false sentiments at his funeral. He would not have Hebrew, the Hebrew he had once embraced, hovering in the air. He did not want to communicate through prayer with God. He wanted no words at all. "Silence," he said, "is the only acceptable way to meet this death." So we were silent.

Perhaps because there was no rabbi, because we were allowed no words to express our sorrow, the burial of the coffin in the wet dirt seemed to take forever. We stood under our umbrellas and the silence filled the universe and each of us heard it in our own way, bitterly, darkly, without comfort. The cemetery was large. We were at the top of a hill. The gravediggers took the shovel from my nephew who had wanted to fill in the grave and had begun but was not allowed to finish. The gravediggers had jobs to protect. The upturned dirt became mud as the rain poured down. The mud came over the top of my shoes. The rain slid down the umbrella sides in sheets. The silence went on and on until we finally turned and left. Back in the car we hardly could speak. Was it all right now to talk? There were no friends waiting at my brother's home. He had wanted no one.

There were no cakes on the table. There were no covered mirrors. The funeral was over. The thing was done. My sister-in-law did not want us back at her house. She had been instructed by my brother to avoid visitors. The silence would not leave my head. My husband and I insisted on taking my sister-in-law to lunch.

We sit in the restaurant. There are voices all around waitresses carrying plates of eggs and muffins, sausage and salad ease past our table. Is it all right for us to talk now? It seems wrong to be at a restaurant with people who did not know that we have just buried a man. It seems wrong to let my sister-in-law be at her home without comforting voices, friends and family, her own parents, her own brother. They had been explicitly excluded from the funeral by my brother's injunction. We are the most alone people in the world. Have we lost our link to others? The silence at the grave site hangs over us, weighs us down, humiliates us.

My brother in his final months when he planned this funeral had been searching for the best way to tell God that he was furious at Him beyond words. This of course is part of a dialogue with God. A true nonbeliever would never have thought of not talking to the deity. In its own way the funeral was profoundly religious, a kind of duel between almost equal antagonists. It was sharply personal. But profoundly unsettling. Who in fact was my brother angry at? I thought perhaps it was me.

There is no way of knowing if God heard the unsaid. But I am sure that we, the still-alive members of the family, felt uncared for, both by God and by my brother, who did not at the end consider that the ceremony around death is not for the dead but for the living.

Did Cain love Abel, did Abel love Cain, the question seems irrelevant to the story. Did I love my brother? I did most deeply. Did I want him to love me? I did most deeply. Did he? I've heard things since he died. It seems he did not, not exactly. Was I angry at him for reasonable and unreasonable reasons? I was. Was he my first rival, was I his? Of course. He won some and I won some. That should have satisfied us but I don't think it did. Did I really love my brother or did I just think I should? I don't know.

My brother kept the secret from me for eight years that he was HIV positive. He did not tell me he was sick until nearly a year after he had a full-blown AIDS pneumonia and then he swore me to deepest secrecy. Of course I considered the fact that I might still not have the full truth. If he did not even then tell me everything about his life and if his AIDS was in fact contracted in the more usual way I would have been heartbroken—heartbroken because he would had lived so long bending beneath the deceptions forged in other ignorant and cruel times. How sad if he believed that he needed to disguise an important part of his humanity. He didn't need to do that, not for me. If he had told me then that he had a parallel life I would have cursed the world that causes some of us to veil our heart's desires and to live out our days in fear that the very most ordinary and truest parts of our souls will be scorned. He did not trust me. Of course I did not trust him which is why the questions linger. The tragedy one way or another was that we missed the opportunity to be with each other, fully him, completely me, not posing not hiding, no secrets, just being.

I think of my brother everytime someone tells me a joke. I think of him when I hear Mozart on the radio. I think of him when I am on the beach, my face in the sun: how much he would disapprove. I think of him when I read a book he would have liked. I think of him when I have no reason to think of him.

the end   Today my Aunt Sylvia breathes in and out with less consciousness than fifty years earlier: but how much less, a really significant amount? What of the next generation? Must our mistakes simply repeat themselves like symphonic themes with variations on and on until the end of time?

Of all of us only my Uncle Sy's widow, who is ninety-three years old, still lives at 1185 Park Avenue. She does not hear very well. She remembers less and less as we approach the millennium. But she does not complain and each day passes and fades into the next one without causing her any noticeable disturbance. The shirt company is no longer in family hands and those who had large blocks of stock sold them to some company in Asia.

One of my children lives near Mott and Elizabeth streets, near Prince and Houston. There are the tenements my grandparents once inhabited as greenhorns and fled as soon as they could. Now these leaning rickety buildings with their sloping fire escapes are filled with fashion models, film students, and art galleries. The cappuccino flows through the neighborhood like the flood-time Mississippi racing through the delta. The old railroad tenements with outdoor privies have been converted into hi-tech lofts. Park Avenue is a very long subway ride away.

My husband and I live on Riverside Drive and in the early evenings we walk in the park and watch the boats float by and the sun hits the palisades and crashes down into sheets of orange and pink. On Broadway there is Indian food and Korean salad bars and cut-rate dishwasher outlets and flower stalls and a popcorn-smelling movie theater. The sidewalks are never swept and the denizens of the halfway houses, people recovering from all the existing ailments of soul and body, mingle with students carrying backpacks and musicians carrying violins, flutes, cellos. I am, I think, at a safe distance from Park Avenue.

Now at 1185 Park Avenue there is an exercise room in the basement where Willow used to hang our wash to dry. In it there are weight-lifting, rowing, stepping, and biking machines. Pedals whirr and cables grind at all hours of the day. Those noises, however, won't fill the silence, won't replace the lost words that spoke of the passage of time, the change of the seasons. It is the absence of ceremony that haunts us, father and mother, child and child. The elevators now rise and descend on automatic power but the ever increasing distance between God and his furless creations remains. We discarded with the trash or we placed in the storage bins the habits of the spirit that once helped us get by. We substituted money for mind, objects for thought.

We have been on an outing. The wind on the hill is blowing hard and the cold has turned Greta's nose red and my cheeks are smarting. My brother is sleeping in his carriage. His navy blue blanket with the gray monogram is pulled up over his mouth and tucked firmly into the sides of the mattress. We enter at the side gates and make our way through the long basement corridors. There I am in my hat with its wool earflaps and coat and leather leggings. I am wearing a sweater under my coat and Greta could hardly get the buttons closed. She stops to talk to a nanny from the A-B section of the building. The conversation is in German. I go into the laundry room where I watch Willow fold the sheets. Bare light bulbs hang down above our heads. Steam rises from the basement pipes, steam floats above the large sinks overflowing with suds that line the far wall.

Redemption: (tred, pend, note, mend, poem, peer, mope, etc.).